THE SMART

SARAH BAKEWELL

❖

THE SMART

The Story of Margaret Caroline Rudd and the
Unfortunate Perreau Brothers

CHATTO & WINDUS
London

Published by Chatto & Windus 2001

2 4 6 8 10 9 7 5 3 1

First published in Great Britain in 2001 by
Chatto & Windus
Random House, 20 Vauxhall Bridge Road,
London SW1V 2SA

Random House Australia (Pty) Limited
20 Alfred Street, Milsons Point, Sydney,
New South Wales 2061, Australia

Random House New Zealand Limited
18 Poland Road, Glenfield,
Auckland 10, New Zealand

Random House (Pty) Limited
Endulini, 5A Jubilee Road, Parktown 2193, South Africa

The Random House Group Limited Reg. No. 954009
www.randomhouse.co.uk

A CIP catalogue record for this book
is available from the British Library

ISBN 0 7011 7109 X

Papers used by Random House are natural,
recyclable products made from wood grown in sustainable forests;
the manufacturing processes conform to the environmental
regulations of the country of origin

Typeset by Deltatype Ltd, Birkenhead, Merseyside
Printed and bound in Great Britain by
Biddles Ltd, Guildford & King's Lynn

Contents

Illustrations

15. Thomas Lyttleton, 2nd Baron Lyttleton., after Thomas Gainsborough, oil on canvas. (National Portrait Gallery, London)
16. Francis Rawdon-Hastings, 1st Marquess of Hastings, attributed to Hugh Douglas Hamilton, oil on panel, ca. 1801. (National Portrait Gallery, London)
17. James Boswell, Sir Joshua Reynolds, oil on canvas, 1785. (National Portrait Gallery, London)

In forgery and perjury owned such art,
She palmed the Gold, while others paid the smart.

William Combe, *The Diabo-lady*, 1777

Introduction

The strange story of Margaret Caroline Rudd and the Perreau brothers fell into my path entirely by accident. My job then was (and still is) cataloguing early printed books in the medical history collection of the Wellcome Library in London. Cataloguing is a peculiar business, half scholarly and half menial. It requires many ant-sized pieces of detective work: to decide which variant printing you have, or to trace a previous owner from an unreadable signature, or to discover whether a picture really belongs to the book or has just been stuck there because it looks nice. Some days this work is as pleasantly soothing as basket-weaving; other days the joys of all the pedantic pottering wear thin. But then there are also days when every so often you stumble across a genuinely fascinating bit of history, which suddenly makes everything worthwhile. This time the story I found was to give me much more than a minute's satisfaction, though. It was to start me off on a quest.

Mrs Rudd and I met between the pages of a slightly battered volume of eighteenth-century pamphlets, of which only the first item was relevant to a medical library. It was a satire on the insanity of King George III, poking fun at his confusion and telling a lot of cheeky anecdotes about his conduct – particularly towards young ladies. Not surprisingly, it was anonymous, and so was the pamphlet which followed it: a compilation of *Maxims in Prose and*

Verse published from inside Newgate Prison by one of its inmates. It included a handwritten note from the Newgate sheriff, declaring that the author had 'behaved himself since he has been prisoner here very properly, and is certainly an object of Charity'.

The third item after this contrasting pair of oddities – the badly behaved monarch and the well–behaved convict – was a short work called *Mrs Stewart's Case, Written by Herself, and Respectfully Submitted to the Enlightened Part of the Publick*. The calm title belied the contents, which were twenty-seven pages of sizzling vitriol distilled from long-nursed grievances and poured over one Lord Rawdon, a wealthy relative who had abandoned the writer in her hour of need. Mrs Stewart savaged him mercilessly and invited him to make amends by handing over a large sum of money as soon as possible.

It didn't take long to find out who this angry lady was. The British Library catalogue listed a 'Stewart, Margaret Caroline (pseud.)', author of *Mrs Stewart's Case*, and revealed that her real name was Margaret Caroline Rudd. When I looked up Mrs Rudd in the Library of Congress's name file, a roll-call of other pseudonyms came tumbling down the screen: Mrs Gore, Mrs Perreau, Margaret Youngson, Mrs Potter, Mrs Porter, Caroline de Grosberg, and more. The source given for all this was a 1776 book, itself anonymous: the *Authentic Anecdotes of the Life and Transactions of Mrs Margaret Rudd*.

I was hooked. What was this woman up to with all these multiple identities and 'transactions'? And what exactly were the agonies and injustices she bemoaned so bitterly in *Mrs Stewart's Case*? The next time I passed by the British Library I ordered up their copy of the *Authentic Anecdotes*. It was a far from reliable book, being obviously written by someone who knew her personally and hated her guts, but the tale it told was extraordinary, and it revealed a very interesting woman indeed.

There was plenty more to read on Mrs Rudd, including transcripts of the Old Bailey trial which I soon learned lay at the heart of her story, and accounts of the two men whose fate was entangled with hers: Robert and Daniel Perreau. They were just as intriguing as she was. Identical twins with lifestyles and personalities that could hardly be more different, they too had been accused of serious crimes and tried for their lives, and were rarely mentioned without a woeful, chilling adjective: 'the *unfortunate* Perreau brothers'.

Addicted, I read my way through everything: pamphlets, trials, newspaper reports, published letters, the *Newgate Calendar*, gossipy periodicals like the *London Magazine*. The more I read, the more I realized that I could not take a single word of it at face value. Almost everyone involved had something to say – even Mrs Rudd's maid wrote her memoirs. They all said it in print at great length and with powerful conviction, but none of them ever quite seemed to be telling the truth – least of all the three stars of the show. On the rare occasions that Mrs Rudd and the Perreaus agreed on the facts of an incident, you could be sure they would disagree about the reasons for it, or the events that had led up to it, or its consequences. Atempting to piece together some sort of consistent picture, I felt more and more like a judge trying a case in which the witnesses were all liars, the documents were all forged and the law was that of *Alice in Wonderland*. Sometimes I despaired of ever making sense of it, but curiosity kept drawing me further in.

Then came another totally serendipitous discovery. I happened to pick up an anthology of Boswell's diaries in a second-hand bookshop, and to my astonishment found a long account of a flirtatious, sexually charged meeting between him and Mrs Rudd in 1776. As I learned more – including the full story of their eventual affair – I found myself starting to see Mrs Rudd through Boswell's eyes. For the first time I could visualize what it might have been like to meet her and be exposed to her formidable charisma. She began to live and breathe in my imagination.

At last, with a stack of papers as tall as an eighteenth-century hairdo, I settled down to shuffle and reshuffle them until a coherent story emerged. Sometimes it was simply impossible to reconcile two conflicting versions and I had to let them both stand, sceptically eyeing one another. But eventually a unified narrative emerged from the chaos and everyone's viewpoints somehow slid into place. I ended up with a story which felt right, and which might even be something like the truth. Only Mrs Rudd herself remained elusive. Vivid though she was to me, she was if anything a more profound puzzle at the end than at the beginning.

As in any court, my judgement is a creature of the floating world and entirely open to appeal. I hope that readers will enjoy playing detective, advocate, jury and judge just as I did – and that they may even arrive at their own quite different verdicts in this case of the long-suffering Margaret Caroline Rudd and the unfortunate Perreau brothers.

I owe thanks to all the libraries and archive repositories I used, especially the British Library, where the vast majority of the published material is to be found and where I spent most of my time – and of course the Wellcome Library, in which it all began. I am very grateful to my editor Jenny Uglow for taking me on and for providing so much friendliness and wise editorial work; I would also like to thank Marina Warner for her kind encouragement. For reading the book in various stages, spotting blunders and suggesting ways of making it better, I thank my parents Jane and Ray Bakewell, Helen Ficai-Veltroni, Alison Eiffe, Bartek Pawlak, John Symons, and above all Simonetta Ficai-Veltroni, without whose faith and enthusiasm it would never have got beyond the dithering stage.

CHAPTER
ONE
——◆——
'NOT A ROBBER BUT A THIEF'

At ten o'clock in the evening of 22 April 1776, the celebrity-chasing writer James Boswell called at 10 Queen Street, Mayfair. It was his third attempt to meet its occupant that day, and each time he'd lost another portion of his nerve. He fidgeted as he waited for the door to open, smoothing his waistcoat and worrying about the impression he would make. Perhaps it had not been a good idea, after all, to spend quite so much of the afternoon idling and quaffing at the dinner table. Still, it was too late to worry about that now.

The coming encounter was the sort of thing Boswell lived for. A mere lawyer and literary dabbler, not yet the famous biographer he was to become, he had a flair for people-collecting. He had already captured some of the biggest stars of his day – Johnson, Wilkes, Rousseau, Voltaire – and he was hungry for more. He was an audacious stalker, an enthusiast, a canny observer of character and a scribbler in notebooks.

And so here he was at the door of 'the celebrated Mrs. Rudd', the woman about whom London had been gossiping since her arrest for forgery the previous year – a charge of which she had been acquitted, while her co-defendants Daniel and Robert Perreau had swung for it. Even the

American revolutionaries had been obliged to jostle with Mrs Rudd for column inches in the newspapers. Was she guilty or innocent? A tragic heroine, or a seductress who could hypnotize men as lethally as snakes do their prey? No one could agree. Everything about her was discussed and marvelled over: her sufferings in Newgate, her cleverness, her glamorous appearance, her past and present lovers, her bewitching powers of influence. And what of those 'unfortunate brothers', the Perreau twins: had they really died for a crime they did not commit? The story was no longer merely news. It had become a part of the city's mythology.

All this was irresistible to Boswell. He traced Mrs Rudd's address and came to call. As a writer he wanted to learn the truth about her – but as a man he was also ready to be swept off his feet should the opportunity arise.

On his first visit, that morning, he had been turned away. The maid told him that Mrs Rudd was out until the evening. Boswell left a message, saying that he was a friend of a Mr Macqueen's, and that he would try later. The day was spent in his habitual visits and conviviality around the town, culminating in a long, leisurely meal with friends. When he returned to Mrs Rudd's house at half-past nine that night, the maid was more forthcoming.

'She is just gone out, sir,' she said. 'But she will be home in half an hour. You will oblige me if you will walk up stairs. I told her that you called.'

Instead of waiting, Boswell went for a walk. He crossed Piccadilly and sauntered through St James's to the river, where he stood on Westminster Bridge and watched the boats on the dark water below. He returned for the third time; Mrs Rudd was still out, but this time he agreed to go up and wait in her apartment.

'I was shown into a dining-room, decent enough, but how poor in comparison of her former magnificence!' he wrote later that evening.[1] 'A couple of tallow candles gave me light. My fancy began to form fearful suppositions in this solitary

2

situation. I thought the ghosts of the Perreaus might appear. I thought that there might be murderers or bullies in the house.' He knew that Mrs Rudd had children, but there was no sign of them.

To ease his nerves, he examined the books on her shelves. There weren't many, and they were an odd mixture: a Court Calendar, two works on logic, a volume of Pope, *Johnsoniana*, a novel called *The Small Talker* and some pamphlets relating to her own case. As Mrs Rudd still did not appear, he sat down and browsed through *The Small Talker*, which he rather liked. It was an amusing but edifying story, warning young ladies against the danger of men who won their affections only in order to seduce and then abandon them.

After a half-hour or so, he at last heard the sound of a lady coming up the stairs, and jumped to his feet. The door opened; Mrs Rudd stepped into the room.

The first impression was not as Boswell had expected. She was 'a little woman, delicately made, not at all a beauty, but with a very pleasing appearance and much younger than I imagined.' There was no grand air of 'dignity or of high elegance.' Her style of dress was quietly tasteful rather than thrilling: she wore a plain black gown set off by a white cloak and hat.

Boswell's disappointment was only momentary. Remembering his manners, he apologized for having disturbed her and repeated that he was a friend of Mr Macqueen's from Scotland.* Although the Macqueen family had not actually sent him, he said, he knew that they would be glad to hear news of her. Mrs Rudd thanked Boswell for his civility and invited him to sit down. He noticed that her voice was pleasant, with an Irish lilt. In some mysterious way she had already managed to put him at his ease, and he began to warm to her.

* Robert Macqueen, later Lord Braxfield. Mrs Rudd claimed Scottish ancestry and had visited Scotland, where she said she had made many new friends amongst the nobility.

They sat in chairs facing each other, a short distance apart. 'How are you now?' he asked, alluding delicately to the rigours of the trial she had just been through.

'As well as could be expected,' she replied, and without further prompting told him the whole story of her sufferings. She described how the Perreaus' relatives had conspired together and still tried to throw the guilt upon her. The family was like a little commonwealth, she said: spread over England and Ireland, and all united in enmity against her. Boswell noticed with surprise that she pronounced the name '*Perreau*' rather than '*Perreau*' or '*Perroo*' as others did.

He sympathized, and said, 'It is shocking that the brothers died denying, as they did.'

'Yes,' she replied. 'It must shock anybody who has any tenderness of conscience. They should have died in silence.'

Her conversation flowed from one thing to another. She spoke of her desire to discover whether her estranged husband, Valentine Rudd, was alive or not. There was a man in Ireland claiming to be Rudd and she wished to go there to find out if it was true. In any case, she thought his long neglect of her set her free from her marriage vows. And she would not think of marrying again after being twice so unlucky – unless perhaps it were someone who could help her, a man of rank and fortune who would bear her up despite all that had happened.

She grew sad and said that her main pleasure lay in reading. Her only resources were in her own mind; without them she should have been very unhappy. Her imprisonment had been harsh. She had been consumptive. And by the time she had emerged from her prison cell into the light, she had been almost blind.

Boswell noticed that her eyes did appear to be weak. Moreover, she had a flushed heat on her cheeks and breathed with difficulty. Yet there was something so attractive about her that he could now see why the newspapers called her an enchantress. Her charms may have been more subtle than he expected, but that only made them more fascinating.

He brought up this subject, saying playfully that she was reputed to possess the power of sorcery. Mrs Rudd smiled, as if to acknowledge that it might have been true in the past, but said that now she could bewitch nobody.

Boswell hastened to object: 'My dear Mrs. Rudd, don't talk so. Everything you have said to me till now has been truth and candour.' He was convinced that she did have such powers, he said, but he begged that she would not enchant *him* too much, nor change him into any other creature, but allow him to remain a man with at least some degree of reason. He was pleased with this turn of phrase, and described himself later as having spoken 'with exquisite flattery'.

By now Boswell was getting into the spirit of the thing: he had forgotten his earlier reservations and felt himself to be in that delicious peril he had hoped for. 'I was as cautious as if I had been opposite to that snake which fascinates with its eyes. Her language was choice and fluent and her voice melodious. The peculiar characteristic of her enchantment seemed to be its delicate imperceptible power. She perfectly concealed her design to charm. There was no meretricious air, no direct attempt upon the heart. It was like hearing the music of the spheres which poets feign, and which produces its effect without the intervention of any instrument, so that the very soul of harmony immediately affects our souls.'

She no longer expected happiness, Mrs Rudd was saying, in tones that moved Boswell's heart. It was enough for her if she could achieve a state of insensibility to suffering. At this, Boswell rose from his seat.

'You must not be insensible!' he cried, and seized her hand to kiss it fervently. There was genuine warmth of feeling in this, but at the same time he could not help but reflect on how splendidly the encounter was going. Writing about the hand-kissing the next day, he remarked, 'This was all experiment, and she showed neither prudery nor effrontery, but the complaisance, or compliance if you please, of a woman of fashion.'

Mrs Rudd gently withdrew and asked about Robert Macqueen's eldest daughter: was she married yet? Miss Macqueen promised to be a fine woman, she added. Then she grew wistful and said she liked Scotland; she would like to visit it again. If she did, she would visit the house of Mr Stewart of Physgill,* to which she had been invited several times. She referred to the Earl of Galloway, whom she did not like, and various members of his family: Boswell mildly took issue with some of her judgements, but on the whole felt that her remarks showed insight into human nature. They touched briefly on the wider question of character and how it is formed. Mrs Rudd said that she believed one could be anything one pleased. Boswell nodded approvingly: his great friend Samuel Johnson was of the same opinion.

In short, Mrs Rudd was 'never at a loss for chit-chat'. Boswell sometimes kept silent on purpose, to see how she would keep the conversation going. 'She never let the pause be long, but with admirable politeness, when she found that I did not begin again to speak and might perhaps be embarrassed, said something quite easily, so as not to have the appearance of abruptness, to make me feel that I had stopped short, but rather . . . as if what she then said had grown out of what we had talked of before.' He was utterly won over. There was no self-conscious effort to be witty. 'She did not dazzle with brilliance, but cheered one with a mild light.' Nor, he considered, did she go on inordinately about her suffering or affect a sad face. Instead, she did all she could to be cheerful and companionable.

He noticed that the light seemed to be hurting her eyes and moved the candles to a table further away from her. Then,

---

* John Hathorn Stewart, of the Stewart family to which Mrs Rudd claimed relationship.

however, he realized that he could not see the 'pretty turns of her countenance' as she talked, and he moved one of them back again, telling her flatteringly why he was doing it.

Mrs Rudd spoke about what she had learned in prison from the experience of solitude. She had chosen to sleep alone in her cell, declining the company of a maid. This was because she wished to spend the time in spiritual reflection. 'I hope I shall be the better for it,' she told Boswell. 'I hope I am wiser.'

'When you speak of insensibility and of solitude', said Boswell half jokingly, 'you might as well be a nun.'

'Oh, yes,' said Mrs Rudd. 'If it were not for my children I would retire to a convent.' But in fact, she admitted, she could not bring herself to retreat from the world altogether.

People told many stories about her, she went on. For example, they were now saying that she lived with Lord Lyttelton, although she did not even recognize the man by sight and he had denied the rumour himself. 'Besides, Lord Lyttelton is not a person with whom one would form a connexion, as he is quite a profligate.'

That wasn't all, said Boswell with a twinkle in his eye. 'I heard today that you and the Earl of Loudoun were very well acquainted.'

'To be sure,' said Mrs Rudd, 'if the Earl of Loudoun were to come into this room, I should know him; but as to any intimacy . . .'

'It is amazing with what confidence people will tell lies,' said Boswell. 'But there is a vanity in being thought to know particularly about a lady so celebrated as you.'

'People are apt to form an idea of one whom they have never seen. A gentleman told me he had imagined that I was old and ugly!'

'Why,' said Boswell merrily, 'that was very extraordinary, though indeed it may have been owing to the reputation of your enchantment, as witches were said to be old and ugly. You are, however, much *younger* than I supposed.'

'But I am not a young woman,' she said, 'I am nine-and-twenty, and I do not think that young.' In fact she was thirty-one.

They talked a little longer, and the conversation again returned to her trial and confinement. As she spoke Boswell noticed that a 'pretty little foot' had become visible, and the combination of this sight with the tale of her sufferings excited him. He rose out of his chair, saying, 'I cannot believe that you have gone through all this. Are you really Mrs Rudd?'

She smiled and said, 'I *am* Mrs Rudd.'

'You must forget all the ill that has passed,' said Boswell. 'You must be happy for the future.' And he ventured to add that he believed *love* was the remedy she needed.

'I do not think so,' she replied gently. And when he began to run on about the happiness to be had from love, she stopped him by saying, 'But I must now be very cautious in my choice.'

At length Boswell realized it was time to go home. He told Mrs Rudd that he hoped she would forgive the liberty he had taken in waiting upon her. He would be very much obliged if she would allow him to call on her again. She consented and said that she was always at home. Boswell thanked her warmly and took his leave at the door with a kiss, which she received with serenity. There was a moment of confusion while Boswell wondered whether to pursue things further, but he thought better of it and left.

He went home in fine spirits and immediately wrote his account of the meeting, setting down as much of the conversation as he could remember – which was a lot, for Boswell's memory for dialogue worked like a tape-recorder. He also thought about his own response to Mrs Rudd. Her subtlety and skill in putting him at his ease intrigued him greatly. The whole time he was there, he wrote, 'I was quite calm and possessed myself fully, snuffed the candles and stirred the fire as one does who is at home, sat easy upon my chair, and felt no confusion when her eyes and mine met. Indeed her eyes did not flash defiance but attracted with sweetness, and *there* was the reason of the difference of effect between the eyes and those of more insolent or less experienced charmers. She was not a robber but a thief.' He was pleased, too, that she had never tried to find out his true identity, which he took as a sign of good breeding.

Yet he was not completely fooled by her talk of nunneries and nights of meditation, and guessed that her true vocation lay elsewhere. Although not completely sure of it, he surmised that she was 'on the town', although her conversation showed that she had little in common with the brash, earthy prostitutes he was used to.

He finished his account by wondering what Mrs Rudd had made of him, and decided that on the whole he had been very agreeable. 'I would not for a good deal have missed this scene,' he wrote. 'We crowd to see those who excel in any art, and surely the highest excellence of art is the art of pleasing, the art of attracting admiration and fondness.'

Boswell's observations normally remained in his journal, but sometimes he posted them to friends for their edification and entertainment. This time he decided initially to send his account as a letter to his wife Margaret. The two of them had discussed the trial and he'd told her how curious he was to meet this 'celebrated Mrs Rudd'. Since the encounter had gone so well, he could hardly resist rattling off the whole story to her. But after reading it through a second time he admitted to himself that it was not wise, and instead sent it to his old friend William Temple, asking him to read it and send it back. (Impressed, Temple wrote back saying, 'You *do* excell in painting *minds*.')[2] By the time the manuscript was returned, Boswell had definitely concluded that it was not suitable for Margaret's eyes. He annotated it 'To my wife – but not sent' and filed it away.

James Boswell was a raw, confusing and extraordinarily

human character. Like Rousseau and Goethe, he occupied an intermediate zone between Classical poise and the introspective turbulence of Romanticism. Frequently he seemed childish and absurd, perhaps only because he revealed more of himself than was usual for an eighteenth-century literary gentleman. Open as he was with acquaintances, he was even more honest in his private journal. There he dissected his own emotions with a pitiless blade, as well as noting the oddities of others. No allowances were made for the petty self-deceptions that bear up most people's vanity. Going to witness an execution in 1768, for example, he found in himself not only horror and pity, but also joy, an emotion which he ascribed to the pleasure of being still alive himself.[3] Another time he marvelled at his own hypocrisy in attending church in a genuinely religious state of mind, whilst simultaneously laying plans for seducing women.[4]

He had been born in 1740 into the Scottish nobility, being distantly related to Robert Bruce and the royal Stuart line on his mother's side and heir to the sober estate of Auchinleck on his father's. At the earliest opportunity he fled all that to go to London, arriving there for the first time in 1762. Boswell fell in love with the city, as Samuel Johnson had done before him, and was lucky enough to discover it at a time when it was going through a particularly vibrant period. London in the 1760s was a city of coffee houses and clubs, of gambling dens and gossip-mongers, of pleasure gardens and theatres, a city in which a young man could fling together a witty poem one day and see it printed in his friend's newspaper the next. It was a city of high-class courtesans in boudoirs and bawdy strumpets on the streets, of dandies, drunkards, seducers, pimps, sharpers and swindlers. It was full of everything that Auchinleck lacked. Boswell adored it, and recorded everything he saw and heard in his journal.

In 1763 he met Samuel Johnson, and after following him around devotedly for a while had the honour of being accepted as an intimate friend. Putting up with constant teasing and abuse, Boswell collected every tic and every *mot* of the great man. After many years he boiled all this material together in a generous cooking pot of a book and in 1791 recreated Johnson as one of the most vivid characters in literature, an eccentric, domineering titan who is at the same time a maze of all-too-human vanities and vulnerabilities.

Boswell was a people person. 'Of so soft and warm a complexion am I', he wrote, 'that I adhere a little to almost all with whom I come in contact, unless they have qualities that repel me.'[5] But in his close relationships he could be callous. His wife suffered more than anyone. He flirted and fornicated indiscriminately, and left written accounts of his adventures lying around where Margaret could not avoid seeing them. From his whoring he caught diseases, which he brought home with him. When drunk (as he often was) he could be aggressive, and once threw a lighted candlestick at her. Yet he did love Margaret and often tormented himself with remorse.

Boswell's debauchery was out of the ordinary even for an era of general sexual brio. In his early diaries he boasts of his talents, notably his ability to copulate five times in one night.[6] He genuinely liked the company of women, although he was no feminist and once wrote, 'In my mind, there cannot be higher felicity on earth enjoyed by man than the participation of genuine reciprocal amorous affection with an amiable woman. There he has a full indulgence of all the delicate feelings and pleasures both of body and mind, while at the same time in this enchanting union he exults with a consciousness that he is the superior person.'[7]

By 1776, the year in which he met Mrs Rudd, his sexuality had developed into a frenzied addiction. Terror of venereal infections warred with a total inability to control himself. Between Saturday 30 March and Monday 1 April of that year, for example, a few weeks before his first meeting with Mrs Rudd, his diary relates an absurd sequence of events in which he set out to find a young woman he'd had sex with on

Friday night in order to reassure himself that she was not diseased. It had worried him so much that he could not sleep, but in the course of lurking around prostitutes' alleys he found himself falling into bed with another one. He now had two women to investigate instead of one, but only managed to get embroiled with yet a third – and so it went on, until he had risked his health with four different women and was still none the wiser about the first.[8]

Boswell's emotions were as volatile as his sexual impulses. He suffered from bouts of depression and could become intensely involved with people and their problems. One such was John Reid, a condemned sheep thief to whom he gave legal help. He presented a series of petitions to the King and others, pleading for mercy for Reid, and even concocted a scheme for spiriting the body off the gallows and resuscitating him should the hanging take place. He visited him frequently in Newgate ('When I got home I found several vermin upon me ... It was shocking. I changed all my clothes.')[9] and arranged for Reid's portrait to be painted while he waited to learn his fate. In the event, all the appeals failed and Reid's execution date was set. Boswell spent the last evening with him and his family, watching as Reid's youngest son Daniel clambered boisterously over his father, too young to comprehend what was happening. At the fatal hour, Reid was fetched for the customary slow procession to the gallows at Tyburn. His last words in front of the crowd of spectators were, 'Take warning: mine is an unjust sentence.' A cap was pulled over his eyes and the noose put around his neck; as he fell he clutched at the ladder for a moment and then let go. The onlookers argued about what they had heard – 'He says his sentence is *just*.' – 'No. He says *unjust*.'[10] Nothing came of Boswell's resuscitation plan and afterwards he became profoundly gloomy, tormented with feelings of worthlessness. 'I was so affrighted that I started now and then and durst hardly rise from my chair at the fireside.'

He recovered quickly from these episodes, but could slip back into melancholy without warning at any time. Johnson, who was also a sufferer, advised him on 22 March 1776 – a month before Boswell's visit to Mrs Rudd – to 'take a course of chymistry, or a course of rope-dancing', anything to occupy his mind with things outside himself. 'I *thought* of a course of concubinage,' remarked Boswell mischievously in his journal, 'but was afraid to mention it.'[11] In fact Boswell's amorous adventures rarely cheered him up, and he worried endlessly about his moral weakness, his excessive drinking and his tendency to make a fool of himself in public. He longed to be more like the teetotal and industrious Johnson, or his own father. Yet both Johnson and the elder Laird of Auchinleck were more feared than liked, whereas everyone had a soft spot for the warm-hearted 'Bozzy'.

Three weeks went by after Boswell's first meeting with Mrs Rudd. He called on her on Monday 13 May, but she was not at home; the following evening he tried again and this time managed to see her briefly. As soon as he got home, he sat down and composed some verses in her honour.

On Wednesday Boswell told Johnson about the encounter. He'd already broached the subject in March, saying that he would like to meet the lady if he could. 'Sir,' Johnson had replied, 'never believe extraordinary characters which you hear of people. Depend upon it, they are exaggerated.'[12] Boswell ventured some mild disagreement – this was the opposite of his own philosophy – but he did not press the point. However, Johnson later said, 'I should have visited her myself, were it not that now they have a trick of putting every thing into the newspapers,' and this time he went so far as to confide that he envied Boswell his acquaintance with Mrs Rudd.[13]

That same Wednesday Boswell had an enjoyable evening introducing his two great friends Samuel Johnson and John Wilkes to one another for the first time. As it happened,

Wilkes was also no stranger to Mrs Rudd. As one of the judges at the Perreaus' trials, he had made a point of excluding her from giving testimony to ensure that she would not escape trial herself. Indeed, rumours were now afoot that she and Wilkes had once had an affair: love nests in Lambeth were whispered of. Since Wilkes was as famous for his libertinism as for his rabble-rousing politics, it is not surprising that the two names were linked. His apparent vindictiveness towards her in the courtroom had fuelled the speculation. Yet there is no convincing evidence of Wilkes having been her lover, and he and Boswell never seem to have compared notes.

Wilkes was clever and charismatic – Boswell's favourite sort of person. Although undeniably ugly, with a twisted mouth and a squinting eye, he was considered hugely sexy by women. His capers with the orgiastic Medmenhamite Brotherhood were the stuff of legend. Boswell was proud of the friendship and wrote, 'When Wilkes and I sat together, each glass of wine produced a flash of wit, like gunpowder thrown into the fire – Puff! puff!'[14]

Introducing Wilkes and Johnson was asking for trouble. Johnson was as passionate about chastity, temperance and virtue as Wilkes was about vice. The two men were political opposites and each of them was every bit as domineering and intolerant as the other. Moreover, Johnson knew that Wilkes had poked fun at his monumental *Dictionary*. (After Johnson unwisely declared that 'H seldom, perhaps never, begins any but the first syllable,' Wilkes observed in print that 'the author of this observation must be a man of quick *apprehension* and a most *comprehensive* genius'.) Yet, as it turned out, everything went swimmingly. Wilkes made a great performance out of charming Johnson, dancing attendance on him all through dinner: 'Pray give me leave, Sir – It is better here – A little of the brown – Some fat, Sir – A bit of the stuffing – Some gravy – Let me have the pleasure of giving you some butter – Allow me to recommend a squeeze of an orange – or the lemon perhaps may have more zest.' The legendary grouch could not resist, being also something of a gourmand, and Boswell was delighted with his social coup. That, combined with Johnson's admission that he envied him his knowledge of Mrs Rudd, really made his day.

The following evening Boswell called on Mrs Rudd again. This time he sang a musical version of the poem he'd written for her. Neither tune nor words survive; we know only the title, 'The Snake', presumably a reference to the hypnotic power of her eyes. Mrs Rudd showed him a miniature portrait of herself, which she said had been done while she was in prison awaiting trial – 'in case of any accident'.[15]

Boswell was shocked. 'What, Madam, do you talk with so much ease? Do you mean losing your life?'

'Yes,' she said.

'What, being hanged?'

'No, I assure you I should never have been hanged. I had taken care of that.'

He took this to mean that she would have committed suicide sooner than go to the gallows. 'What! had you resolution to destroy yourself?'

'I promise you, I am not afraid of death,' said Mrs Rudd. 'This is no affectation. I am above it. As I said to a gentleman, "I have too much virtue to be a prude, and too much sense to be a coquette."'

'The latter is very true,' said Boswell. 'As for virtue, one cannot answer for another's. One can hardly answer for one's own. But why too much virtue to be a prude? I've seen a virtuous prude.'

'No, they have only the affectation of it,' said Mrs Rudd.

Boswell then became somewhat incoherent. He said, 'You could make me commit murder. But you would be sorry afterwards to have made so ungenerous a use of your power. You have no occasion to be convinced of your power over the human heart. You know it. I dare say you could make me do anything – make me commit murder,' he repeated. Then he was overcome with emotion, and cried, 'Is a pretty ankle one of your perfections?'

'Yes,' said Mrs Rudd.

'Your eyes . . .'

'Poets and painters have made enough of them,' said Mrs Rudd coolly.

He kissed her, and she said, 'I have heard I have a fine mouth.' Again and again he kissed her, with passion. Then, as he wrote in his journal: 'Twice [I said] "Adieu"; at last, "God bless you."' After leaving her, he went to Johnson's house.

An afterthought, scribbled in his journal above the heading for that day, reads, 'Like water corrupted and grown fresh again, her art is become purest simplicity.'

Yet Boswell cooled off abruptly after this and made no further attempt to see Mrs Rudd that year. Now that there seemed to be a real chance of something more than pleasurable flirtation, he lost his nerve. Certainly, she was a formidable proposition. If she was indeed 'on the town' she carried a health warning, but more importantly, she had a reputation for being quite literally *fatale*. She had also made it clear that an intimate connection with her would involve financial responsibilities. Boswell may have stopped seeing her out of loyalty to his wife, but on the other hand he may simply have decided that she was more than he could handle.

When they met again nine years later, however, it was to be a different story. He was older, in his mid-forties rather than mid-thirties, and had a greater sense of his own substance. She had aged too and had more modest expectations. This time Boswell did not back off, and for several months in 1786 he and Margaret Caroline Rudd were to be lovers.

CHAPTER
TWO
◆
ADVENTURES

Something neither Boswell nor Mrs Rudd seems to have known is that they were related to one another – that is, if her own descriptions of her family background are to be given any credence.

All accounts agree that she was born Margaret Caroline Youngson, in 1744 or 1745, in the small town of Lurgan near Belfast in northern Ireland. Her father was an apothecary of genteel appearance and education, with a small but respectable income.* Her mother was born Isabella Stewart and was also from a family of modest means. However, she had a secret claim to nobility.

There was later to be a lot of confusion about Margaret Caroline's origins, most of it generated by herself in her attempts to claim direct descent from the noble – indeed royal – families of Scotland. She acquired a certificate from the Lyon Office, authenticator and issuer of Scottish pedigrees, showing descent from a whole line of Stewarts reaching back to one Alexander Stewart, who was 'progenitor' of the Stuart

---

* Most contemporary sources give him the name Patrick Youngson, but the pedigree which Caroline herself had issued names him James. There is a similar disagreement about her mother's name: it is usually given as Isabella (including in the pedigree) but sometimes appears as Marjory. The Lurgan parish registers have nothing to say on the subject.

royal family.* This much-disputed claim was not entirely imaginary. The name Stewart was certainly in her lineage, but it may not have got there in the way she implied. Alternative sources[1] claim that its probable origin was a Scottish officer related to the Earl of Galloway, Major W. Stewart, who had a long affair with her unmarried grandmother while he was stationed in Ireland; the relationship was stable, at least until he was transferred away from the area a few years later, and their two children – Margaret Caroline's mother and a boy named John – were given his name.

If this was the case, then Margaret Caroline was descended through Major Stewart from James Erskine, Earl of Buchan, whose brother Sir Charles Erskine of Alva was James Boswell's great-grandfather – and so the two were distant cousins.[2] She was indeed loosely related to royalty, as was Boswell. The fact that it was on the wrong side of the sheets was something she was less keen to emphasize. Cleverly fudging the issue, she wrote in one of her pamphlets: 'It has been erroneously said in the newspapers, that on my examination I declared myself the daughter of a Scotch nobleman; I never said or intimated the like ... I am the daughter of an untitled man of fashion, in the true signification of the word, and am infinitely too proud even to wish myself descended from any other family than that which I have the honour to derive my birth from, being convinced that there are very few so noble ... none more.'[3]

The childhood of Margaret Caroline, or simply Caroline as she was often to be known,† was lonely and full of sudden

---

* The pedigree describes a splendid set of arms as well as an extraordinarily inappropriate motto: 'Prudentia Praestat'.

† In fact, in earlier life she probably used Margaret. One source has her husband calling her Peggy, and the vicar who married them was apparently unaware that Caroline formed part of her name. However, people who knew her in later life (apart from Boswell, who used both her names together) called her Caroline or Carrie.

upheavals. She had no brothers or sisters. Her father died while she was a baby, and then her mother when she was eight. The family property, never much to start with and mortgaged to the hilt, was lost. The young orphan was sent to be raised by her maternal uncle John Stewart. He was a fairly prosperous farmer, who rented out land and made a good living from the kelp trade. Uncle John treated Caroline generously but sternly, and when she was older he sent her to a boarding school in Downpatrick to be educated and made suitable for marriage upwards into the gentry. In her pamphlet the following affectionate reminiscence is attributed to him: 'I was the guardian of her youth (an orphan at eight years old) – she knew no other parent; I ever loved her as such, and she was all the fondest one could wish: sensible, an elegant accomplished mind, graced with every female virtue; beautiful, well-bred, and to use the poet's words, "of gentle manners, as a soul sincere".'[4]

This was not quite the impression she created at school. According to one account she caused so much trouble there that the other children's parents threatened to take them away if she were not removed. The anonymous author of this report tiptoes with gleeful squeamishness over the specifics of the offence: 'It would be too indelicate to relate the particulars of a criminal incident that happened between her and one of the servants belonging to this school. The fact, with all its aggravating circumstances, is well known in the town of Downpatrick.'*[5] Caroline was expelled; her uncle

* Most of the information in this chapter concerning Caroline's early life in Ireland and London is assembled from somewhat dubious sources, for they are the only sort that exist. The most detailed are three anonymous works published when Caroline had already acquired a reputation for wickedness, which they are only too happy to confirm. They agree on many facts and the chronology they present is internally consistent. The titles are: *Authentic Anecdotes of the Life and Transactions of Mrs Margaret Rudd* (1776), *Genuine Memoirs of the Messieurs Perreau* (1775) and *Prudence Triumphing over Vanity and Dissipation* (1776). The last-named is an anthology compiled from different sources and wavers between sympathy and antipathy towards Caroline. The first two books show occasional

refused to have her back, and she was sent to live with her grandmother, who was no more able to control the teenage tearaway than anyone else.

Before her expulsion Caroline had been doing well at school, and she certainly learned her letters well enough to wield a formidably eloquent pen in adulthood. Throughout her life she displayed an acute intelligence, and the modest curriculum of girls' schools was insultingly easy for her to master. But even more striking than her academic attainments were her blossoming powers in the gentle arts of coquetry and charm. She was barely fourteen, claims another anonymous writer, before she was 'throwing out lures to every young fellow she met with' – with a high success rate.[6]

Popular as she was with the young men of Lurgan, Caroline was an outcast in the eyes of the respectable members of the community, especially the female ones. Wherever she went, there was barely concealed pointing and whispering, and everyone knew what she had done – or was rumoured to have done – at the school. She responded defiantly and began plotting her escape. The obvious route out of town lay with the English soldiers of the 62nd Regiment of Foot, currently garrisoned there. A nomadic population of susceptible youths, they had no ties to Lurgan life and did not disapprove of Caroline in the slightest. At seventeen she ran away with one of them, but did not get far before the young man's commanding officer sent her home. Her second rescuer appeared early the following year, and this time she was more successful. His name was Valentine Rudd.

Rudd was a young lieutenant posted to Ireland on recruitment duty. The son of a prosperous tradesman of St Albans in Hertfordshire, he had risen smoothly through the

---

flashes of understanding, but otherwise maintain a tone mingling sensationalism with disapproval. All three authors claim to have known Caroline personally.

ranks, buying his way from promotion to promotion according to the usual practice. Despite his success in army life, his
personality was far from militaristic. He was easy-going,
impulsive and irresponsible; he liked a drink and enjoyed
good company. Caroline's flirtatious vitality perfectly
matched his character. She swept him off his feet completely.

The courtship was not a long one. The couple announced
their intention to marry just ten days after meeting. Uncle
John Stewart gave his formal consent and on 4 February
1762 Valentine Rudd, Lieutenant, and Margaret Youngson,
spinster, both giving their residence as the parish of Shankill
in the diocese of Dromore, were married in the Anglican
church in Lurgan.

As with almost everything in Caroline's life, there were
later to be dramatically opposed interpretations of this
whirlwind romance. Some thought that Valentine Rudd was
an adventurer who married her in the hope of gaining some
benefit from her family – she was already boastful about her
noble pedigree. Others said that Caroline was after *his* family
wealth. Whatever the colder motives, it seemed a good
match. Rudd was undoubtedly charmed by her, while she
was more than eager to be whisked away by a dashing
officer.

They did not leave Lurgan immediately, however. During
the first year after their wedding they remained there, living
in army quarters as a couple. For Caroline it was at least
more fun than living with her grandmother. She continued to
flirt with her former admirers, as well as acquiring new ones
amongst her husband's fellow officers – to the displeasure of
the other regimental wives.

One of the benefits of married life, she quickly discovered,
was spending her husband's income. She threw herself into
this task with gusto, and Rudd also developed a taste for
flamboyance and luxury. They both spent freely, although
Rudd knew his income could not support it for long, and by
the end of their first year the pair were in serious financial

difficulties. The solution was clear and suited Caroline very well. Rudd's wealthy and generous father in St Albans was keen to meet his son's new wife. He had been told that she was a lady of quality, related to some of the best families in Scotland and Ireland, and he was glad that Valentine had done so well for himself. And so, in 1763, Valentine took temporary leave from his regiment and Caroline said good-bye to her relatives and her home town – which she was never to see again – and the Rudds set sail together for England.

Valentine's family welcomed them warmly, as expected, and gave them all the money they needed. Caroline turned up her charm to full blast, conversing fluently and entertainingly about the nobler branches of her family and hinting to her delighted father-in-law that Valentine was on the brink of getting command of a regiment of his own. Everyone was happy. Caroline enjoyed the novelty of the environment and the opportunity to invent a fresh character for herself in a world where no one knew her past. Best of all, they had money again.

Rudd could not stay away for ever, though; eventually he had to return to his regiment. He left Caroline at his father's house, where she was supposed to settle down in rustic tranquillity for a few years while he built up his career. He visited occasionally, when he could get leave, but most of the time Caroline was left alone with her in-laws.

Things soon turned sour. The pleasure of entertaining the family and being adored by them wore off. There was nothing to do in St Albans, at least nothing that appealed to a woman of Caroline's temperament. Country walks and evenings by the fireside were not for her. Having money was all very well, but there was precious little to spend it on. It seemed as if she had left Lurgan only to find the same scenery in a different land. She was desperately bored, and boredom was the one thing Caroline could never endure for long.

Every time Valentine came home, she begged him to let her

live in London instead. He prevaricated, mindful of the dangers and temptations of the big city for a wife alone – and of its expenses. Caroline grew more and more frustrated and rebellious. At last, in the summer of 1766, she either persuaded him, or simply took matters into her own hands. With or without Rudd's agreement, she left St Albans and set off by herself for London. Valentine was to join her there whenever he next had leave.

When one thinks of eighteenth-century London, one pictures Hogarthian scenes of gin-drinking and merry squalor, but by the 1760s a process of gentrification had begun and a new mood was in the air. There was money in the city: a great deal of it. Gin was passé, though addicts could still be seen around. The public thoroughfares had recently been widened and many ramshackle old houses cleared away, to be replaced by fine new ones. There were pleasure gardens and grand rotundas, all vast and refulgent. Instead of the torrents of 'dead cats and turnip-tops' that used to tumble down watercourses in the streets in Swift's day, there were proper waste pipes and well-regulated sewage systems. Overhanging house signs, which had obstructed the light and groaned like lost souls in the wind, had been removed and replaced by sensible door numbers. Street lighting was so dramatically improved that when the Prince of Monaco came on a state visit to George III he mistook the ordinary lamps of London for a spectacular grand illumination in his honour.[7] London had become, in every sense of the word, a more enlightened city.

At the same time, filth and poverty still existed on a terrifying scale. Crime was rampant, despite the ferocity of the punishments designed to prevent it: death for most felonies, branding, hard labour or the pillory for lesser offences. Muggers and pickpockets prowled the city and gangs of street urchins followed anyone who looked foreign or was dressed too fancily, mocking and taunting. The public

executions at Tyburn were attended by violent and unpredictable mobs, of whom the gentlefolk lived in fear.

London in the 1760s and 1770s was a city full of
contradictions, poised between grimy chaos and a new,
glittering elegance. While some commentators fretted over
the crass materialism and extravagance of the era, others
relished it as an 'Age of Pleasure'. Dickens was later to
describe the instability of the late eighteenth century in simple
terms: 'It was the best of times, it was the worst of times.'

It was also an age of urban expansion, and Caroline joined
a great influx of immigrants to London – many of them from
her own homeland. Life for the Irish in London was a
struggle for survival in difficult conditions, amidst a population who viewed them askance. They were distrusted by
native Londoners for their perceived criminal propensities,
although many also admired their resilience and quick wits.
'Throw an Irishman into the Thames at London Bridge,
naked at low water', went a saying of the time, 'and he will
come up at Westminster Bridge, at high water, with a laced
coat and sword.'[8]

Caroline and London were made for each other. She put
her memories of St Albans and Lurgan behind her and threw
herself into urban life. The first task, finding accommodation,
was not difficult. The city was full of small lodging houses at
all levels of comfort and respectability. Over the next few
years Caroline was to live in a great many of them, some
luxurious, others low and squalid. For the moment she found
one in the upper middle of the range, in the house of a tailor
named Mr Marseilles in Princes Street, just off Hanover
Square – a fashionable address in a modern part of town.

Once settled in, Caroline set out to discover London,
thrilled by its vastness and promise just as Boswell had been
on seeing it for the first time six years previously. She was
alone for a few weeks, but it wasn't long before Valentine
arrived to join her – bringing a surprise announcement. This
time it was to be more than just a holiday. With typical

impulsiveness, he had decided to accept a form of semi-retirement from the army, giving up active service and going on to half-pay.[9] It meant that his time would be his own and he could live with his wife in London. It also meant, however, that they would have less money.

This move sorely disappointed Rudd's father, who had been convinced that his son was on the verge of promotion and glory. An idle life in the lodging houses of London was not at all what he had expected for the boy. Soon after this unpleasant shock, Rudd senior died – of a broken heart, some said.

His death was not a complete tragedy as far as Valentine and Caroline were concerned, for they found themselves the beneficiaries of a generous inheritance of cash and property. For a while they consoled themselves for the bereavement by spending lavishly, and as a result soon became poor again.

And now, four and a half years into their marriage, their relationship began to founder. Much as they each liked London individually, it was a bad influence on them as a couple: there were so many amusing things to do, so many distracting and sophisticated strangers, and so much to buy. Regrets over the squandered inheritance and disagreements over where it had gone took their toll. Paying off debts became a constant, tedious struggle. And then they had never been used to living together twenty-four hours a day. For most of their relationship Valentine had not been there; now he was around all the time, nagging Caroline every time she brought home a new gown or necklace – even though he too was far from frugal. Caroline lost patience with the sight of her not-so-dashing officer lying around doing nothing all day, and she was contemptuous of the way he let himself be manipulated by her; she could always win arguments by sheer winsomeness and charm. He was weak-spirited: he could fly into rages, but rarely exerted any real force over anything. Caroline found him boring and, again, this was not a feeling she could endure passively.

More to the point, there was a good-looking young Irishman upstairs. His name was Benjamin Bowen Read, and he lived alone in the room above them on the second floor. He was a soldier too, a cavalry officer, and he was much more entertaining than Valentine Rudd. Read and Caroline became friends and before long the friendship developed into a full-blown affair. They carried on the liaison behind Rudd's back for a while, but with debts climbing and the marriage getting more and more abrasive, Caroline came to the conclusion that her husband wasn't worth the effort of deception. In November 1766 she abandoned him and ran away with Read.

This was a rash step. Divorce then was virtually impossible, even for wealthy men; for a penniless woman it was out of the question, especially when she was the one who had absconded. The only alternative was to give up all respectability and live as a social outcast, alone or with a lover from whom no guarantees could be expected. Caroline was a pariah again. The anonymity of the big city made this fate at the same time easier and more dangerous than it had been in Lurgan.

Read and Caroline went to the East End and found lodgings first at Ratcliff Highcross, above a tripe shop owned by one Mr Crosby, and later at the house of an apothecary named Bradshaw on the Ratcliff Highway. They were a long way from the gentility of Hanover Square: this was London's port zone – the wildest, saltiest, sleaziest part of town, reeking of bilge water and rotten vegetables and raucous with drunken sailors and prostitutes. Caroline readily adapted, and she and Read led a flamboyant life in this chaotic new setting. She began spending Read's small store of money with just as much enthusiasm and flair as she had Rudd's larger one. As a result Read got into debt for the first time. Before long he had as many creditors on his heels as Rudd, who was now being pursued both for old debts which he and Caroline had contracted and for new ones: while living off Read she continued to charge bills to her husband, giving his address and solemnly assuring merchants of his creditworthiness.

Like separation, debt was a serious matter. To be indebted, and unable either to flee your creditors or to persuade them to accept a friendly instalment plan, meant prison. And prisons were places of vermin, discomfort and overcrowding, dangerous to enter because of the deadly diseases that regularly swept through them. If you were lucky you would be given bread and water, but there was no legal obligation on gaolers to feed debtors and often they did not. If you could not afford to pay for a pallet of straw, you slept on the floor with the rats.

For the moment, both Read and Rudd somehow managed to keep their creditors at bay. At the same time Rudd was energetically trying to trace Caroline, as much because he wanted to stop her spending his money as because he wanted her back as his wife. He found out that she was living at Crosby's tripe shop and went to visit but was not allowed in. Worse, when he told Crosby that he was her husband, the landlord demanded the rent that she and Read had failed to pay for the room.

Rudd refused and left, but his escape was short-lived. Crosby continued to chase him and on 26 February 1767 he had Rudd arrested for debt. He wanted £96 for Caroline's accommodation since November – a very high rent for lodgings in the East End, which should normally be less than that for a whole year. Rudd could not pay it. He still had some property inherited from his father, but was unable to sell it quickly enough. He was sent to prison: first to the Poultry and then to the King's Bench gaol, where – since he had no money for bail – he remained for over three months, until 7 May.

Rudd's problems did not end with his release. Other creditors were on his trail and he still had no money. He took refuge by lodging in a 'spunging house' run by a Mrs Kennedy. Such houses were a compromise between prison and freedom, offering shelter from the demands of the world while doubling as a minor punishment. Rudd stayed in his retreat until August, brooding over his wife's wicked ways and making arrangements to have the rest of his inherited property sold. He also hired a lawyer to embark on the near-impossible task of getting a divorce. The grounds were to be that Caroline had abandoned him for Read; for this it was necessary first of all to get evidence of infidelity and then to serve an affidavit on the other man. But the plan came to nothing and the divorce suit had to be abandoned because, by the time Rudd traced them to Mr Bradshaw's, Read had disappeared.

Caroline's lover had apparently decided on a sudden holiday on the Continent. Prudence dictated escape from Rudd and the burden of debt which the deserted husband was trying so hard to transfer from his own shoulders. In addition, there had been some sort of falling out with Caroline – who would otherwise have gone with him – although it cannot have been too serious because he continued to write to her from abroad.

Now on her own, Caroline moved back into the West End and look lodgings above an oil shop in St Martin's Lane. This part of Soho was hardly more salubrious than the Ratcliff Highway: it was a rundown maze of streets haunted by beggars and streetwalkers. Still, it was closer to the heart of town, and promised more interesting kinds of fun.

It was almost certainly at this period of her life that Caroline embarked on a new career, utilizing the very considerable talent which she had discovered in herself for making 'an impression on the hearts of some dignified persons'.[10] Or in the words of another account, 'rendering feeble and aged lovers exceedingly enamoured of her'.[11]

Her first step into prostitution was probably inspired by necessity. With Read gone and Rudd's name no longer bankable, Caroline had no means of support. She needed to live. Once she had started, however, it became clear that she had discovered her true vocation. Gifted by nature with sharp wits, good dress sense, and a formidable capacity for flirtation, and having at the same time an appreciation of money and what it could buy, she was made to be a *grande horizontale*. She knew how to make men not merely lust after her, but fall deeply in love, which was far more lucrative. As we know from Boswell, she was a pleasure to be with. In her company a man felt strong, agreeable and sophisticated. If he was elderly, he felt young again. She could entertain him with amusing and eloquent conversation and laugh charmingly at his own faltering attempts at wit. And if the gentleman suddenly found the beguiling stream of gaiety and companionship replaced by a wall of ice, a small present would usually melt it: perhaps some jewels or fifty pounds in cash. It was all very easy.

Life was not all wealthy clients and valuable presents: Caroline was destined to experience the whole spectrum of prostitution, including the miserable existence of the cheap and homeless hooker on the streets. For the moment, she started at a modest level in the middle of the scale, but she quickly built up a high-class client base of affluent men who were happy to give her whatever she desired.

Some stories suggest that she was now starting to try her hand at other skills too, though as yet with little success. In one tale, a landlady took pity on her because she had (or appeared to have) no money, and vouched for her creditworthiness to a Long Acre haberdasher so that Caroline could obtain four guineas' worth of goods from him on credit. The haberdasher, Mr Hogard, never received the money he was owed and when Caroline went back to his shop he refused to sell her anything further, particularly not on credit. He accused her of being a 'woman of the town', and not at all the respectable young lady her landlady had said she was. Caroline replied haughtily that she was a lady of wealth and fortune, but was simply short of ready money for the moment. She produced a promissory note for £100 payable to herself thirty days later, and said that all she wanted Hogard to do was to take the note, subtract the value of the goods she had bought earlier as well as the ones she wished to take now, and give her the difference in cash. It would all be paid off, she assured him: there was nothing to worry about. Wisely, Hogard asked her to leave the note while he prepared the things she wanted. He then showed the note around to several friends, who agreed that it was a forgery – and not a very good one. The names of the drawer, the accepter and the endorser were all obviously in the same hand. Hogard tried to trace more information about these names, and found none. They seemed to be imaginary. Caroline got wind of the fact that he was making enquiries about her and never returned. Hogard kept the note until the end of August, when he succeeded in tracking down the long-suffering Valentine Rudd, who paid him what he was owed.

Another story of this period claims that Caroline became involved with a group of con men whose speciality was swindling money out of rich gentlemen by various impostures. Her contribution was to pose as a woman of noble Scottish parentage and great fortune, who was temporarily short of money while she waited for her wealthy husband to come to London and pay all her bills. It worked, to a limited extent, but the gang was caught shortly after she joined them and the scheme ceased, although Caroline herself was never arrested.

Rudd was still living at Mrs Kennedy's spunging house at that time. However, with Read off the scene, Caroline now renewed contact with him. That summer she humbly presented herself to her husband saying that she had finished with Read, was destitute and helpless, and needed help. Rudd stood on his dignity for a while, but eventually his heart melted. In August 1767 he helped her move into new lodgings in Charles Street in Mayfair – a much better part of town – and granted her a maintenance allowance out of the money left from the sale of his property. Now that they were on friendly terms again, Caroline soon returned to Rudd's bed. She assured him that she had mended her ways and that she loved him just as before. He allowed himself to believe it, and moved his own belongings out of Mrs Kennedy's and into her rooms. They enjoyed a second honeymoon.

This pleasant state of affairs did not last. After a few weeks a letter arrived for Caroline from Read. It said that he would be passing through London on his way to Ireland, where he intended to take possession of a large estate he had inherited from an uncle, and that he wanted her to join him. Caroline instantly abandoned the reconciliation with her husband and ran away to join Read. She took a coach to meet him at Guildford in Surrey, bringing one of her landlady's young daughters along with her for the ride. Something nefarious may have happened to the girl, although the only hint of what it might have been is provided by the anonymous author of the *Authentic Anecdotes*, who writes, '*here* the rules of decency and other considerations oblige us to draw a veil, and to omit the particulars of a barbarous transaction'.[12]

This was to be a fleeting episode. Either the reunion with Read was a failure, or Caroline never intended to stay more than a few days anyway. He went on to Ireland and she returned to London, where she acted as if nothing had happened. Rudd now refused to have anything more to do with her. He cleared all the debts at the Charles Street lodgings, but warned the landlady never again to trust her either with the rent, or – more importantly – with her daughters. In November he inserted a notice in the *Daily Advertiser* advising readers not to give her credit in his name: 'Whereas Margaret, wife of Valentine Rudd, gentleman, has withdrawn herself from her husband, this is therefore to caution all persons against giving her credit on her husband's account, as he will not pay any debts she contracts.'[13]

Turned away from the Charles Street house, Caroline moved back into her old lodgings in St Martin's Lane, but was ordered to leave when the landlady found out that her husband would not pay the rent. She must have been on better terms with the man of the house, for she was able to persuade him to vouch for her reliability to the owner of another lodging house, a cider merchant named Mr Hyde. Hyde took her in on the understanding that she was a married lady who was in town for a few months on 'legal business'.[14]

She moved in, but there was no sign of either lawyers or rent, and Caroline went out every evening and stayed away until late at night. Hyde became sure that she was not as described and fretted about getting his money. When he asked her for it, she prevaricated. Then he learned from a neighbour or friend that she had an estranged husband living at Mrs Kennedy's; he tracked Rudd down and demanded the money he was owed. Rudd referred him to the disclaimer published in the newspaper, but Hyde scoffed at it and threatened Rudd with the law. He was an intimidating fellow and Rudd wanted above all else to avoid going back to prison, so he offered to clear the debt by paying a guinea a week. That was no good, said Hyde; he would not accept less than a guinea and a half. It was more than Rudd could afford. He was only earning £32 a year as a lieutenant on half-pay, plus £60 a year interest from the capital left from selling his estate, and paying what Hyde asked would have left him without a penny of his own to live on. So he answered that this was not in his power and Hyde promptly had him arrested.

The case was heard at Westminster Hall several months later, on 26 April 1768. Rudd produced his newspaper advertisement and also explained to the court that he was only in this position because he didn't have enough evidence against Read for 'criminal conversation' with his wife; otherwise it would not be himself but Read who would be responsible for her. The judge declared both arguments worthless. A husband was liable for his wife's debts and that was the end of it: it could not be signed away by a mere notice in the paper. As for the unsubstantiated story about Read, that was simply irrelevant. The court ordered Rudd to pay his debt. He obediently scraped together all the cash he had and gave it to Hyde – but it was not enough, so he was sent to prison anyway.

As a result of these battles, meanwhile, Caroline had been evicted from Hyde's, and she had nowhere to go. The early winter months of 1768 found her completely homeless. There is no telling how she would have rescued herself, but with perfect timing Read came back from Ireland, managed to track her down and took her off the streets into his own lodgings in Soho. There they lived under the name of Captain and Mrs Shee, putting it about that they were people of great property in Ireland. A local Italian hairdresser later said that she knew Mrs Shee was Mrs Rudd because she recognized her from a tiny scar on her neck.

Read and Caroline went on for some months, spending freely and enjoying all the most expensive entertainments around town. In truth they had very little money, and Read was surviving by borrowing from friends. When some of those friends clubbed together and wrote to tell his family in Dublin how Read was living, his father – a respectable alderman – came over to England in March to see for himself and to sort matters out. What he found at Read's apartment was his son in bed with Caroline. Alderman Read ordered him to throw Caroline out and have nothing further to do with her, and Read obeyed, either because he was easily intimidated or because he desperately needed to have a placated father to clear his debts. The alderman stayed on in London for two months, paid off what his son owed and spirited him away to Ireland. Just one debt was reputedly left outstanding, to Mr Marseilles, the landlord of the house where Read had been staying when he first met Caroline.

Alderman Read did not succeed in reforming his son altogether, although he did manage to separate him from his spendthrift mistress. They probably never saw each other again; if they did it was just the once and not for long.* Benjamin Read died a short while later in prison in Dublin, still £300 in debt to Mr Marseilles. It was generally felt that his decline and ruin were entirely to be blamed on Caroline.

Meanwhile, she had gone back on to the streets, to work and possibly to live, but it was only a brief interlude. With Read out of the picture she returned to Rudd, now freed from prison and re-installed at Mrs Kennedy's. She begged his forgiveness and pleaded for another reconciliation. Once more Rudd allowed himself to be won over; he accepted her back and they moved into new lodgings together. They were thrown out by a rapid succession of landladies, but eventually managed to settle down with a Mrs Cranston in Park Street, Mayfair.

Accounts of their life at Mrs Cranston's make it clear why they had been evicted from other places. Caroline went out every night in her finery and brought clients back to the rooms, while Rudd waited fuming in his bedroom next door. The two of them fought constantly and Rudd became more and more violent. 'Great riots there used to be', and once, 'when she came home one morning at daylight, he fired a pistol at her out of the window; and at times he beat her, not moderately, but very severely.' Her body was always covered with bruises.[15] Rudd drank heavily, and for a while suffered from an unidentified illness which kept him bedridden while he listened to Caroline carrying on next door. Even after he recovered he was still weak both physically and mentally, and now began to show signs of real psychological disturbance. His violence intensified.

At last, in March 1769, Caroline ran away from him, determined to endure no more of what she later described as 'his insanity and personal abuse'.[16] In a helpless fury, the abandoned Rudd fled to France.

* See page 40. She claimed to have visited Dublin a few years later, but it is not certain either that she went there or, if she did, that it was to see Read.

Caroline now went through an even harder and more chaotic time. She was often penniless, borrowing money from the daughters of her new landlady and from other people in the house. Even the milkman gave her milk on credit. She passed a few spells in spunging houses, lying low to avoid arrest for debt. As the author of *Authentic Anecdotes* remarks, in a rare burst of generosity, 'To do justice to the philosophy of Mrs Rudd, it is readily allowed that she has experienced the extreams of good and ill fortune; has known how to want as well as to abound.'

She continued to earn money from prostitution and now started working for a pimp, who visited her every day at noon to make arrangements for her evening customers. Occasional wealthy patrons came along: one elderly lord escorted her to fashionable entertainments around town for a few months before becoming worn out and retiring from the scene with 'exhausted finances and debilitated constitution'.[17] Most of her clients, however, were almost as poor as she was. She was repeatedly thrown out of her lodgings and each time she descended a step further down the social scale. At last she ended up living in houses which could be more accurately described as brothels. She reached her lowest point when she moved into an infamous place in Lambeth known as the Coffee House, a filthy warren inhabited exclusively by down-at-heel prostitutes.

However, living in the Coffee House caused her fortunes to take a turn for the better, for there she met a new pimp called Andrew White, with whom she found an immediate rapport. White took her under his wing and set her up with several regular and lucrative clients, including an 'enamoured dotard' from the West End who showered her with clothes and jewels and believed that he was her only true love. Caroline was still 'peculiarly dextrous in making herself agreeable to enfeebled lovers',[18] and her finances improved accordingly. More dotards followed.

Caroline moved into a better house and she and White

experimented with various financial frauds to supplement the prostitution, ranging from impersonation to blackmail. On one occasion a group of thugs came in pursuit of them both in revenge for an unidentified scam; White and Caroline were forewarned and escaped out of a window. They found new accommodation and started up afresh, but not for long; they moved from house to house and had no fixed abode for a while. White often lodged with her in shared rooms; in other places Caroline lived alone and went by the name of Mrs Read or Mrs Gore. Thriving on this unpredictable life, she recovered all her old panache.

In one house, with the rent far in arrears as usual and no money forthcoming, the landlady lost her patience and confronted Caroline, demanding to be paid.[19] Appearing profoundly shocked, Caroline told her that she was astonished at being importuned for such a trifle. However, if it was really so important, something could be arranged. She summoned her footman and ordered him to go to her husband – a wealthy lawyer currently detained on business in the provinces – to obtain the cash, and also to tell him to send his carriage for her at once so she wouldn't have to stay another night in the house of such an ill-bred person. The footman (who was very likely White) duly departed. The landlady now became apologetic. She had no choice, she said: she was poor and needed the money, but had never meant to cause such offence.

The footman knew his job. That afternoon he returned bearing a note to Caroline, which she showed to the landlady. It was signed by the husband and contained an elegant apology. He was obliged to remain in the country for the rest of the day, he wrote, but if he could possibly get away in time he would call at the banker's and bring three times the amount of money owed. In any case he would come to collect his wife, either that evening or the following morning. The landlady was completely reassured and more embarrassed than ever.

The next day, however, no husband had appeared and the landlady's suspicions were rekindled. Caroline and the footman had been packing all morning – 'and probably more than they well could call their own'. They would neither open their door nor answer the questions the landlady called through it. She consulted with a neighbour, who advised her to call an officer into the house. All day she and the officer sat waiting, but there was nothing but silence from upstairs. At midnight, Caroline thought the coast was clear and sent the footman to tiptoe down and get a carriage. The officer overheard everything and they were caught in the act of sneaking out with their baggage.

Caroline apparently spent 'a few hours' in prison for this incident – but she managed to extricate herself very quickly. Not for the first time, her combination of sharp wits, charm and audacity got her out of trouble.

Her finances began to pick up after this: she started lucrative relationships with a number of regular clients, including a 'noble Nabob of immense wealth'[20] who reportedly gave her £800 a year for just an occasional visit. She also continued to dabble in blackmail, once brazenly following home a Lord who had been visiting a married lady in another room of the house she lived in, ringing the doorbell and demanding money from him to keep her mouth shut.

Among the gentlemen rumoured to have connections with her was John Manners, the Marquis of Granby. He was a rollicking military man, brave in battle and greatly loved by the soldiers under his command, but prone to flinging around money at the gambling table and elsewhere. Having fallen into debt in his youth, he married an heiress for her wealth, but the young lady squandered most of it before the wedding. He died relatively young, of gout, leaving behind a debt of £37,000 – a colossal amount.[21] That some of this money had gone into Caroline's pocket is suggested by various sources. 'It is well known', said an article about him in the *Morning Post* at the height of Caroline's notoriety, 'that [he] lavished away very considerable sums upon women of easy virtue, and that Mrs R—dd, whose name makes such a conspicuous appearance in the Newgate Chronicle, participated, in no small degree, in his generosity.'[22]

Another name linked with Caroline's by the gossip-mongers was that of the Duke of Cumberland,[23] also a notorious rake. She herself allegedly boasted of involvement with 'two royal personages', of whom Cumberland may have been one.[24] And then there were the rumours concerning Boswell's friend John Wilkes, though little ever came of these.

During this period Caroline met a man who was to become one of her best clients. Joseph Salvador was a wealthy Sephardic Jew in his early fifties whose main distinction was an extraordinary naïveté. A lover of variety, he liked to maintain regular arrangements with a number of women at the same time. He could become quite besotted with one he liked, such as Caroline, but at the same time 'was of such an amorous disposition, that every woman was alike to him'.[25] Caroline catered to this undiscriminating enthusiasm single-handedly by passing for as many as four different women. She changed the colour and style of her hair and dress – and also, significantly, changed her handwriting: a skill that was to come in useful later on. Often she simply pretended to be her own sister, but sometimes she went further afield. On one occasion she arranged a meeting with him in Paris in the guise of a French countess. Even though a servant of Salvador's recognized her when he saw her again in London and tried to enlighten his employer, Salvador refused to believe it. It was blind love, wishful thinking, stupidity, or all three.

He continued to be Caroline's most devoted regular for some years. 'She condescended to appear abroad in her friend's equipage, had her apartments new furnished by his tradespeople, and passed whole weeks with him occasionally at his villa' – a glorious house in the pastoral village of Tooting.[26] She kept him dangling on her string with the greatest of ease, performing additional swindles whenever the need or desire arose.

She thus 'played upon him so artfully that in a short time she squeezed from him near fifteen hundred pounds', wrote someone going by the name of 'An Old Observer' in the *Town and Country Magazine*.[27] 'Not contented with his cash, she fixed her mind upon several pieces of his most valuable furniture; and took a great fancy to some of his most costly plate and curiosities. These she carefully packed up, and sent to town . . . She often did him the honour of her visits, in one of which she took with her, for convenience, a couple of carts, and brought away as much furniture as would equip a genteel house.'

Once Caroline announced to Salvador that she wished to give up the London life and retire to a convent in France. Although he was heartbroken, he gave her the money to pay for the journey. She took it, but travelled to Scotland instead. From there she arranged to have letters posted to him purporting to be written from the convent. At first they described the tranquil charms of the retreat, but as time went by she sounded increasingly lonely and eventually she sent a message saying that she had had enough and was missing Salvador too much to stay: she wanted to come home but could not afford it. He had a messenger send the money to her at once. She contrived to have it brought to her in Scotland, and returned to London pleasantly refreshed from her holiday.[28]

The schemes continued, each more daring and openly contemptuous of his intelligence than the last. She told Salvador that she would marry him if he wished, so he bought her a splendid array of clothes and jewels for the wedding – but at the last minute it was called off. A few years later she blackmailed him with a pregnancy, saying he was the father when he almost certainly was not. When cleverer schemes failed, she was not above simply having a note delivered saying, 'Send me fifty pounds now, or you will not see me tomorrow.'

A typical tale about Salvador reveals as much about his mixture of generosity and folly as it does about Caroline's wiles.[29] She told him that she wished to go to Ireland to see her relations, who needless to say were of the highest nobility. (The true reason could have been to visit Read.) According to Caroline's story, her family had disowned her after her disastrous marriage to a man of whom they disapproved and who had indeed turned out to be cruel and neglectful. Now that she had left him, they were willing to renew contact. However, she could afford neither to pay for the trip nor to present herself in the style that would be expected by a family of quality. Salvador accordingly gave her money for the fare and took her to a jeweller, who fitted her out with a beautiful set of jewels for the occasion.

Caroline was away for some weeks; when she came back and met Salvador she was visibly distressed, wringing her hands and weeping. Salvador begged her to tell him what was the matter, but she would not say. He persisted and eventually extracted the story. On the very last day of her stay, she had run into her dreaded husband at the docks in Dublin. He had chased her and seized her by the waist as she tried to escape, and had felt the outline of the jewel box in her pocket. When he demanded to know what it was, Caroline reluctantly showed him the jewellery. It belonged to him as much as to her, said the wicked husband, and whatever she chose to do with her person he was entitled to a share of her property. He grabbed at the box. There was a tussle and the jewels were accidentally knocked into the water, where they sank to the bottom at once. And now she could not forgive herself for the loss of Salvador's precious gift, nor could she expect him to pardon her carelessness.

Salvador was only too delighted to find that her misery had such a trivial cause and was so easily mended. He wiped away her tears and sent a servant to the jeweller to buy replacements. And so Caroline became the richer by two sets of jewels instead of one.

Margaret Caroline Rudd was now at the height of her powers. She was twenty-five years old, energetic, bold and clever. Although neither more nor less beautiful than many other fashionable young women in London, she had made herself irresistible. 'Her powers of pleasing in a certain degree, have been well attested by many martyrs,' wrote one author. She was articulate, with a 'happy, insinuating flow of language', at ease with herself and able to take control in almost any situation. 'Airs of address, gentility and importance are distinguishing features of our heroine's character; and it is allowed to her credit, that she is perfectly acquainted with every sphere of life, and never at a loss how to behave in company of the peer or the porter.'

Caroline owed her success, as well as her later disasters, to an extraordinary combination of intelligence and sheer nerve. Both were in full bloom at this stage of her life, and although they frequently got her into a great deal of trouble they never let her down when she needed to get out of it again.

We leave her in the spring of 1770 as she once more moves into new lodgings, this time under the name of Mrs Gore. The new house was that of Mrs Johnston, in Wardour Street in Soho, and it was there that she met the man who was to become the most important figure in her life.

CHAPTER
THREE
—— ◆ ——
THE MACARONI

The Perreau brothers were identical twins; Daniel was the elder of the two, his brother Robert younger by just a few minutes. They came into the world on 22 July 1733 on the island of St Kitts in the West Indies.[1]

The history of their family was one of fortunes alternately made and lost. The twins' grandfather, whose name was also Daniel Perreau, was a Huguenot refugee who fled France after the Revocation of the Edict of Nantes in 1685 and joined the large community of exiles in London. Although he had been a wealthy man in France, he was forced to abandon everything in the rush to escape and never regained any degree of prosperity. He settled down well in his new country, however, marrying a woman named Esther Perdriau and having four children: a boy who was also christened Daniel as well as three girls, one named Susannah and two named Esther.[2] One of the latter died before the other was born – recycling names in this way was common practice. On the death of Daniel senior the family was left with very little money and the three children were all set to learn trades. The two daughters became respectively a milliner and a maker of the women's gowns known as mantuas, while Daniel studied banking. He had no vocation for it, however: there was 'a vivacity in his composition which plainly indicated his disrelish of the dry study of figures'.[3] Instead he managed to get himself a job in the Windward Isles, and set sail for St Kitts in search of excitement and success.

He found both, and also a wife: the Attorney-General's daughter Elizabeth Breton. Her family was well off and Daniel was able to buy a small plantation from which he quickly built up a sizeable fortune, reversing the Perreau family's decline. However, perhaps spurred on by exhilaration at their success, the couple proceeded to produce a family so enormous that the silver spoon had to be divided into ever-diminishing shares.[4] Most of the children were sent to England as they reached school age, to be lodged with relatives and apprenticed to various trades. On reaching adulthood they generally chose to stay where they were; some of the girls found husbands and embarked on genteel provincial lives.

The twin brothers were the eldest in the family, so they were the first to leave home and set the pattern. They were separated and sent to learn different occupations. Daniel went to Coventry and was trained in the traditional Huguenot line of silk trading, while Robert was apprenticed to an apothecary called Mr Tribe in London.

Robert did very well in his field. Tribe had a successful business in Pall Mall, and when he died a few years later the still youthful Robert was entrusted with its control. At first he worked as a manager, with the profits going to the master's widow, but later she sold the business to him and he ran it on his own behalf. He moved premises to Oxendon Street, off Piccadilly Circus, where he developed an increasingly loyal, high-class clientele. It was a great success story for the young man and he was well thought of by all who had dealings with him.

Genuine Memoirs of the Messieurs Perreau supplies a romantic version of Robert's courtship and marriage, whilst throwing in a little entertaining sleaze for good measure.[5] In St Kitts, the Perreau family had been friendly with a neighbour named Walter Thomas, who had two daughters of similar ages to Robert and Daniel. The girls had also been sent to London, where they lodged with the twins' aunts, Esther and Susannah – the milliner and the mantua-maker. Robert was a frequent visitor there and soon became friendly with the elder Miss Thomas; the younger girl, Henrietta, was usually away at boarding school and he saw her less frequently. During this period the older sister became embroiled in a drama. A Welshman called 'W——s' (most likely Williams) made up his mind to marry her and, when he was rejected despite tireless pestering, attempted to abduct her by force. He was defeated by the mantua-maker, 'a fine tall woman', who physically wrestled him out of the door. Williams then claimed that he had in fact already married the girl in a 'Fleet marriage' – a form of instant wedding usually conducted for financial convenience – and that the Perreau aunts had kidnapped her from him. He took the case to court, producing witnesses claiming to have been present at the wedding. Since these witnesses were unable even to identify Miss Thomas in the courtroom, however, they were discredited at once and he lost the case. Williams fled back to Wales, managed to get himself ordained as a clergyman and later died in a shipwreck on his way to the West Indies.

While she was being besieged by this unsavoury character, Miss Thomas had developed a crush on her friend Robert Perreau, who was now an extremely handsome young man. But her feelings were not reciprocated. Sadly for her, he had instead taken a fancy to her younger sister, now returned from school. The elder girl bowed out of the contest gracefully and later married a Welsh lawyer – the courtroom drama with Williams apparently not putting her off the Welsh so much as giving her a soft spot for lawyers. The wedding of Robert Perreau and Henrietta Alice Thomas took place on 2 February 1758 at the church of St Martin-in-the-Fields.

The young couple moved into the moderately fashionable

address of Golden Square, not far from Robert's shop. Their first child, Susannah, was christened in St Martin-in-the-Fields on 1 January 1759; a boy followed and was christened Robert Samuel Perreau on 29 December 1760. They were to have more children – seven in total – but four of them did not survive infancy and were buried in the same church, creating a substantial family tomb. Only three lived long enough to see their father become the 'unfortunate' Robert Perreau.

While Robert consolidated his business and established his family, Daniel struggled along much less successfully in the silk trade. The work bored him and he hated Coventry. He wrote to his aunts in London and begged them to let him come to live with them instead. The reply was curt – he should stay where he was and work hard at establishing himself. Daniel left Coventry anyway and 'fairly walked it to London'.[6] He had very little money at the start of the journey and his pockets were completely empty by the time he breasted the hill at Highgate and saw the city spread out before him – standing on the same spot where James Boswell was to gasp at his first view of London a few years later. Daniel 'hummed a tune during his downhill walk', and by evening had reached the centre of town.

Having nowhere else to go, he turned up on his aunts' disapproving doorstep. As it happened they were away for a few days, and the only people there were two of his own sisters, Henrietta and Susannah – usually known as Hetty and Sukey. They let him stay, and by the time the milliner and the mantua-maker returned home Daniel had settled in. The aunts agreed that he could live with them if he would tidy up his appearance and look for work, and Daniel was prepared to do anything rather than go back to Coventry.

The aunts arranged a job for him, still in the silk business. Working in the Huguenot area of Whitechapel, Daniel's task was to 'beat the round of his master's customers, with a bag full of samples under his arm'.[7] He liked neither the customers nor the samples and complained about it to his aunts: wasn't there anything else he could do? They conferred and decided that he might make something of himself if he went abroad. This idea pleased him, and it was agreed that he should train as a merchant in order to seek his fortune overseas. He signed up at an academy near the Haymarket to learn accounting and other necessary mercantile skills.

At the academy he began to show signs of 'a strong passion for such gaudy trifles, as only served to please or gratify a weak mind':[8] gambling, fine clothes, theatre-going and all sorts of dissipation. According to *Genuine Memoirs*, which makes up in detail and verve for whatever it may lack in accuracy, he now became the toy-boy of a notorious lady by the name of 'Miss la R——he' (presumably Roche). Daniel was as good-looking as Robert – they were, of course, identical – and if anything had a more charismatic air than his brother. He and Miss la Roche wasted no time in commencing an affair, for 'bashfulness was not his vice, nor delicacy hers'. She improved his dress sense, took him to expensive tailors and hairdressers and taught him 'all the gallantries of a smart fellow'. In short, she supervised Daniel's metamorphosis into a 'macaroni', the contemporary term for a dandyish young man of fine plumage and loose morals.

When her work was complete, Miss la Roche lost interest in him, as she was 'accustomed to change her lovers with the same ease as she changed her clothes'. But Daniel retained his taste for high living, although without her patronage he could no longer afford it, and became impatient with the dull life he was leading in the academy and at home with his aunts.

Genuine Memoirs provides an entertaining account of how eventually he managed to break away and sail for exotic shores. One day, after waiting for a cart to pass so that he could cross the street, Daniel saw a gold watch glinting in the dust near the wheel tracks. A young woman on the other side of the street saw it too and they rushed to pick it up at the same time. Exercising his new-found gallant's skills, Daniel offered to share the find with her and asked for her address so he could sell the watch and bring her half of the money. She hesitated at first, but eventually told him where she lived.

Before he had a chance to sell it, Daniel saw an advertisement in the newspaper offering a reward of five guineas for the lost watch, describing its appearance and the area where it had disappeared. He took the advertisement to show the young woman that evening, and told her he would collect the reward the next day and bring half of it to her. The next morning he called at the address provided in the paper, but there discovered that the man who had lost the watch was someone he knew, an eminent merchant from the academy. Now Daniel had a problem. It would be ungentlemanly to claim a reward from an acquaintance, yet the young lady was expecting two and a half guineas from him.

He decided to give the watch back for free and try to explain matters to the young woman as best he could, hoping that she would not only give up the money willingly, but would also admire his honourable behaviour. She did neither. Instead, she simply assumed that Daniel had decided to keep all the money for himself and berated him loudly, being 'firmly and pertly resolved' to have her share. There was only one way out for Daniel: he had to pay her the two and a half guineas out of his own pocket.

Yet the story had a happy ending after all. The owner of the watch was so impressed that Daniel had waived the reward that he sought the young man out at the academy, and offered him a job on the fleet he was currently equipping to sail to Guadeloupe. So Daniel quickly got his affairs in order, bade farewell to his family and set off for a new life.

Once arrived in Guadeloupe, Daniel established himself in a trading partnership with a Scotsman bearing the auspicious name of Martin Jollie.[9] The business boomed at first and Daniel threw grand parties and entertainments, which were lapped up by the fashionable colonial crowd. But the profits were squandered, the business died and Daniel became penniless again. During the decline he acquired a serious gambling habit born of desperation, which contributed to his further ruin. The socialites lost interest. Daniel lingered on in Guadeloupe uncertainly for a while, then moved on to try again elsewhere.

For several years he drifted around the West Indies, then went up into North America to try his luck as a trader on the Canadian frontier. Even in the remote wilderness he managed to fritter away profits and he failed there too. There was something about Daniel that attracted disaster. Besides his extravagance and addiction to gambling, he suffered from bad business sense, lack of realism and a naïve tendency to trust the wrong people.

At last, after several years of wandering, he returned to England, partly to chase some old business debts from Guadeloupe days and partly because all else had failed. However, he had as many creditors as debtors in London and so plunged straight into a sea of troubles. His aunts were displeased with him and showed no inclination to help. 'A broken merchant, and with very slender finances, he met with a *freezing* reception from his relations.'[10] And, despite being a hunted man, Daniel did not protect himself by lying low. He spent any money he could raise on living it up in fashionable theatres and coffee shops, making himself visible and gambling recklessly.

His gambling now mainly took the form of 'stock-jobbing', or betting on economic and political events. This form of speculation, although essentially similar to trading in today's stock market, was then considered just as disreputable as gaming at the card table. Indeed, it was regarded with even more suspicion because of the huge sums of money involved and the aggressive atmosphere in the coffee houses where trading took place. Daniel's favourite was the best known of these, Jonathan's Coffee House, in Exchange Alley, Cornhill.

Jonathan's was a tumultuous, feverish place, where fortunes could be blown in moments. The writer George Stevens[11] visited it out of journalistic curiosity and described how his ears were assailed by a deafening clamour as he walked through the door: rude young men who looked like schoolboys ran back and forth yelling: 'Long, Long, Long – Navy, Navy, Navy, Navy – 4 per cents. 4 per cents – India bonds, bonds bonds, bonds.' There was a thick fug of smoke and a babble like Billingsgate fish market. When Stevens and his companion finally managed to struggle through the crowd to a table and tried to order some coffee – since it was, after all, a coffee house – the waiter said, 'No, Sir, no coffee here; and if you don't like to stay here without coffee, you must go out: you don't belong here, and there's nobody wants to have you here.' The faces Stevens saw around him were distorted by greed: the upper lip of one was 'drawn up by an involuntary grin' so that his mouth resembled 'an old wound, the edges of which were shrunk back, and the bones left bare'. Another had 'a large bushy bob, frizzed out as stiff as so many entangled wires' and a face 'not above the dimensions of a twelvemonth-old infant'. It was a grotesque, thrilling environment.

Cynics deplored the way in which speculation in Exchange Alley influenced international relations and matters of life and death:

> Here the daily Lie encreases;
> Now it's *War*; and now it *Peace* is;
> Judge you for what this is meant, Sir?
> To get Things up Ten per Cent, Sir.[12]

Daniel's luck was such that if he gambled on a peace treaty there would be war, and if he bet on war, peace would break out instead. Nevertheless, occasionally he made good and he got lucky just often enough to survive his more catastrophic losses. When things went well he was flamboyant with his earnings, and even when they went badly he dressed smartly and attended fashionable parties. He was a full-fledged macaroni now: his wits were nimble, his conversation sparkling, his manners impeccable. He was always the centre of attention. Women adored him.

His only problem was the posse of creditors on his trail, and it was not long before they caught up with him. Debtors' prison threatened – but he succeeded in having himself formally declared bankrupt on 4 May 1770. This was a gift. With his debts wiped out at a stroke, Daniel buried the bankruptcy statement in a bottom drawer and carried on exactly as before.

During Daniel's absence in the West Indies, Robert had been steadily thriving in his apothecary's business and enjoying a modest but comfortable domestic existence with his wife and children in Golden Square. If most accounts are to be believed, this virtuous life was now blown out of the water by Daniel's reappearance in London. The more reckless brother tempted Robert off the straight and narrow, mocking his dullness, flaunting handfuls of cash and enticing him into whatever get-rich-quick plan was currently uppermost in his mind.

Not everyone agreed with this picture. Robert's enemies were later to claim that Robert's bourgeois life had only ever been a hypocritical veneer over a secret tumult of vices, from compulsive gambling to fornication. A putative mistress, Miss Matthews, was pointed to.*[13] Some even said that it

* A gossipy piece entitled 'Histories of the tête-à-tête annexed; or, Memoirs of the E. of A——m and Miss M–th–ws' in the *Town and Country Magazine* linked Miss Matthews primarily to the Earl of Ancram, who was later rumoured to be a lover of Caroline's as well, but the article also indicated that Miss Matthews had previously been the mistress of Robert Perreau. The latter had apparently 'hired an elegant lodging near Portman-square, and furnished it in a costly manner; he also made her a present of a black servant, and she lived in a most luxurious stile'. Miss Matthews met Caroline, believing her to be Robert's sister-in-law. However, when she found out about Caroline's 'real character' she decided no longer to associate either with her or with Robert himself – strange, since Miss Matthews herself was supposed to be a prostitute in all but name.

was Robert who lured Daniel into Exchange Alley, not the other way round.[14]

Whichever interpretation is followed, Robert's personality must have been a peculiar mix of caution and recklessness: he generally proceeded much more sensibly in life than the ne'er-do-well Daniel, but there was something darker under the surface, even if it was nothing more than a susceptibility to temptation. The two brothers, looking so alike that people could tell them apart only by their style of dress, shared a complex, Janus-headed nature.

With Daniel living in London again, they became deeply entangled in each other's lives. They lent each other money, collaborated on financial schemes and frequently dined together in Golden Square. A day rarely passed in which they did not see one another at least once, and it was common for there to be several visits in one day.

The fateful first meeting of Daniel Perreau and Margaret Caroline Rudd occurred in April 1770. There are various versions of exactly how it happened. According to the *Authentic Anecdotes of the Life and Transactions of Mrs. Margaret Rudd* and Daniel's own account of events,[15] they were introduced by an acquaintance called Garret Burton, who was living in the same house as Caroline. *Authentic Anecdotes* goes on to say that the attraction was instant and that the very next day they went together to a masquerade party, from which they adjourned to 'a certain retreat in Leicester Fields, always open for the reception of both sexes', where the affair was inaugurated without further ado.

Genuine Memoirs, more poetically, portrays them meeting at the masquerade itself. It festoons the encounter with so much premonitory symbolism that it is almost certainly a fantasy.[16] According to the story, Daniel appeared in 'an extraordinary garb, one side of which represented a skeleton, the other a proper handsome figure'. It was a marvellous costume: 'Everyone was struck with the oddity, and the cry of "it is he," "it is he," was at length re-echoed by some dozens, males and females, from all quarters of the room, who were too well acquainted with his voice and abilities to be mistaken.' Caroline, dressed in 'an elegant domino' – a masquerade cloak with a hood to cover the face – surreptitiously followed him for a while, but at last he spotted her and, as was the custom at masquerades, challenged her to identify him. 'One half of you seems no ineligible acquaintance' she replied elaborately, 'but the horrid memento of mortality you bear about you on the other, is an insuperable impediment to my gratifying a curiosity I own your expressions have excited.' If he wished to speak to her, she said, he should 'assume a less terrible shape'. Daniel accordingly divested himself of the skeletal half, 'and soon a handsome domino whispered such things in the lady's ear as were best calculated to win her heart'.

The next day Daniel made enquiries of all his friends about the mystery woman. The general rumour was that she was a mistress of a 'Mr S——' (presumably Salvador), from whom she had earned a considerable fortune. Daniel went to visit her and found that her lodgings were 'rather commodious than elegant; their situation somewhat obscure, in a little street not many miles from Soho' – not a setting that implied the possession of a great fortune. Still, he was sufficiently impressed with her personal qualities and her elegant manner to pursue the relationship.

Caroline soon told him all about herself, omitting the fact that she was married but going into great detail about her pedigree. 'Her history, when told in her own words, was not a little romantick.' Daniel 'condoled, he sympathized with the amiable lady, who, on a single hour's acquaintance, had been so abundantly communicative; and before he took his leave, such an everlasting friendship was settled between them, that they were to share each other's future prosperity or adversity'.

Caroline herself said that their 'union' did not take place

until 20 May 1770 – just sixteen days after the date on his bankruptcy statement, as she later discovered when she was snooping through his possessions.[17] By the end of that month, they were living together at Mrs Johnston's as a married couple. 'From the moment we lived together I considered myself in every sense his wife,'[18] wrote Caroline later.

Daniel's family did not take to Caroline at first. The aunts turned up their noses and Robert's wife Henrietta disapproved as well, although she concealed her opinion under a veneer of courtesy. Robert himself had reservations, but he was very close to Daniel and could not avoid getting to know Caroline; eventually he grew to trust her. It was hard, especially for a man, to feel cold towards her for long. 'Her person . . . was exceedingly agreeable, her manners engaging: she surprised, she pleased, she interested him in her welfare,' says *Genuine Memoirs* of her conquest of Robert. Once he had been won over, his wife came to accept her as well – or at least to pretend to. Later Daniel's sisters Hetty and Sukey also became friendly. To some extent, Caroline was able to charm women as well as men, or at least to present the appearance of respectability which a ladylike acquaintance demanded.

From the start the relationship between Daniel and Caroline was financially complicated. They each later wrote descriptions of their early years together, giving completely opposite accounts of who was borrowing from whom. In Caroline's version Daniel was desperately short of cash when she met him, and she immediately began bailing him out. She was very willing to do this, she said, and even took care to do it delicately so he should not feel embarrassed at being supported by a woman. 'My feelings on this point have ever been so refined,' she wrote; 'I studied to know his wants to relieve them unasked.'[19] According to her, this money was then squandered by Daniel and his brother on reckless gambling and stock-jobbery. He even pawned her possessions without her permission, to raise money.[20]

Daniel told a different story. In the account written by him for presentation at his trial, he said that he realized soon after meeting Caroline that she was indebted to a number of people. A silk merchant called Ryder came to demand £60 from her, and a milliner by the name of Smith also claimed £80. Daniel was alarmed and wanted to break off the affair, but she persuaded him otherwise and he cleared her debts just in time to save her from gaol. He also paid her rent for July, he said, as well as 39 shillings to a mantua-maker and 23 shillings to her porter James Lacey.[21]

In October Daniel was to have a severe shock. Valentine Rudd came back from France.

Daniel did not know there was a husband in the case at all, and certainly not one as violent and irrational as Rudd, who was now seriously deranged. His months drifting around France had done nothing to improve his sanity and he was also destitute, having used up every last penny of his inheritance. Friends supported him in London, giving him food and letting him stay in their houses, and one of them must have told him that his wife was living with Daniel at Mrs Johnston's. He came after them in a murderous rage.

Fortunately Daniel and Caroline were out at the time; when they returned home the servants told them of the madman who had been pounding on the door. Caroline hastily filled Daniel in, detailing the beatings she had suffered from her husband and the way in which she had been forced to flee for her life. She warned him that she believed Rudd capable of anything and said that they should hide for their own safety. They hurriedly packed up their possessions, and Daniel used a windfall from a recent gambling win to rent a fine, secure apartment for them in Pall Mall.

Rudd never did track them down. In May 1771 his friends clubbed together to buy him a ticket to Ireland and he left London for good. He was to live in Dublin for many years in miserable circumstances, apparently never seeing Caroline again. An acquaintance who visited him in October 1775 found him occupying a small garret room 'in the most abject condition, loaded with filthy rags designed as bedcloaths, covered with vermin. His person all squalid and foul, and the apartment of such a putrid smell that it was impossible to remain there.'[22]

Whether he was suffering from delusions or was in fact the victim of Caroline's vengefulness, Rudd was to claim that her network of friends and relations wielded a sinister power over his life even in Ireland. A letter purportedly written by him in March 1776 claimed that he had had 'Mrs Rudd's friends to combat with' on arrival there, and that they were the cause of his poverty. 'I have been robbed, cheated and persecuted from place to place where-ever I have been,' he wrote.[23]

After his departure, Caroline considered herself entirely free from her marital bond. By 1776 she was telling Boswell that she was curious to investigate a man in Ireland who might be her husband,[24] but nothing seems to have come of that. Rudd went on in his degraded state for twenty years. At some point he moved back to his home town of St Albans, where he lived in an almshouse. Many years after the first rumours of Caroline's death, he remarried,* and died in 1809.[25]

Back in 1771, Daniel and Caroline continued to have a fine life together. Their relationship was flourishing and Caroline was now pregnant. They spent March to June of that year in Paris, supposedly setting up a small bank in partnership with a gambling colleague of Daniel's, Colonel George Kinder – a man who was later to become viciously inimical towards Caroline. The scheme fizzled out and the bank was never mentioned again, but they had a pleasant holiday – partly financed by Caroline's client Joseph Salvador.

She still had Salvador well and truly under her control, and

---

* He married a widow by the name of Judith Briggs on 8 October 1798 and they lived in the almshouse together until he died.

continued masquerading for his benefit as a number of different women. A servant working for her at the time, Mrs Dickinson, delivered letters from Salvador to Caroline, some addressed to Mrs Gore and others to Lady Caroline Gower. Mrs Dickinson watched as Caroline replied to the letters in two different styles of handwriting. She warned Salvador about the deception, but he refused to believe her.

Far from being obliged to give Salvador up because of her pregnancy, Caroline turned it to lucrative effect by telling him that he was the father. Salvador was delighted, and celebrated by renting and furnishing an apartment for her. She gave every appearance of taking up residence there and he came to call almost every day.

Daniel was supposed to have heard Salvador's name mentioned when he had first enquired about Caroline, but accounts differ as to whether he knew she was still seeing him. Some writers claimed that the couple conspired together to come up with schemes for fleecing Salvador, referring to him contemptuously as 'the old woman'. Daniel once allegedly pretended to be Caroline's husband and to have discovered that Salvador was writing letters to his wife. He challenged Salvador to a duel, but when Salvador turned up in Hyde Park at dawn as appointed no one was there. A few days later Caroline told him that her husband was planning to take out a lawsuit for 'criminal conversation'. Salvador panicked and Caroline said that in reality her husband cared only for money. If a large quantity of it was sent to him he could easily be persuaded to abandon the claim. Salvador gladly paid up and Daniel and Caroline enjoyed the proceeds together.*[26]

This was one version. Daniel, instead, said that he knew nothing about Salvador until he accidentally opened a letter

---

* *Town and Country Magazine* tells the same story, but instead of presenting it as a scam asserts that Daniel did intend to fight Salvador. Caroline persuaded him to take money instead.

from him to Caroline. It was a fairly innocent communica-
tion, merely requesting another woman's address, but he
confronted Caroline with it. She told him that Salvador was a
man she'd received letters from in the past, and who had
'afforded her more pleasure and amusement than any
comedy or novel she had ever read',[27] but that she now had
no further involvement with him. Daniel ambushed Salvador
and demanded to know what was going on; Salvador
muttered something about wanting the address of Caroline's
sister (very probably one of Caroline's alter egos). Daniel
knew that she had no sister and was suspicious, but could
prove nothing further, and eventually the incident was
forgotten.

On 30 July Caroline gave birth to a daughter, whom they
named Susan. Salvador received a message saying that
Caroline had gone into labour, but when he arrived he was
told that the baby was already born and had been sent to 'a
great personage's nursery'. Caroline never allowed him to see
this child, whom he believed to be his own, and it is a
measure of her dominance over him that he was unable to
insist on his paternal rights. Apparently she herself had no
doubts that Daniel was the father. She almost certainly
employed some form of contraception with her clients;
condoms were widely used in the profession at the time.
Presumably she told Salvador that it had broken on this
occasion.

The relationship eventually died out, either because Caroline lost interest when money became available from other
sources or because Salvador finally wised up. One day, some
time after the end of their relationship, he met her by accident
in the street. He followed her home to the apartment in Pall
Mall, which she had not told him about, and knocked angrily
on the door. When she answered he demanded to know if she
were not 'his lady Caroline'. She replied that she had never
seen him before in her life, and scolded him for his
impertinence. But perhaps, she said, you're that old villain

who ruined my sister? She threatened him with the law and rang the bell to order the servants to take him before the magistrate. Outwitted once more, Salvador ran off and never dared approach her door again.

A detailed portrait of Caroline's life with Daniel is given by a woman named Christian Hart, who was employed by her as a maidservant and who was later to figure importantly in her trial – after which, like many of those involved, she published a book.[28] Born Christian Mackay, of parents who had played a glorious role in the Jacobite uprising of 1745* – a fact of which she was very proud – she had grown up to marry a carpenter and settle down into a servant's life. She came to work for Caroline just before the move to Pall Mall. Mrs Hart's account of their first meeting at Mrs Johnston's lodging house is rhetorically addressed to Caroline in the grammatical form which might be called 'second person contemptuous':

> I had the misfortune of being hired your servant: at which time, I affirm to the world, you had not the least appearance of a person of fortune . . . When I came to you Mr. Perreau was sitting by Mrs. Johnston . . . You was then looking through a long deal box and taking out some shabby cloaths, two dirty sacques and petticoats trimmed with gauze, two or three old washing gowns, &c.[29]

Mrs Johnston's mother introduced Christian Hart, mentioning her family heritage and saying that she deserved to be employed as a lady's maid rather than as a lowly kitchen

---

* According to Mrs Hart's account, both parents had been actively involved. Her mother had handed down a collection of twenty-four fragments of bone which she had extracted from the wound of an injured rebel named Nairn. Whilst living with Caroline, Mrs Hart heard that Nairn was now a wealthy gentleman living in India and she tried to post the bone shards to him in the hope of eliciting some sort of reward in memory of her mother. However, she claimed that Caroline diverted both letter and bones and used them to extract money from Nairn herself.

servant. Mrs Hart looked around and asked which of the ladies in the room was to be her mistress. Mrs Johnston pointed to Caroline and said, 'This sweet creature, ay, you will soon get all these cloaths, and it will prove the best place you ever had.' (The handing down of expensive cast-offs from mistresses to maids was considered a great perk of the job.) Mrs Hart put her nose in the air and said she hoped the lady was not 'one of the grand ones', for she would never serve such a person. Mrs Johnston scolded her for speaking vulgarly, but later took her to one side and whispered that Caroline was not married, for particular reasons which could not be helped, but was pregnant by, and would probably soon be married to, the gentleman who had been sitting with her.

Then came the first mention of Caroline's boldest claim yet: Mrs Johnston said that she 'had a great fortune being the Pretender's daughter, though [she] then went under the disguised name of Gore'. Apparently Caroline was putting it about that she was not merely descended from the Stuart line but was actually the daughter of Bonnie Prince Charlie. Nothing could have impressed the proud Jacobite more. Mrs Hart forgot her reservations at once and accepted the job.

Other servants also lived in the Pall Mall apartment. One, a Scottish manservant of Daniel's who was 'very faithful to his master', told Mrs Hart that Caroline was a 'common ——' who was married to another man, and that she would be the ruin of Daniel. His dislike of Caroline was entirely reciprocated. Mrs Hart overheard her saying to Daniel, 'My dear Dan., if you keep that blackguard Scotchman in your service, every wretch will find me out, for you know the fellow hates me.' The servant ignored Caroline's commands, obeying only his master's, and at the end of each day he rushed away home saying 'he could not bear to be a long time together in the house, as it was filled with such a set of strumpets'.

At that time Mrs Hart was fiercely protective of her

mistress. She had complete faith in Caroline's genealogical claims and defended them to anyone who expressed doubt. Looking back after the trial, however, she remembered things differently and wrote that she had always secretly distrusted Caroline, knowing her to be a bad woman at heart. Whatever her true sentiments about Caroline, Mrs Hart certainly adored Daniel. 'His looks, his person, his delicacy and his uncommon tenderness and sweetness of temper, would have made the first lady in England happy in a cottage,' she wrote.

The clothes which had been promised to her never materialized. Caroline even told Mrs Hart that she would have to reduce her wages because they were short of money, and would make it up in the form of clothes – but 'I never got any one article except an old petticoat, for you gave them all to Miss T—— and other *amusing* misses.' This Miss T—— seems to have been a companion and friend of Caroline's for a while, although Mrs Hart thought it a mystery what Caroline could see in her: she 'could lay not the least pretensions to beauty or sense, and was very troublesome'. Mrs Johnston regarded Miss T—— as mentally subnormal, 'almost a natural', and Mrs Hart agreed. Caroline's retort was that this only made her more entertaining when she felt in need of someone to cheer her up. When Daniel asked Mrs Hart why she disliked Miss T—— so much, she replied that she 'had no patience to see her sit continually ornamenting her ordinary features with my mistresses beautifying wash,' and was 'very much diverted to see her pencelling her forehead, and endeavouring to form eyebrows, which nature had forgotten to give her: in short, for her affectation of copying every thing she saw my mistress do'.

On one occasion a former maid of Caroline's came to call, but Caroline told Mrs Hart that she would not see her. The maid would not take no for an answer, and hung around the servants' quarters making meaningful remarks for some hours. Did such and such a gentleman still come to call, and was Caroline sufficiently recovered from her recent illness to 'see company'? Mrs Hart warily gave 'indifferent answers' to these questions. The maid warned her 'never to go out with you [Caroline] at nights, or to any of the intriguing houses, as you would certainly draw me in, for there is nothing you would stick at if you wanted money'. Daniel's servant came in and the two of them fell to swapping Caroline stories. The maid talked about a grand entertainment once laid on by Caroline for Daniel, his friend Garret Burton, and a man named McLean. Caroline had flirted openly with McLean, who turned out to be one of the rare men able to resist her allure. When Caroline asked him how he liked her dress and the entertainment, he said, 'Every thing was very gay, only too much so, and too many dishes for three men; that [Caroline] was too bountiful a lady: as for his part he liked nothing to excess: he loved natural simplicity, if it was as deformed as his face' – for he was pitted with smallpox scars, though still a good-looking man. As a result of this snub, Caroline took a dislike to him and called him a 'dirty fellow'.

Daniel's servant left in 1773 – 'through your machinations', wrote Mrs Hart. Caroline herself later described him as 'an ignorant footman, whom I made Mr. Perreau turn away, because he was a slovenly bad servant, and continually making disturbances with the servants, by his lyes and tattles of them to his master'.[30]

The servant who took his place was an Irishman named John Moody, and he was a very different proposition, for he warmed to Caroline greatly and tended to prefer her to Daniel, whom he called a 'mean stingy fellow'. Caroline won his loyalty by being generous towards him from the start, 'now and then dropping a guinea into his hand' and making him feel that he was her confidant and that she relied upon him. She encouraged him not to respect Daniel. As Mrs Hart wrote, 'You took every method you well could to make him [Daniel] look as contemptible as possible in his servant's eyes, and render yourself beloved.' However, Moody was to turn against Caroline in the end, just like Mrs Hart herself.

Moody was less gullible than Mrs Hart, and when she told him that Caroline was the daughter of the Pretender by a Scottish 'lady of quality' he laughed and replied that he was sure she was Irish – 'for he never saw a Scotch person so noble and generous, without they had been born in Ireland'. Mrs Hart did not record her opinion of this remark, but she was quite generous in her assessment of Moody, describing him as 'polite, likely, and exceedingly active' and adding that 'his appearance like the generality of his country was graceful'.

Her book recounts numerous tales of Caroline's extravagance. One day Caroline sent her out to an expensive shop to buy a cap, giving her an old one to use as a pattern. On the way, however, Mrs Hart saw a cheaper one which perfectly matched the style Caroline wanted. She bought it and took it home. At first Caroline was pleased, but she flew into a rage when she found out that it did not come from the right shop. She threw it in the fire, scolded Mrs Hart and dispatched Moody to buy another. He came back with one that cost five shillings – 'but this expensive cap was scarcely soiled, before you was tired of it, and gave it to Miss T——'.

'Your clear-starcher's weekly bill was never less than ten shillings and six-pence,' goes on Mrs Hart, 'your washing extravagantly and beyond conception dear; sattin shoes thrown aside after once or twice wearing; your hair dressed at ten shillings and six-pence a week . . . Several pieces of silk continually coming in, so that Mrs. C——, the mantua-maker, had at one time nine beautiful silk sacques, besides petticoats to make for you. The best of linen and the finest of laces was got for you: jewels were bought which you told me were diamonds, though Mrs Johnston and I suspected them to be French paste.' Another interesting expense mentioned by Christian Hart amidst these baubles was bribery to servants 'for relating you news out of Mr Robert Perreau's family, which you inveterately hated at that time, and was your perpetual laughing-stock'.

'When you went abroad,' she continues, 'it was in the most splendid dress, and you painted with such consummate art, as might easily deceive, and even tempt his holiness to sin.' There was often money to burn – literally.

When money was as plenty with you that you minded not how it went, you carelessly wrapped a seventy pound bank note in the paper that had been put round your pot of rouge, and with the greatest absence of mind intended to throw it into the fire; luckily it fell under the grate, and I afterwards found and gave it to you, which my fellow-servant blamed me for, and called me a cursed fool for not taking an advantage of your carelessness.

Sometimes it was all too much for Daniel. 'He would often throw himself on the sopha, in a desponding attitude, look wishfully [sic] at you with watery eyes, and sighing, say, "My dear Carry, this will never do"; you then would smile, raise him gently in your arms, and bid me quit the room.'

Christian Hart did not stay in Caroline's employ for much longer. Shortly after Moody's arrival, another position came up, and she left: 'and I thank God I left you, I hope, without the least stain on my character'.

The life of Caroline and Daniel now entered a new phase. From now on, the expensive lifestyle described by Mrs Hart was to be supported not only by Caroline's high-class prostitution and Daniel's hare-brained stock-jobbing schemes, but also by a new and far more lucrative activity, which utilized the handwriting skills developed so effectively by Caroline in her pseudonymous letters to Joseph Salvador.

CHAPTER
FOUR
━━ ◆ ━━
DANGER

After a number of prosperous and tranquil years, in early 1775 Daniel and Caroline were suddenly thrown into terrible danger. The following account appeared in the *Annual Register* for that year:

> On Saturday evening, March the 11th, a gentleman came to the Public Office, in Bow Street, in company with a woman elegantly dressed, and inquired for one of the Magistrates. William Addington, Esq., being then in the parlour, the parties were introduced, when the man, after a short preface in which he acquainted the Justice that his name was Robert Perreau, and that he had lived as an apothecary, for some time in Golden Square, in great reputation, said he was come to do himself justice, by producing the person who had given him a bond for £7500, which was a forgery. The woman denying the circumstance, and the parties mutually upbraiding each other, Mr. Addington thought proper, as there was great appearance of an iniquitous combination, to commit them both to Tothill-Fields Bridewell for further examination. On the next day, from a variety of circumstances, there being a strong foundation to believe Robert Perreau's brother Daniel was also concerned in the forgery, he was

detained in Tothill-Fields, upon his going to pay Robert a visit.[1]

Caroline and both Perreau brothers were thus abruptly thrown into prison and set to face trial for their lives. The peril was extreme. Not only was forgery a capital crime, but conviction was far more likely to lead to actual execution (rather than to a commuted sentence) than with any other felony except murder.[*2] Financial fraud, undermining the brave new economic order of the eighteenth century, was judged and punished with the utmost harshness.

How had Daniel and Caroline progressed from the relatively minor sleaze of their earlier lives to this catastrophic moment, accused of swindling an amount that represented over a century's earnings for a poor man? And how on earth did the respectable Robert come to be caught up in it?

All three participants were only too eager to answer these questions, but their explanations were wildly contradictory. Even the most straightforward facts were inconsistent: to begin with, there was no single version of the scene in the magistrates' office. The newspapers said that Robert and Caroline went in together, but Caroline's story had the two brothers going in while she waited outside, while Daniel put all three of them in the office at the same time. The newspaper reporters might have garbled the details, but at least their mistakes can be presumed genuine, while the protagonists' disagreements were motivated by a desire to twist matters in their own favour. And if they could not be consistent about the arrest, Caroline and the Perreaus were hardly likely to agree about the events which caused it.

The basic outline of the story is clear, however. The arrest

---

* Approximately two-thirds of those convicted of forgery were executed; John Howard's survey of prisons indicated that of 95 forgers convicted at the Old Bailey between 1741 and 1771, 71 were hanged. The rate for murderers was 72 out of 81.

followed an attempt by Robert Perreau to obtain a cash loan from a bank using what turned out to be a forged promissory note as security. The bogus document was later to be produced in court, supporting the accusation, and the victims of the fraud came forward with accounts which implicated one or more of the three principal characters. No one accused Robert of actually executing the forgery, and it was open to debate whether he knew what he was doing in 'uttering and publishing' it, but he was definitely the one who took the document into the bank. How he came by it was a harder question to settle.

During the years from 1772 to 1775 a great deal of money flowed into Daniel and Caroline's household. They had always acquired money through strange channels; very little of their income can ever have been from sources other than disreputable. But these were particularly flush years. The couple settled down in Pall Mall, undisturbed by difficult landlords or importunate creditors. They managed a trip to Paris and a lengthy spell in the country, and Caroline enjoyed a leisurely tour of Scotland. A small team of servants was kept busy looking after them. Their existence was so well padded as to seem positively bourgeois, and they lacked only one thing: complete social respectability. Few people had any idea that they were not married; but still, prosperity was not the same as propriety, and even those who knew nothing of their true situation sensed that they were short of that.

Their family had become one of substance in numbers as well as income. Two more children had arrived, bringing the total to three: a son named Stewart was born in October 1772, and on 25 April 1774 came a daughter whom they named Elizabeth Caroline. Caroline was slow to recover after this third childbirth, so her doctors advised her to convalesce in the countryside. Daniel rented a house in Mill Hill, which at that time was still a green and rustic retreat, and the family enjoyed a summer idyll there. The house was grand and elegant; they were waited on by 'servants in rich liveries'. The anonymous *Prudence Triumphing over Vanity and Dissipation* supplied a list of provisions purchased by Daniel for their cellar:

Cyder 72 Bottles.
Port 167 Ditto
Claret 136 Ditto
Madeira 105 Ditto
Champaigne 170 Ditto
Burgundy 115 Ditto
White Wine 36 Ditto[3]

Yet it could not have been all relaxation and claret-sipping, for it was during this pastoral period that peculiar financial activities began to occur in London.[4] As the *Prudence . . .* author archly remarks, 'Fresh air is certainly beneficial to persons in a bad state of health; but this is not all; for persons who want to contrive new schemes, ought always to go for a little time into the country. The noise and hurry of the town leads off the mind of the student from attending to things of an important nature.'[5]

In fact the 'new schemes' at Mill Hill were refinements of old ones, rather than completely novel inventions, for the first of the transactions had taken place in the spring – just before the move to the country and while Caroline was still heavily pregnant (a fact which she later adduced as proof that she could not have been involved, although in truth she could have arranged the whole thing from the comfort of her sofa, with the help of a few servants and – wittingly or not – of Daniel). One day that April Daniel* went into the office of a banker named Mills and asked to borrow money. As security he offered a promissory bond for £5000, drawn up formally

---

* Or according to one source, Robert. One must bear in mind the difficulty of telling the two brothers apart except by style of dress.

in a scrivener's office and signed by a guarantor named William Adair – a retired army agent and respectable businessman. There was a remote connection between Adair and the Perreaus, for Caroline was friendly (*very* friendly, said some) with his cousin James, but neither she nor Daniel seems to have known William personally. The bond was also signed by two witnesses: a conveyancer called Arthur Jones and one Thomas Hart, who described himself as William Adair's clerk. The bond looked sound: Mr Mills accepted it, and lent Daniel the sum of £3290 in cash.

He was fortunate enough never to discover that the bond was a forgery, although he probably guessed it was when reading about the Perreaus in the newspaper the following year, long after he had retrieved his money. The loan was paid off in good time. There is little doubt, however, that the bond was a complete fabrication – and it was to be the first of many.

In the eighteenth century bonds were widely used, and abused, for raising cash; in many ways they were the credit cards of their day. Just like credit cards, their purpose ranged from serious business investment to the financing of spend-thrift folly, and they were easily employed for fraud. London in the 1770s was pleasure-oriented, optimistic and in the midst of an economic boom: like any such society it developed a strong appetite for credit, together with an army of people ready to feed this appetite at suitably usurious rates. The resulting dance of interests was complex and energetic.

The bond system worked according to a simple formula. It began with a person who wished to borrow money but did not have anything to use as security for the loan. This person (call him 'Spender') persuaded an acquaintance of solid reputation and financial substance ('Guarantor') to sign a written bond which promised to pay a certain large sum by a certain date. Spender then used this promissory note to borrow a sum of cash from a banker or other loan dealer ('Lender'). Lender kept the bond in his coffers while the loan was outstanding. When the due date came, either Spender paid off the loan and reclaimed the bond, or he failed to do so and Lender presented the bond to Guarantor and demanded the amount of cash specified.

The system rested on the goodwill and trust between Spender and Guarantor – the latter having nothing to gain from it all and acting only out of friendship. As in any type of loan scheme, the one who really benefited was Lender, who made a good living through such operations. He charged interest and, if Spender defaulted, stood to gain a much greater amount on Guarantor's bond than had been lost in the original loan. There was therefore no shortage of Lenders ready to co-operate, and the newspapers were full of advertisements enticing clients with offers of larger and larger sums, like this example from the *Gazetteer*:

> Money lent on Bond. The nobility, gentry, ladies of fortune, and others, may be supplied with sums to any amount, on their bonds or other securities, with secrecy and the utmost despatch . . . Nothing under £500 will be advanced . . . In cases where it is required, any sum from £500 to £7000 may be had, in six hours after the application.[6]

The amounts mentioned in these notices have to be seen in the context of a world in which most people struggled to survive on incomes ranging between £25 and £50 a year. The rich were not merely richer than the poor; they were richer by whole orders of magnitude. Of course, the poor were not the target market. No one wanted to lend several thousand pounds to someone who had no hope of ever paying it back, nor were such people on hobnobbing terms with suitable guarantors. Instead the bankers aimed their advertisements at the idle aristocratic youth whose inheritance was slow in reaching the pocket, or at the gambler who had lost a thousand or so at the table the night before and wanted to try his luck again,* or at the foolhardy entrepreneur who fancied his chances at a new scheme and needed a wad of capital. Such people were still a minority, though becoming more numerous as the prosperous century went on. The chasm of difference between them and the massed poor now seems almost unimaginable, but in the eighteenth century it was taken for granted – and people like Caroline and Daniel knew very well on which side of it they wished to stand. Both had glimpsed life on the opposite bank and they did not care for it at all.†

The bond system, then, was a finely balanced structure of debts and promises, and it relied upon a sense of honour and friendship between Spender and Guarantor. If Spender defaulted and Guarantor was forced to pay up the larger sum, that would probably be the end of the friendship, and no doubt this happened regularly. However, the architecture of the arrangement would collapse far more dramatically (at least from Lender's point of view) if Spender disappeared and it then turned out either that Guarantor denied having signed the bond, or that he simply did not exist. That meant that the security was imaginary and it was Lender who had been giving away money on trust alone – not something that bankers and loan sharks are ever likely to do. Such things did occur and lenders learned to be cautious. By the 1770s they were wise enough to take some care in checking bonds

* In 1770 Horace Walpole observed that it was common for young men to lose £5000 to £15,000 in an evening, and gave as an example the 21-year-old Lord Stavordale, who had 'lost eleven thousand last Tuesday, but recovered it by one great hand at hazard'.

† The usual method of equating eighteenth-century monetary values to modern ones is to multiply by sixty; the loan for which Caroline and the Perreaus were caught would then be worth £300,000. However, this method does not really capture the extreme gulf between the amounts squandered by the rich and the pittance scratched by the poor. Analysing the figure of £5000 in terms of an annual £50 wage gives a hundred years' earnings, or a figure equal to considerably more than £1 million for a British worker today.

offered to them and they generally lent only on bonds signed with names they knew well. They also preferred Spender, as well as Guarantor, to be someone of good social standing. Yet, on the whole, sophisticated credit fraud was still a new crime and it was not until the end of the decade that a few high-profile cases – not least the one involving Caroline and the Perreaus – woke lenders to the danger and inspired greater vigilance.

In cases of fraud, the scheme was usually haphazard and ill-planned, and ended with the defaulting Spender disappearing back into the underworld, never to be seen again. However, the process could be extended and the inevitable collapse of credit postponed if a respectable-seeming Spender paid off each loan as it became due, using cash obtained from yet another loan, itself secured by another fraudulent bond. In theory such a chain of ever-increasing debts and loans could go on for ever.

In practice, a link in the chain was bound to snap eventually. All it took was one suspicious banker – and getting caught and convicted of forgery was not a good idea at all. However exhilarating the ride had been, and no matter how clever Spender had been in prolonging it, the landing would be a very rough one. As the author of *The Life, Trials and Dying Words of ... Robert and Daniel Perreau* melodramatically put it, the chain of forgery 'might postpone, but it could not prevent, the hour of discovery; and when that hour should come, with what accumulated horror was it infallibly to be accompanied?'[7]

A forger – especially a serial forger – was likely to be treated not as a mere casual trickster, but as a traitor who had attacked the very foundations of society. The then Ordinary of Newgate Prison, Stephen Roe, had described forgery in 1759 as 'a complicated *falsehood* and *injustice*, confounding the distinction of *true* and false', and he added, 'It is one of the worst and most dangerous kinds of *theft*, bereaving a person of his nearest and most undoubted property, even his hand-writing, which is the key of all he possesses or enjoys; and destroying all mutual credit and confidence amongst men.' So destructive was it that God himself was liable to take offence: 'The same wise and powerful hand by which the human frame is amazingly formed, who . . . hath made a wonderful variety in men's faces and handwritings, is concerned to detect and punish the base impostor who dares to defeat the great and glorious scheme of his dominion and providence over human affairs.'[8]

This almost suicidal course of topsy-turvydom was what the case of Margaret Caroline Rudd and the Perreau brothers was all about. There is no knowing which, if any, of them understood what they were risking, and all three claimed to have been led into it unawares. One thing is certain: whoever did deliberately set off on this path must have been either completely blind to the future, or else relying on a clever evacuation plan. This might involve hoping for a splendid gambling win with which the accumulating loan could at last be paid off (perhaps Daniel's style), or else the idea could have been to ride the wheel of fortune just long enough and no longer, leaping clear at the perfect moment and starting again elsewhere, probably with a new identity. This has more the air of Caroline about it.

Either way, things did not work out as planned. The riders clung to the spinning wheel for almost a year – a long time – but when disaster came they found themselves still stuck to it, with no escape possible after all.

A couple of months after the first loan from Mills, in May 1774 – with Caroline and Daniel freshly installed in Mill Hill – a second sum of £3000 was borrowed from another lender. This time a bond for £6000 was used, signed by the same guarantor as before: William Adair. It was Robert rather than Daniel who procured this loan. Despite the usual difficulty in telling the difference between the brothers, we can be more sure than usual that it *was* Robert, because the lender knew him well. He was Sir Thomas Frankland, a close neighbour and regular customer of Robert's, and a character who was to have a particularly lively role to play in the dramas to follow.

Sir Thomas Frankland was a crusty and miserly former admiral, who kept himself occupied in his retirement by amateur loan-sharking. His naval career had been distinguished by punctilious disagreements with his colleagues, notably his own predecessor in the post of Commodore in Antigua, Thomas Pye. At the changeover between the two of them in 1755, Pye had committed the offence of keeping his broad pennant flying in the presence of Frankland, who was the senior officer, and of showing no embarrassment about it. In revenge, Frankland had Pye officially accused of everything from financial fraud to neglect of duty. The unfortunate man was sent to England to be court-martialled, and although he was acquitted of all the more serious charges, few dared to cross Frankland once the story got around. The incident became the foundation of a formidable reputation for meanness and combativeness.[9]

By the time he became the victim of the bond scheme, Sir Thomas was safely settled back in England. His home was in Old Bond Street, not far from Robert Perreau's shop, and Robert became his family's local supplier of pills, potions and general medical advice. Frankland thought Robert a reliable businessman and an upright fellow. He was more than happy to oblige when Robert came to him asking for a loan on bond. As the author of *Prudence Triumphing over Vanity and Dissipation* comments, 'When a man has lived nearly twenty years in credit, when he gradually, to all appearance, rises to affluence and even grandeur, what man would suppose that he had any intention to deceive, and much less to commit a crime that would subject him to capital punishment?'[10] And Sir Thomas was very much in the habit of granting loans to anyone who could produce a modicum of security. It was a tidy, easy income for a retired man of means. All he had to do was parcel out negligible portions of his fortune and then sit back and wait for the profits to come in. If anything went wrong, he could always find ways of compensating himself. Pressure could be applied; amounts could be re-extorted and counter-swindled in various ways. 'He has been called a common usurer,' says *Prudence* bluntly.[11]

A few days after his first loan from Sir Thomas, Robert returned to him and borrowed another £1000, this time on the security of a promissory note from his brother Daniel. Whatever Frankland might have thought of this as security under normal circumstances, he was quite willing to follow up the earlier loan, for that had seemed beyond suspicion.

There was now £4000 in cash to play with. It immediately came in handy, for it was undoubtedly used to pay off the earlier loan from Mills, which was just reaching its due date. The method was then applied the other way round. At the end of July 1774 Sir Thomas left for a long stay in Yorkshire, lodging Robert's two bonds with his bank. They were due at the end of August, but Robert paid them off in full five days before the deadline, using another loan from Mills, who this time had lent him £6000. There had been a slight shortfall, since interest was due to Sir Thomas, but this was made up from other sources: 'during the same month, Daniel and Robert between them had used bonds to borrow amounts of £1300 and £600 from Mr Vaughan, a laceman, and £600 and £300 from Mr Bailey, a perfumer. These figures may seem small compared to the others, but one has to remember that even the trifling sum of £300 represented up to a decade of a working man's wages.

That summer Daniel and Caroline were still ostensibly rusticating at Mill Hill, but in practice Daniel was commuting regularly into central London – and by now Caroline, too, was pining for the bustle of the city. In September the family gave up the country house for good and Caroline and the children returned to the Pall Mall apartment. 'I could never endure the country to live in,' she wrote afterwards. 'It would have been the very last thing I should have proposed.'[12] She added that, regardless of what the doctors said, the dampness of the countryside was certainly bad for the health.

Now the family was reunited; and the shuffling to and fro of funds and bonds continued exactly as before. In early November Robert wrote to Sir Thomas in Yorkshire saying that he wished to borrow another £5000, once again using a bond from William Adair, this one to the value of £6000. If Sir Thomas privately wondered why Adair should be sanctioning all these loans, he refrained from asking. The previous debt had been paid promptly and in full, so there was no reason to hesitate. Sir Thomas had his banker give Robert the £5000. On 19 November Frankland returned to London and Robert dropped in to thank him for the new loan. He promised that he would pay it off before the due date, which was early in the following year.

Daniel had also been keeping busy. On 1 November he took an Adair bond for £3100 to his doctor and friend, Thomas Brooke, asking to borrow money on it. Brooke wished to help but was temporarily short of cash himself, so instead he gave Daniel £1500 worth of bank bonds from the Ayr Bank in Scotland, keeping the Adair ones in exchange. The Ayr Bank bonds were readily cashable, and Daniel used them to raise money from elsewhere.

It was a lucrative business and Caroline and Daniel's lifestyle improved accordingly. The Pall Mall apartment, which had once seemed so luxurious, felt cramped after Mill Hill, and so in December Daniel spent £4000 on a new house – a very fine one, at the Cavendish Square end of Harley Street. He did not have the money to pay for it entirely in advance, but agreed to transfer the complete sum to the vendor, a builder named Thomas Collins, by the end of that month.

Daniel's lack of cash was quickly remedied. On the day before Christmas Robert went back to see Sir Thomas

Frankland. The admiral was pleased to see him, thinking Robert had come to pay off the £5000 early, but instead Robert asked him for another loan of £4000 – exactly the amount owing for Daniel's house. Frankland agreed, subtracting £110 to cover the interest on the earlier loan; Daniel made up the difference from his own money and paid Collins £4000 on the last day of December. And so, in January, the happy family moved in to their elegant new home: Daniel, Caroline, their three children, and a number of servants.

The delicate financial gavotte continued into the early months of 1775. In January Robert Perreau borrowed £1400 from the bankers Henry and Robert Drummond of Charing Cross. This time he used as security not a bond but the title deeds of Daniel's Harley Street house, which the Drummonds retained in their vaults. They did not hesitate to accept the transaction any more than the other bankers had, and the Perreaus and Caroline could little have suspected that the Drummond brothers were to prove their undoing, just two months later.

The following account of what happened next comes from the testimony of the two Drummonds, as told at the trial of Robert Perreau.

According to the two bankers, Robert Perreau came to see them on Tuesday, 7 March 1775, bringing a bond for £7500 signed by William Adair and the usual witnesses. He told Henry Drummond that he wanted to borrow £5000, and that this was at the request of William Adair himself. Out of this money, Robert proposed to pay back the amount he already owed to the bank, leaving £3600, which he would take away with him in cash.

Henry Drummond knew and respected William Adair, and would normally have honoured any financial request made by him without question. However, he had a bad feeling in his banking bones about this bond. He scrutinized it for a long time and asked Robert whether he had been there himself when Adair signed his name. Robert said no, but added that there could be no question about the signature's authenticity.

Henry called his brother Robert and the two bankers inspected the bond together. Robert Drummond at once said, 'Why, this is not his hand. I have seen his draughts, and seen him write a great many years ago.'[13]

'Oh,' said Robert, 'there is no doubt but it is his hand; it is witnessed by Mr Jones, Mr Adair's solicitor, and his servant.'

'It is very odd,' said Robert Drummond. 'I have seen his hand formerly; this does not appear to be the least like it. I think, if I were to take my oath, I would rather swear it was not his hand-writing.'

Robert Perreau repeated that he was sure it was Adair's bond even though he had not seen it signed: Adair was his 'particular friend', and there were 'family connections' between them. The Drummonds were not convinced. Robert seemed unperturbed, but took back the bond and went away. The two bankers agreed between themselves that if he came to them again they should ask him to leave the bond so they could investigate it.

Robert did return, just two hours later. This time only Henry was there; Robert Drummond had gone out. Robert Perreau told Henry that, being alarmed by what the bankers had said, he had gone himself to see William Adair, catching him just as he was going out for his daily ride. William had looked again at the bond and said that it most certainly was his usual signature, but that his handwriting might have changed slightly since the Drummonds had last seen it. He told Robert to pass on the message that they should trust him and let him have the money; moreover, he would pay off the bond in May even though it was not due until July.

Henry coolly reserved judgement, and merely asked Robert to leave the bond with him overnight. They would let him have their decision the next day. Robert agreed – 'very readily', as Henry reported in court.

At eleven o'clock the next morning, Wednesday 8 March, Robert Perreau once again called at the bank. Both the Drummonds were there this time. Henry was less polite than the day before, for the two bankers were now sure that they were on to a forgery: they had shown the bond to a colleague, who agreed that it looked false. Henry accused Robert Perreau of trying to take advantage of them. Robert protested. There could be no doubt of the bond's authenticity, he said: indeed, he had just received a letter from William Adair, which was plainly in the same hand. It had been signed with initials only, proving what intimate friends they were. He showed the Drummonds the initials, though not the entire letter.

The Drummonds proposed that they all go together to see Adair, to resolve the question for once and for all. Robert consented quite happily – although he did look at his watch and say 'if he is not gone out', as if hoping or believing that he would be. He took Henry with him in his own coach, which was still waiting at the door, while Robert Drummond went separately.

William Adair was at home. He received his visitors in a strange manner, according to Henry Drummond's testimony: 'Mr Adair took me by the hand, but he made a bow to Mr. Perreau, as a person he had never seen before.' This was as Henry had suspected, and William Adair now confirmed the fraud directly. The signature on the bond, he said, was definitely not his.

Robert Perreau appeared incredulous. 'Surely, Sir, you are jocular,' he said to Adair.

'It is no time to be jocular when a man's life is at stake,' said Henry Drummond.

'Well, then, I have been sent on a fine errand!' exclaimed Robert, and asked for the bond back, saying that he wanted to take it back to the source and find out what was going on. But Adair and the two bankers – for Robert Drummond had now arrived as well – would not give him the bond. They demanded to know what sources he was talking about, and threatened to send for a constable and have him hauled before a magistrate. Tempers ran high: voices were raised. William Adair was bemused and cross. Robert Drummond shouted at Perreau, 'You are either the greatest fool, or the greatest rogue, that I ever saw; I do not know what to make of you.'

Badgered for the names of his accomplices and the source of the bond, Robert told them at last that if they talked to his brother's wife – Caroline – they would find out all they needed to know. He said she could be found either at her home in Harley Street or visiting his own wife in Golden Square. A servant was dispatched to locate her; another was sent to bring a constable.

While they waited, the questions and accusations continued. Henry Drummond asked how it came to be that Adair, who was such a close friend and who wrote Robert Perreau such familiar letters, did not appear even to recognize his face. Robert did not answer. Henry demanded to see the letter again, with its 'intimately' signed initials. Robert handed it over and Henry put it in his pocket, securing it together with the bond itself as potential evidence. Robert offered no further explanation. 'We could get nothing from him but that he was an innocent man, and he did not mean to impose upon us, and that his sister could explain all,' said Henry Drummond in his testimony.

As Robert had thought, Caroline was with his wife. The servant brought her from Golden Square to William's house, where the four men were waiting to hear what she had to say.

She immediately did her best to take charge of the situation. First, she asked to speak to Robert Perreau alone. This was denied. Then she requested a private interview with William Adair, but he declared that she could have nothing to say to him that could not be said in front of the others. 'You are quite a stranger to me,' he said coldly. Finally, she was allowed to speak to the two Drummonds. She asked that her 'husband' Daniel be sent for, and she and the bankers went to another room.

While they were there Daniel and the constable both arrived. Daniel seemed remote and insouciant, merely expressing mild surprise at the whole affair and offering neither an explanation nor any support of Caroline. He denied knowing anything himself and did little but lounge around looking elegantly bored with the whole business. Even his own version of events states only that he waited with the others until Caroline and the bankers came back. What he also wrote in his account was that Caroline later told him that she had successfully convinced the Drummonds, in their private conversation, that the bond was genuine after all and that William Adair had simply disowned it out of embarrassment.

Instead, what had happened was that Caroline had confessed to being the forger. She told the Drummonds that Robert was entirely innocent: it was she who had written out the documents and then persuaded Robert to try to obtain cash on them. It was nothing but a girlish adventure; she had never wanted anyone to be hurt by it. Robert was a family man with children to look after and he had been acting in good faith: he could not be allowed to take the blame for her actions. She begged the bankers not to have him arrested. Her performance was marvellously vivid, full of tears and eloquence.

The Drummonds could not believe it at first. How could a woman fake a masculine signature? It was unthinkable.

She could do it, said Caroline, and she offered to prove it. But she asked them to promise that they would immediately destroy the evidence so that she need not fear its being used by others to hang her. They agreed, and Caroline took a piece of paper and produced a perfect copy of the signature on the bond. She handed the paper to Robert Drummond, who examined it, showed Henry and then threw it into the fire.

Caroline's plan worked. The Drummonds were touched by her appeal, convinced by her demonstration and impressed by her moral courage in risking her own life to save that of her brother-in-law. When they came out, the bankers persuaded William Adair that Robert should be considered innocent and allowed to leave undisturbed. As for the idea of having Caroline arrested instead, that was not to be considered. Their gallant instincts had been too deeply moved.

Adair appeared reluctant, still wanting to turn Robert – though not Caroline – over to the magistrates. He did not seem to believe Caroline's confession, although he did not say so outright. But Robert was lucky: the bankers won the day. Adair agreed gruffly to do nothing further, the constable was sent away, and Caroline and the two Perreaus left unmolested in Robert's coach.

Robert perked up on the way out, and his parting words were that he hoped he was now 'sufficiently acquitted' in the Drummonds' minds. But Henry replied that he had better not enquire into that; he could say nothing to it. Said Robert Drummond, 'Mr. Perreau immediately upon that, for the first time, expressed great uneasiness. He said, I would sooner have cut my right hand off, than have injured any man; and then, and then only, did he seem the least agitated.'

It had been a risky ploy. Caroline's later detractors either mentioned the incident without comment or ignored it. The modern commentator Horace Bleackley wrote, 'In all the sordid history the one bright spot is the loyalty of charming, wicked Mrs Rudd to her grimy confederates, for the scene in old William Adair's parlour on that stormy March morning might well have cost her life.'[14] Her supporters – and she herself – naturally claimed it as proof of her innocence and her devotion to the Perreaus.

This devotion may have been real, and it was certainly courageous of her to have seized the nettle so boldly. But the fact was that saving all three of them was the best way for her to save herself. She would have thought it all through carefully in the coach on the way to William Adair's. Since she was being summoned, that must mean that Robert had already pointed the finger at her: if he was formally arrested he was bound to continue to do so. She would then be accused of forgery before men professionally trained not to be easily moved by personal appeals, excuses, nobility, tears or charms of any sort. It was better to take control before matters reached that stage.

Even if the plan had failed and she had been arrested at William's house, she had an ace still up her sleeve. That was Daniel, conveniently positioned in the reception room should he be needed. But as it turned out, she would not have to play that card until later.

For the moment, the plan had succeeded brilliantly and all three emerged unscathed from the confrontation at William Adair's house. However, they could not now simply relax and carry on as before. They sat discussing the problem for some time that afternoon; all the accounts agree that it was Caroline who took their predicament most seriously, although they disagree about almost everything else. In particular, they differ as to how much Robert knew of the true situation. Since his supporters claimed that he knew nothing, they naturally portrayed him as being puzzled and frightened at this point, having no idea what he had got into and still continuing under the delusion that the bond was genuine.

Caroline was right to be concerned, for there were several things to worry about. First, William Adair had seemed disgruntled at their being allowed to go. He could change his mind at any moment and decide to report them to the magistrates after all. Second, the Drummonds were still in possession of hard evidence against them. They had in their pockets not only the bond itself, but also the letter Robert had given them – which was, of course, a forgery.

Finally, there were still three other forged bonds out there, which could surface at any time – and almost certainly would, if word got out in the banking community. One was in the hands of Thomas Brooke, who had lent Daniel the Ayr bank bonds. The other two were with the bank of Sir Thomas Frankland – and there was no question about it: he would never let them off as lightly as the Drummonds had. That wouldn't be his style at all. If Caroline and the Perreaus could only pay off what was owed to both men before the story got around, they would be all right: the bonds would be handed back to them and could then be destroyed. The difficulty was that the amount owing on them totalled over £10,000, and they did not have anything like that kind of cash. Nor could they risk approaching their usual banking connections to get it – and they certainly dared not forge any more bonds.

The first of the three problems – the fear that William Adair might still prosecute them – was at least something that Caroline could investigate further. It would be unwise to approach William directly, in case it antagonized him, but she could try to probe his state of mind through an intermediary. The next day, according to her own account (which for once does not conflict with anyone else's), she called on William's cousin and her 'friend', James Adair, hoping to persuade him to visit William and find out which way the wind was blowing.

But James declined to have anything to do with Caroline and her tribulations. Even if he believed her version of events, he had no wish to get more deeply involved than he already was. He was elderly, respectable and thoroughly married, and his connection with Caroline was probably based on sex or blackmail – or both. It was not something he wished to advertise. If there was to be a scandal, his head would be down and all hatches would be battened, and he would be using all his influence to keep his name out of the papers and himself out of the courtroom. Helping her now did not fit in with this at all. He refused even to listen; if she attempted further blackmail he simply ignored it.

Caroline gave up, but later that same Thursday someone else knocked on James Adair's door: Robert Perreau. There is no evidence that they had ever met before, and Robert may have been sent by Caroline. If so, it did not work out as she expected: Robert's visit actually made things worse for her. In the course of explaining himself to James, Robert mentioned that although Caroline had pretended to confess to the forgery to save him, she still maintained that she *had* received the bond from William – and therefore he could not understand why William persisted in denying that it was his. But that afternoon Caroline had told James that the writing on the bond was her own, although she had also hinted that she was not ultimately to blame for the forgery. Now James knew that she had been lying to Robert and therefore probably to everyone. Convinced of her guilt, he was less inclined to help than ever. Like Caroline, Robert left the house none the wiser.

Both visits appear to be confirmed by some letters which turned up much later and were reprinted in the newspapers.[15] The letters were never presented in court, presumably because James succeeding in suppressing them. How they eventually found their way into the press is a mystery – unless of course they were a fabrication intended to incriminate Caroline. The first was addressed from her to James and dated Thursday 9 March, the day of the two visits:

Dear Sir,
Fully persuaded of your goodness, and under the greatest torture of mind, particularly at what passed to-night between you and my brother, I take the liberty to conjure you to let me know on what I am to depend, as I apprehend your conversation with Mr. [William] Adair must let you see what his intentions are, and also what opinion Mr Drummond has of the affair, and how far my

brother is justified, or otherwise, in their opinion; for that, superior to any consideration about myself, gives me the greatest misery, as I have, and ever shall most *truly* and *firmly*, declared his perfect innocence, and been the unintentional cause of his integrity being suspected, and the train of evils which must necessarily flow from it to him and his family.

She went on to allude to things she had mentioned in her conversation, veiled accusations against one or both of the Perreaus:

As to myself, I can only say I wish you candidly to consider what I urged to and told you to-day. The dupe I have been unfortunately made of is the least evil to me; for if I can't prove my innocence to every one's satisfaction, infamy must attend me to all that has or may hear the story; I therefore conjure, implore you to adjust this affair with Mr. Adair, so as to make my brother's mind somewhat easy, and relieve me from the necessity of vindicating myself to the dishonour of those whom it has hitherto been my duty and inclination to love and respect most.

Pardon the strong importunity, and allow me to see you by ten to-morrow, either at your house or here.

I am,
Dear Sir,
Most respectfully your obedient
M.C. Perreau.

James Adair remained unmoved. He wrote:

Madam,
Your brother told me yesterday, that after you had been with me, you persisted in assuring him, that Mr. Adair had given into your own hand the bond to raise the money for your husband's immediate relief: after this you must

excuse my declining any further intercourse or correspondence with you.

I am,
Madam,
Your humble servant,
James Adair,
Soho-square, March the 10th, 1775.

Following this snub, Caroline again assessed the situation.
There was still no knowing whether William Adair was going
to prosecute Robert or herself, and the bogus promissory
notes with Brooke and Frankland still lurked in the under-
growth. Money was desperately needed, to buy these bonds
back. According to Caroline's account, she tried to fix up a
quick sale of some of her jewels, but without success. The
lawyer who was supposed to be helping them to arrange the
sale, Henry Dagge, struck her as untrustworthy, and she was
afraid that he would betray them. She even suspected that he
was in cahoots with Robert and his wife against herself. The
deal was called off.

And so, walled in on all sides, they floundered ineffectually
for a couple of days – until one or more of them lost their
cool altogether. Giving up the idea of calmly buying their
way out of danger, they all three bundled themselves into a
carriage on Saturday 11 March and set off pell mell to try to
flee the country.

Before they had even left central London, however, Robert
changed his mind – or perhaps he had been planning it this
way for some time. He stopped the carriage on the pretext
that he had forgotten something. Then he darted around the
corner and into the magistrate's office in Bow Street, where
he announced that he wished to give evidence against
Caroline in a case of forgery.

Robert might have thought that Caroline would be able to
talk her way out of trouble, just as she had in William Adair's
house. Or, having been alerted to her duplicity by James

Adair, he might have been busily plotting against her ever since. In either case, he would certainly have reasoned that things would look better for him if he turned Crown's evidence than if they were all caught sneaking away together. Besides, he had left his family behind: the idea of running to France could never have held much appeal for him. (The less domestically-minded Caroline and Daniel had also left their children; in her lengthy narrative of the escape Caroline did not mention what was supposed to happen to them, although she vividly described her grief at the parting.) Robert had every reason to hope that he would be granted complete immunity as a voluntary prosecution witness and would thus avoid facing any legal action at all. His logic was impeccable. The only trouble was that things didn't work out quite that way.

Caroline blamed Robert's treacherous turn on the lawyer Dagge. 'I clearly saw now', she wrote, 'that Mr Dagge's whole attention and care was fixed upon Robert . . . there was a *particular distinct* understanding between them.'[16] She also suspected that Robert's wife Henrietta, whom she had always despised, had conspired against her. 'There was a *selfish something*, an equivocal duplicity in Mrs Perreau's whole discourse and manner . . . as much as to say, "My husband must, and is determined to take care of himself at all events."' In any case, Caroline was not amused to find herself lured or dragged (accounts differ) into the magistrate's office. Her fury at the betrayal was incandescent: 'Enraged at this flagrant baseness,' she wrote, 'I protested I would no longer show them any favour; that, I would vindicate myself, and tell the truth, however fatal the consequences might be to them; that, my eyes were now open to their infamy.'

Unlike Robert, she had no illusions about their predicament. The magistrates would not be as easily manipulated as the Drummonds. When Robert cheerfully suggested (as Caroline claimed he did) that she should just confess as she had done before so that they would all be released, she knew he was quite wrong. She treated the situation very differently. Although she did admit, when asked, that Robert had received the bond from her, she thereafter maintained a stubborn silence, refusing to answer any further questions until she had legal counsel.

Robert Perreau was more forthcoming. He told the magistrates that Caroline had given him a bond and had fooled him into thinking it was genuine. He also added that she was not Daniel's wife but merely used his name. This was a legal point of great importance, for if she had been married she would have been assumed by law to have been acting under Daniel's complete control and influence. Instead, she was held to be culpable for her own actions, while Daniel was allowed to go free since there was no evidence of his direct involvement. He went home, where he spent an unsettled night with his uncomprehending children. As he must have realized, while turning things over in his mind that night, however, his freedom was to be short-lived. Two days later Robert and Caroline told the magistrates a more detailed story and Daniel too was arrested.

The inevitable had happened: the wheel of fortune had spun out of control and thrown them off. The game was over. An editorial in the *Morning Post* – a paper which was to follow their case very closely over the following months – opined that these forgeries were 'the most remarkable of the kind that ever appeared in this country, or perhaps in the whole world'.[17] Not only were the protagonists glamorous and fascinating, and the relationships between them of the greatest emotional poignancy, but their motivation was unfathomable. 'All other forgeries were commonly a grand stroke at raising of money and running away with it, but these adventurers appear to have forged one bond to pay off another, and raised it at last to something like a regular branch of trade; how their profit or advantage was at last to arise from this trade is difficult to conceive, for their lives were at stake.'

Or as *Prudence Triumphing over Vanity and Dissipation*
summarized the story: 'Of all the women who ever lived in
the world, Mrs. Rudd was the most extraordinary, and she
was connected with men, namely the Messrs. Perreau, whose
characters were equally singular.'[18]

CHAPTER
FIVE
◆
SUFFERING MERIT

During the hearings and interrogations which followed, Caroline and the two Perreaus all struggled to exonerate themselves and throw the blame on to each other. Each side claimed to be the victim of a plot.

On Monday 13 March Caroline and Robert were brought back to Bow Street to make a formal appearance before a panel of magistrates. Lawyers were present; Caroline was approached by a dandyish and youthful one named John Bailey, who said he had once met her socially at a party. She did not remember him as well as he did her, but readily accepted his offer to be her counsel. Once taken on, Bailey's advice was to follow the course of action she must already have worked out for herself: to turn the tables on Robert by offering herself as a prosecution witness against him. It would be her word against his – and only one of them could be offered immunity.

Caroline's testimony before the magistrates was brief but effective. She stated that she had *not*, after all, written the bond, but had only confessed to the Drummonds in an attempt to save Robert's life. Now, she said, she wanted to tell the truth: it was Robert who had been the true source of the forgery. He had come to their house a couple of weeks previously and given her a paper which he said was very important, and which he asked her to keep for a while. Caroline obeyed him and did not look at the paper; four days later Robert took it away. She now realized that this paper must have been the bond, but other than that she knew nothing about it.[1]

Once her evidence was given, Caroline was remanded back into custody in Tothill Fields. Robert was then interrogated, and he repeated his version of the story as he had first told it to the magistrates. He blamed Caroline for everything and also gave details of the other forged bonds held by Brooke and Frankland – it was this that spelled the end of his brother's brief freedom, since it was Daniel who had passed the bonds to Dr Brooke. As soon as the hearing was concluded, Robert was returned to prison, and he was soon joined there by Daniel. The three then waited for the next stage: the hearing which would consider the matter of bail and would also decide who – if anyone – would be admitted as King's evidence.

By now the newspapers had picked up the story. They reported the arrest and the Bow Street hearing in detail, emphasizing the most curious aspects of the case: the striking similarity of the two brothers, Caroline's chic appearance, and the swiftness with which the conspirators had turned on one another. As a result there was a great crowd of spectators waiting to see the suddenly famous trio at the magistrates' court on Wednesday 15 March, when the next session was to take place. The onlookers were of all sorts and conditions of life, including 'a great number of persons of rank and distinction';[2] as was customary many of them paid bribes and entrance fees to get a good view. So great was the pressure of numbers at the door that the room in Bow Street was deemed too small and the hearing was adjourned to the larger Guildhall in Westminster. 'As soon as this news was circulated in the office,' said the following day's *Morning Post*, 'every coach in the neighbourhood of Covent Garden was taken, and the street lined on both sides with persons of every denomination, hurrying down to Westminster, where the court was filled in ten minutes.'

Once the excited crowd had settled down, the prisoners were brought in. Caroline had had a selection from her wardrobe brought to her in prison: she was elegantly dressed in a gown of striped silk, an ermine cloak and a black bonnet. The Perreaus were also well turned out: both wore fine frock coats, one brown and the other slate-coloured, topped by hats laced with gold. The three magistrates were duller to look at, but bore an impressive air of gravitas and substance. The famous Sir John Fielding presided. Half-brother to the novelist Henry Fielding and his successor in the post of magistrate and police chief, he was completely blind, yet rumoured to be able to recognize three thousand London thieves by their voices alone.

The first part of the hearing concerned the accusations made against Robert. The Drummond brothers described the events of 7 and 8 March, and two scriveners testified that Robert had employed them to draw up the bonds. On the basis of this evidence the Drummonds were formally bound over to prosecute Robert for two distinct crimes: causing the bond to be made and 'publishing' it (making use of it) knowing it to be forged. William Adair did not appear in court: like his cousin James, he was keen to keep out of the limelight, and had presumably used his influence to extract himself from the list of witnesses.

Sir Thomas Frankland, by contrast, was far from bashful. As soon as he had heard about the arrests he had presented himself at the magistrates' office in a mood every bit as peppery and litigious as Caroline had anticipated. He now delivered his testimony, detailing the two loans which were still outstanding, of £5000 and just under £4000 respectively. His prosecution was ordered to be added to that of the Drummonds – although in fact it was never pursued, for mysterious reasons: Caroline was to claim that it was because

Robert bribed him not to press the case. No mention was made of the immunity for which Robert had been hoping.

Next to be considered was Daniel, who was accused of defrauding Dr Thomas Brooke of £1500. Brooke stated that he had lent Daniel this amount in the form of Ayr bank bonds, taking a bond supposedly signed by William Adair as security; the loan had never been paid off. The same two scriveners testified again, this time saying that Daniel had had them draw up the bond. Daniel was formally charged with this fraud. Like Robert he was accused both of causing the bond to be made and of making use of it knowing it was a forgery.

In the afternoon Caroline took her turn on the stand. 'She gave her testimony with a great deal of modesty, and without hesitation,' said the *Morning Post*, although the *Daily Advertiser* considered that 'Mrs Rudd was in great agitation during examination.'[3]

She went over some of her history, saying that she was the daughter of one of the most important noblemen in Scotland and that she had been married to a Mr Rudd, who had been violent and cruel but had also given her a great deal of money, which she said totalled £13,000.* This sum had since gradually transferred itself to Daniel's pocket. She told the magistrates about Daniel's dealings in Exchange Alley, describing how he had dissipated her fortune, and she admitted that they were not married. Robert, she said, had always been kind to her – at least until now – and she would have given her life to help him. Indeed, she *had* risked her life for him at William Adair's by confessing to the forgery, although she was quite innocent of it.

She then explained that even after the meeting at William Adair's she had still been afraid for Robert's safety, because it

---

* It is unlikely that Rudd gave her as much money as this, but being absent he provided a convenient alibi for the large amounts which had come into her and Daniel's household over the last few years.

seemed that Mr Adair was not satisfied, and that was why they had taken the coach together in an attempt to flee – a coach which she had paid for, she added. But then Robert, unbeknown to herself and Daniel and having no regard for her attempts to save him, had come into Bow Street and betrayed her.

It was now late in the day, so the hearing was adjourned. The brothers were both moved to the New Prison at Clerkenwell for the night; Caroline was sent back to Tothill Fields.

The next morning the hearing continued, not at Guildhall this time but back in the Bow Street offices, which had now been better organized to accommodate the crowds. Caroline continued from where she had left off, and this time her story took on a new complexion.

She elaborated on the theme of Daniel's greed and carelessness, describing her discovery that he had been declared bankrupt and adding that he had sometimes pawned her possessions without her permission. She also said that it was he who had told friends they were married, and that he had claimed to know the Adairs when obviously he did not. Then, speaking in a 'faultering, pathetic voice',[4] she related a dramatic story. The following version comes from one of her own accounts, published shortly afterwards, and it fleshes out the briefer version reported in the newspapers.[5]

A few days before the Drummonds became involved, she said, Robert Perreau had come to her saying he was in financial difficulties, and he asked her to copy the signature of William Adair. In one hand he held a bond ready to be signed, in the other a letter bearing a signature to be used as a model. Caroline was surprised and shocked. Robert explained that the person who normally did this sort of thing for him and Daniel was away, and that if it were not done they would both be in danger. He swore that he intended no fraud by it, and that he would pay it off as soon as he had the money, but that everything depended on his having cash that day. 'I utterly rejected having any concern with such an affair,' said Caroline. She even offered Robert her jewels instead, but he said that he wouldn't be able to turn them into cash quickly enough. He begged her to consider it and said he would leave the letter and the bond with her. She allowed him to do this, but told him she would have to discuss it with Daniel.

Caroline told Daniel about the incident when he came home – but he astonished her by saying immediately that she had better do as Robert had asked. It was quite safe, he assured her: Robert was an honest man, and it was a very important business, affecting the whole family. Still, Caroline did not want to do it. She would give her life if necessary, she told Daniel, but she could not bring herself to take part in anything dishonest. 'My dear Caroline,' he replied, 'the superior rectitude of your heart, and the exquisite sensibility of your nature, leads you to refine and feel too much on this matter – let us drop the subject.'

Two days later, on Sunday 5 March, Robert came back to see what she had decided. The two brothers conferred together out of her earshot and their discussion must have 'inflamed' Daniel's mind, for afterwards he was transformed from a supportive husband into a ferocious bully. 'He swore if I did not do it, he would break my arm, cursed me, and in his passion, threw a shirt at me which he happened to have in his hand. I was now equally incensed, rang the bell with violence, and declared that I would expose him and the affair to the whole house; but, on the footman's coming to the door, he rushed past him; saying, "It is your mistress wants you," and directly went out.'

The next morning she spoke to Robert again, still refusing to give in. Daniel asked for the bond and seemed to be on the point of signing it himself. Caroline begged him not to, for his own safety. Did that mean that *she* would do it, then? he asked. She said no. He lost his temper again, said he 'might as well be hanged for one thing as another', and pulled a knife from his pocket. He brandished it at her with murderous violence.

And so, at knifepoint and in terror of her life, she gave in and signed the name 'William Adair' on the bond. Then she ran to her room and threw herself on the bed, where she remained all night in emotional anguish.

The next morning – Tuesday 7 March – she got up early and found that Robert had come to breakfast. Daniel picked up the bond from the table and said, 'I think it will do, I suppose you'll be with Mr Drummond this forenoon.' Robert said yes, and left. And the next Caroline knew of it was on the Wednesday, when she was summoned to William Adair's house and confessed to the Drummonds because she saw that Robert's life was in danger.

This shocking story impressed the magistrates profoundly. They were struck by 'the plaintive tone of Mrs. Rudd's voice; the artless manner in which she told her story, and decency of her whole deportment'. Nor were they the only ones – her tale of woe 'produced a scene so truly pathetic, as drew tears from many of the spectators'.[6]

Caroline was granted bail, for the amount of £200 provided by herself as well as £100 each from two men who volunteered to act as guarantors for her, a poulterer and a butcher.[7] Even more importantly, she was admitted as King's evidence against the two Perreaus. She would be immune from prosecution. And so Caroline walked out of the magistrate's court a free woman, not only for the waiting period before the trials but – she had every reason to believe – for ever. It was a splendid result. She went home in triumph to be reunited with her children, who were waiting in the care of the servants in Harley Street.

The Perreau brothers, on the other hand, were denied bail and sent back to Clerkenwell, to languish for several months waiting to be tried. They had not seemed so plaintive or artless; their stories drew tears from no one. Robert, in particular, must have been horror-stricken. The immunity on which he had gambled was not his after all, but Caroline's. Had he kept quiet, they could all have been in Paris by now, congratulating themselves on their escape. This thought was perhaps even more tantalizing for Daniel, who could have adjusted to a fugitive's life more readily – but, if he brooded along these lines, he never reproached Robert in print.

Indeed, Daniel continued to display nothing but the limpid, almost blank composure which had been observed in him during the visit to William Adair's house. William Hickey, who had known Daniel slightly before the arrest and had always envied him his debonair lifestyle, went to visit the twins in prison. He saw the dramatic difference in the two physically identical men's responses to their situation. As Hickey entered the cell, Robert 'covered his face with his handkerchief, and bursting into tears, sobbed aloud'. Daniel, instead, merely stepped forward to greet him, 'with as much apparent ease and nonchalance as if receiving company in his own elegant mansion in Upper Harley Street'.[8]

To counter Caroline's story, Daniel now wrote one of his own, presenting things in a very different light.[9] He set out to clear Robert of all suspicion while avoiding taking any blame on to himself. Instead, he declared that Caroline had masterminded the entire nefarious plan. Later he expanded his narrative to fill a thick pamphlet, telling the whole history of his relationship with her in great detail.

According to Daniel's account, *he* was the one who had had the £7500 bond drawn up at the scriveners, not Robert – but it was not his own idea. He did it only because he had received a letter from William Adair telling him to.

This letter, passed to him by Caroline on 3 March 1775, had given him detailed instructions concerning the amount for which the bond was to be made out, the route through which it should be cashed and the purposes for which the money was to be used. Daniel obeyed all this, having the bond drawn up and giving it to Caroline for her to return to

Adair for signing. A few days later, he noticed a paper on Caroline's bedside table. She told him it was the bond, signed and ready to be taken to a banker – a job which the letter had said was to be done by Robert.

The following morning, Tuesday 7 March, Caroline rose at eight o'clock, 'a very unusual hour for her, who was seldom up before ten'. Daniel went downstairs shortly afterwards and found her talking to his brother. As Daniel came in, she passed Robert the bond folded in a piece of brownish paper. Robert read it, and said, 'This is a very unpleasant business, I wish Mr. Adair would not trouble me with it.' Daniel remarked that it was indeed disagreeable to borrow money, but that Mr Drummond 'would not dislike such a paper', for Mr Adair's name was trustworthy. All the same, said Robert gloomily, it was an unpleasant business. He reluctantly put the bond in his pocket and left. And that was all Daniel knew, until he was summoned to the scene at William Adair's the next day.

This, then, was Daniel's explanation for the events surrounding the bond. And according to him, these commands from William Adair were nothing at all out of the ordinary – for his extraordinary claim was that Caroline had been controlling every aspect of his life by means of such letters for years.

It had all begun back in 1772, he wrote. That year, a long-lost cousin of Caroline's called John Stewart – son of Caroline's uncle of the same name – came to stay with them. Cousin John and Caroline went out every day on mysterious errands; the former rather overstayed his welcome and Daniel did not care for him. However, he did bring one great benefit, for Caroline told Daniel that John had engineered a rapprochement between her and someone she described as an old family friend of great wealth and generosity: James Adair.

Adair and Caroline's uncle had apparently known one another in Ireland, where they were neighbouring land-owners, although Adair was normally resident in London.

When Caroline had first left for England, Uncle John gave her Adair's address in Soho Square and told her to seek his help whenever she needed it. Adair had in fact helped her at first, but had then disowned her in disgust when she left her husband. After that there had been no contact until Cousin John's intervention.

Having melted Adair's heart, John left London. Caroline continued to see Adair regularly and soon started coming home from each meeting with pursefuls of money. She told Daniel that Adair wanted to assist both of them as much as he could, clearing their debts and establishing them in the world. These first small gifts were just tokens of what was to come. She added, too, that Adair wished her to take Daniel's name, although he knew that they were not married, so that she could become a respectable 'woman of fashion' suitable for introduction into 'the most polite circles'.[10] Indeed, she did begin to call herself Mrs Perreau, and most people who met them after 1772 assumed that the family was everything it appeared to be.

Daniel was quite happy with this situation, he admitted in his account. There was no reason to doubt Caroline's story, and she was bringing home plenty of welcome money – why question it?

He told his brother, and Robert was impressed too, but his wife Henrietta viewed the matter with suspicion. She did not think that an upright family man like James Adair was likely to do so much for Caroline, let alone for a man who was not her lawful husband and whom he had never met. Robert conveyed this thought to Daniel, who quizzed Caroline about it. She assured him that there was nothing odd in it at all.

On several occasions Daniel was told that he had narrowly missed meeting Adair, either coming home just after Adair left or leaving moments before he arrived. Daniel wanted to see the man and thank him, but when he suggested arranging a definite appointment, Caroline told him that the near-misses were not accidental after all. James had an eccentric attitude which they should humour: he did not want to meet Daniel until he had fully accomplished his benevolent intentions. Not wishing to disobey someone who was doing so much for him, Daniel concurred.

During that year Caroline continued bringing home regular sums of money: £500 in July, another £400 a few months later. She said that these were inheritances which had been held in trust by Adair, or gifts for the imminent baby. (This was while she was pregnant with Stewart; Daniel actually wanted to name the baby James in their benefactor's honour, but Caroline was afraid that Mrs Adair would hear of it and get the wrong idea.) She told Daniel that Adair intended very soon to give them another £2000, which would be held in trust for the children, but that she and Daniel should enjoy the interest on it in the meantime.

At the end of 1772 Caroline took a five-week trip to Scotland by herself, which she said was financed by James, who wanted her to meet her long-lost relatives there.* At the same time she gave Daniel £1500, donated by James for family expenses. The year 1773 then passed peacefully, their coffers being continually topped up by similar gifts.

If Daniel was telling the truth about this cash and the explanation Caroline gave for it, one cannot help wondering what its true source was – for Henrietta Perreau was surely right in guessing that James Adair wasn't supporting Caroline out of pure philanthropy. He may indeed have been paying her for some other reason, either for sex or because she was blackmailing him – contemporary accounts regularly describe her as a practised blackmailer. It could also have been a combination of the two: they go very well together when one partner is a rich, married gentleman with a great deal to lose, and the other an unscrupulous schemer.

* Caroline's own writings also mentioned this trip: 'I went to Edinburgh, in December 1772, where my uncle Stewart and his family met me; there I not only saw, and was caressed by my relations, but also acquired many friends.' *Facts, or a Plain and Explicit Narrative of the Case of Mrs Rudd*, p. 11.

Alternatively, the money could have come from quite another source: Joseph Salvador, perhaps, if he was still involved with Caroline despite her assurances to Daniel; or it could have been any other gentleman of means. The name of one in particular, Lord Lyttelton, cropped up in the gossip columns very soon after the trials, and she may have already had an arrangement with him during these years. James Adair, the elderly family friend, would have made a convenient alibi for the money.

In any case, Daniel was content to accept her story. It was not in his nature to probe too deeply when money was tumbling so easily into his pocket.

In late 1773, continuing Daniel's account, Caroline announced to him that James wanted to give them a large capital sum to set them up in business, but was obliged to do it in a roundabout way because his wife would jump to conclusions if she knew where the money was going. Therefore, she said, he had arranged for his cousin William Adair to make the payments, though the true supplier of the money would continue to be James. This was the first mention of William Adair. *Prudence Triumphing Over Vanity and Dissipation* remarked of this development: 'She had for a long time made so free with the name of Mr James Adair that she was obliged to shift the scene, by changing it to that of his kinsman William.'[11] At the time Daniel did not give it a moment's thought, but he later came to the same conclusion: that she had merely used William's name, having little or no personal knowledge of him.

The first fruit of this new arrangement was £150 in cash to pay for a new coach, and there was a further promise of £800 a year to be used for business investments. Daniel was also encouraged to involve Robert in these affairs: it was suggested in one letter that the two brothers should set up a bank together. A few days later, Caroline added that William was now to act as James's agent in *all* matters concerning herself and Daniel, and all payments would be authorized by him in future.

With William in the picture, affairs took a fateful turn. Daniel was told by Caroline early in 1774 that serious capital sums were now to come to them, but that James and William did not have the cash ready to hand. William would therefore enable them to get it themselves, by signing bonds which they could use to raise money on loan. The Adairs would take care of repayments when the time came.

Regular instructions now allegedly began to arrive for Daniel, telling him to fill up bonds for specified amounts and use them to obtain cash. He obeyed unquestioningly. As for the Perreau Bank, it was often mentioned in letters – it was this, Robert later claimed, that lured him into using the bonds – but nothing actually came of it.

More exciting ideas were raised. Daniel was now told that the Adairs would use their influence to have him made a baronet and to buy him a seat in parliament, the latter being a desirable status symbol, the mark of a true gentleman and yet (like army commissions) a readily tradeable commodity. A letter reproduced in *Prudence Triumphing Over Vanity and Dissipation* shows that, if Caroline was indeed the secret puppeteer behind this deception, she was taking care to shore it up with well-placed hints elsewhere in the family, in this case with Daniel's sister Hetty – now living in Carmarthen in Wales and about to get married. In the letter Caroline plays the whimsical fantasist to the hilt. Indeed, she may well have half-believed the pipe dream even while using it for her own purposes:

Dear Hetty,
I am so much overjoyed at the prospect of approaching grandeur, that I embrace this opportunity of writing to you. I hope you are not going to be married to a common vulgar fellow who has no taste for elegance, for if so you will be forever discarded by your brother. What, Hetty,

would you bring dishonour upon a baronet and a lady allied to the greatest families in the kingdom? But I am just now called to wait on his majesty; the splendour of the drawing room, with which I have been long acquainted, will revive my spirits with new vigour. What an honour to be introduced by the chamberlain to his majesty, and caressed by the greatest sovereign in the world. I am only afraid that the ladies of the bed-chamber will become jealous of me, and consequently I shall create myself many enemies; but what is all that to grandeur, seeing that I shall be admired by the lords in proportion as I am hated by the ladies. When I have made a low curtsey to his majesty, a nobleman of my own family will conduct me to an elegant seat in the drawing room, and nothing will then be heard from the drawing room to the bottom of the stairs, than *Lady Perreau's servants! Lady Perreau's servants!* For some time I will affect not to hear them, till at last with an easy elegance peculiar to myself, I will rise up, and eight or ten lords will conduct me to my coach . . . Ah! what is money to grandeur! I really cannot say more, for my head is almost intoxicated with the thoughts of being able to vie with the first ladies at court. We are to dine to-morrow at the Earl of Galloway's, where all my noble relations will be present, and every thing will be settled . . . Mr. William Adair has almost completed the election for the borough, and in a few days Dan will be sworn in a member for the House of Commons. For shame, my dear Hetty, don't live any longer in that contemptible place, but come to London, for Wales is as bad as the Highlands of Scotland, or the abominable bogs of Ireland. In Scotland nothing can be procured besides brimstone and oatmeal, in Ireland nothing but whisky and potatoes, and in Wales cheese and goats flesh is the most delicious entertainment that can be set before a stranger.

Adieu, dear Hetty,
M.C. Perreau.[12]

However, the baronetcy and the seat in parliament went the way of the banking scheme. All three wild ideas had served their function: to keep Daniel and Robert hooked long enough to cash more bonds. That, at least, was to be Daniel's line. Caroline proclaimed the whole tale to be the product of his lying, fevered imagination.

The two positions were now clearly stated. Daniel was to present himself as an innocent dupe, an Adam tricked into sin by a wicked, calculating Eve. Robert would claim to have been similarly tricked, but at an even further remove from the true source of the crime. Caroline, on the other hand, would invoke an equally powerful, opposing archetype: the naïve young woman lost in the woods of men's financial affairs, intimidated into compliance by threats of physical violence. The world's preconceptions would help her, she hoped: for how could she be expected to understand the masculine details of promissory notes and loans? And who could fail to be moved by the thought of a knife held threateningly at that pale, delicate throat?

After her release on bail Caroline did not simply sit around playing with her children and recovering from her ordeal in the courts. Instead she immediately got to work on an extended 'Case of Margaret Caroline Rudd' to be serialized in the newspapers, setting out her version of the events in detail and feeding the public hunger for information. She worked fast, and her pen fairly smoked with passion and righteous eloquence. The first episode of the 'Case' appeared in the *Morning Post* on Monday 27 March, and was reprinted in full the following day, 'on account of the great demand' and 'at the desire of many friends' who had missed the previous issue. Since the paper was only four pages long and other news had to be left out to make room, this is a measure of the public's enthusiasm for the story. The 'Case' was also serialized in the twice-weekly *London Chronicle*, starting that same Tuesday.

This level of interest was not to wane for a considerable time, and whenever it showed signs of flagging during the summer it was quickly revived by news of some dramatic development: a trial date set, or a new propaganda attack launched from one side or the other. The volume of newsprint devoted to the case during 1775 rivalled that expended on the contemporaneous events in America: the beginning of the war with the rebels at Concord and Lexington on 18 April, the battle of Bunker Hill with its Pyrrhic victory for Britain in June, and the long months of debate and fighting leading up to the following year's announcement of independence. Which story the average reader was likely to turn to first and read more avidly is anyone's guess.

The 1770s were a decade in which newspapers had just discovered a refreshing new sense of populist fun, abandoning the gentleman's-club prose and refined satires of an earlier generation for a snappier, bloodier and grittier approach to news. The dailies were full of true-crime and human-interest stories, as well as political gossip, advertisements, promotion of upcoming galas and festivals, and page after page of readers' letters ranting about pet subjects (the preposterousness of the latest hairstyle, the three-foot-high plumed beehive, was a favourite in 1775). Above all, attention was paid to a newly discovered species: the media celebrity. Dandies and society figures such as Lord Sandwich, beautiful and fashionable women of debatable morals like the Duchess of Devonshire, flamboyant criminals and glitterati of all sorts became highly marketable, and their antics were encouraged accordingly.

Caroline Rudd and the contemporary press were made for each other. Not only did the editors fill their pages with trial accounts and opinion pieces, but both Caroline and her opponents treated the newspapers – particularly the *Morning Post* – as a private arena in which to indulge in extended and furious ink fights. Far from objecting to being used in this way, the papers and their readers loved every word of it.

There was something about this case, and the players in it, that fascinated people beyond all measure. Apart from her elegance and poise, the ambiguity of Caroline's nature was deeply intriguing. Her air of wounded virtue blended oddly with a hardcore *femme fatale* reputation which even her supporters made no attempt to deny. The combination was a powerful one, especially for the excitable sensibilities of the mostly male readership. The Perreaus were extraordinary too: men of education and style, eerily alike in appearance. They were also ambiguous figures, but in their case their equivocal nature was shared, and their single face divided like a masquerade costume into two halves. One was modestly dressed, the other flash; one bourgeois and successful, the other feckless; one tame and the other wild. And of course, the natural assumption was that the first was innocent and the second guilty – even though it was Robert, not Daniel, who had been caught red-handed.

'The public curiosity for the perusal of facts is every day more abundantly excited,' wrote the compiler of *Genuine Memoirs of the Messieurs Perreau*. Horace Walpole noted that the town was 'very busy about a history of two Perreaus and a Mrs Rudd, who are likely to be hanged for misapplying their ingenuity'.[13] Nor was it only London that was busy with the story. The author of *Genuine memoirs* added, addressing an imaginary country correspondent: 'I do not wonder your little village rings with the big villainy, or that its inhabitants should receive such erroneous accounts of the matter.'[14] Indeed, the newspapers teemed with such debate and speculation that its writer considered it pointless to delay production of the book, despite acknowledging that it might fuel prejudice in the minds of the public before the trial.

Caroline put this very issue to use as a propaganda point. On the day the final part of her 'Case' was due to be published, she instead sent a letter to the *Morning Post* announcing that she had decided to withhold it for the moment, since the final instalment was the most incriminating and she did not wish to prejudice the Perreaus' case – even though her enemies showed no such consideration for *her*. 'I defer it from motives of compassion,' she wrote, adding: 'I know at this moment the Perreaus are concerting abominable falsehoods, whereby they hope to blacken my character, and devising every possible scheme to further distress and ruin me.'[15] In truth she was herself planting a number of anonymous missives in the papers which set out to 'distress and ruin' her opponents every bit as much as they did her. She thus managed to score moral points, sacrifice nothing and create even more consumer impatience for the deferred episode of the 'Case'.

It was true, however, that the papers were full of letters devoted to Caroline's undoing. Typical was one in the *Morning Post* of Wednesday 29 March, which opined that 'her story appears extremely contradictory and evasive. If newspaper intelligence tell truth, this woman had been in *gay life* (worse I ought to stile it) long before she became acquainted with these malefactors, and was ever esteemed as artful a woman as any in England.' A peculiar argument was then advanced: 'As she was no wife to *Perreau*, she was subject to no controul,' and therefore 'the fear of *Perreau's* cutting her throat, which compelled her to forge the Bond, is a farcical affair'. Thus, from the axiom in law that a wife is presumed to act under the control of her husband, combined with the fact that Caroline and Daniel were *not* married, the writer illogically deduced that Caroline could not have been coerced in any way at all.

The letter also pointed out that she had exerted upon the magistrates exactly those womanly wiles that ought to make her notorious, and mocked the newspaper's reporting of the hearing. 'It seems, she has always been remarkable for her great powers in moving the passions, therefore it is not the least object of admiration, that the *tone of her voice*, the artless manner in which she related her story, and the decency of her whole deportment was so *truly pathetic*, as to lull the wisdom of the Magistracy that examined her, and make them give credit to all she said and unsaid.'

Caroline was particularly irked that the person behind a number of the anonymous attacks appeared to be a figure for whom she had always felt a lofty contempt: Robert's bourgeois wife. Henrietta Perreau was now loudly claiming that she had never before known that Daniel and Caroline were not married and would have had nothing to do with the strumpet if she had. She also threatened to reveal ghastly details which she had since learned about Caroline's past indiscretions with other gentlemen. Caroline angrily replied that Henrietta had known all along about her and Daniel: 'her affecting now to be affronted at my being introduced to, and living with her in the familiar intercourse of a sister-in-law, together with the vile falshoods she reports of my having lived with a gentleman and tricking (for that is her elegant phrase) him out of considerable sums, is both weak and wicked'.[16]

The greatest insult of all was that Henrietta refused to surrender two items of clothing belonging to Caroline, which had been left at her house. 'The detaining of the two gowns left by me at Mr Robert Perreau's last summer, and the *mean* injustice of Mrs Perreau refusing them to my written order sent, by Mr Bailey my council, needs no comment.'[17] The gowns were haughtily returned the following day, as a notice in the paper reported.[18] However, Caroline's problems with Henrietta were to continue.

The affair of the gowns paled into nothing by comparison with what was to happen a few days later. The first sign of trouble was an anonymous notice in the *Morning Post* on 28 March, summoning Daniel's creditors to a meeting that evening. The outcome of this council of war was a concerted move by Sir Thomas Frankland, Dr Brooke and the Drummonds to strip Daniel of his property, including the house in

Harley Street and all its contents. Daniel humbly co-operated with the manoeuvre, and a few days later was once again declared bankrupt.[19]

Caroline and her three children now found themselves suddenly homeless. Besides the apartment, she lost furniture, household goods, a great deal of expensive china and silverware and almost all her clothes and jewellery. Sir Thomas turned up in person to assist in the eviction, presumably in order to see what valuables were there and to ensure that none was overlooked. There was a tempestuous scene between him and Caroline. She demanded to know what was supposed to happen to the family. Destroying her home and throwing her out on the street was one thing, she said: she could look after herself. But why should three innocent children be made to suffer? She insisted that Sir Thomas provide for their care and housing. He waved her arguments aside, but Caroline refused to give in. A furious dispute ensued and it was eventually Sir Thomas who crumbled. The combatants agreed that the children would be temporarily lodged at the home of their nurse, Hannah Dalboux, and that Sir Thomas would foot the bill of five shillings per week for each. In fact, only the two younger children remained at Mrs Dalboux's. The eldest daughter Susan went to live with a friend of Daniel's, Mrs Jacques – an arrangement made by Daniel himself from his prison cell. Caroline was angered by his interference: 'The glaring partiality he showed Susan, in placing her (in preference of the two younger and more helpless) with Mrs Jacques, has not escaped my notice,'[20] she wrote.

At least the children now had homes of sorts and Caroline could go her own way. Some mysterious 'friends' gave her a roof over her head, and she was financially supported by 'two humane people'.[21] Had it not been for their help, she later wrote, she would have starved.

Frankland did not keep his side of the bargain for long. According to Caroline, he paid the charges for just one month before defaulting. In early May he sent a message to Hannah Dalboux announcing that he would pay nothing further and that if no one else took over the payment the children could go to a workhouse.[22] To Caroline's horror, when she had this development conveyed to Daniel he reportedly shrugged and said they *could* go to a workhouse for all he cared – a statement for which she never forgave him. It was his favouritism again. 'Poor Stewart and Caroline was more like their mother,' she wrote bitterly in a letter to his sister Sukey – 'of course a workhouse was allotted them.'[23] She vowed that in return she would teach them to 'curse and abhor' the name of Perreau. The payments were continued by Caroline herself, using money from her 'humane people', and the children remained with Hannah Dalboux.

Meanwhile, she was still being attacked by anonymous writers to the newspapers, each more vicious than the last. A letter signed 'S.L.' proposed that, as Caroline would eventually be obliged to refute the unjust charges brought against her, she might benefit from seeing a comprehensive list of them. S.L., whose identity is a puzzle but who apparently knew a lot about her link with Joseph Salvador, proceeded to lay out the litany of accusations both for her and for the scandal-hungry readers of the *Morning Post*, adding with heavy irony that there was no doubt 'but I shall receive her warmest thanks for thus giving her an opportunity, in one single relation of her story, to clear her character from all calumny, and hold it up to the world in all its former purity and innocence'.[24]

There followed a list of questions, referring to many familiar stories.

> Whether she did not elope ... with an officer who frequented the house where she and her husband lodged and boarded? Whether she did not as a foreign Princess submit herself to the embraces of a noted amorous son of

Levi, and get from him the many thousands mentioned in her case? Whether she did not afterwards personate the sister of this Princess, and again impose upon the Levite? Whether she did not, in conjunction with Mr. D.P. who on that occasion passed for her husband, under pretence of *crim. con.* [a lawsuit for adultery] extort a further large sum from him? Whether she did not pretend to be with child by this Jew, go through the farce of a mock lying-in, actually hire a child for the purpose, and under these pretences get large sums for child-bed linen, nurse, &c? . . . Whether she has not, at different times, personated many and various Ladies of the first quality and fashion in town, and in *their* names prostituted *herself*? And, Whether she has not, at considerable expence, at different times, hired and procured persons to pass for her mother, aunt, and other relations, in order to give colour to such impositions, and the better to carry on such intrigues?

If Caroline answered even this small selection of the many questions clamouring to be addressed, said S.L., then the public would be satisfied.

A letter in reply appeared in the same newspaper just over a week later, on Saturday 8 April, this time signed 'Candour'. It may have been written by Caroline herself, and was certainly complimentary towards her. The writer opined that 'the tender feelings of which she is possessed are very evident, from the prudent conduct she has shown in so distressed a situation; her behaviour truly engaging, and the woman of quality visible in her deportment', and then went on to return to a tough list of counter-questions to S.L.

Whether he did not rob a man on Hounslow Heath, and take from him a purse, containing seventy guineas? Whether he did not, under the assumed character of a man of fortune, obtain goods to a large amount, for which he never paid a single shilling to this hour? Whether he is not at present in the most intimate friendship, and strongly connected, with a gang of common imposters? Whether he did not rob his ready furnished lodgings of a considerable quantity of furniture? Let him clear himself of these charges before he meddles with the character of a woman who has suffered enough already, from the misery into which she is plunged, from her unhappy connection with a man in whom she placed the most unbounded confidence; and whose imprudencies have brought on these calamities.

On 4 April Caroline had written to the *Morning Post* under her own name, saying, 'Did I wish myself revenged of the Perreaus, I should be amply so in the base, contemptible lyes they daily propagate and get conveyed to the public by anonymous letters. Such conduct must to every intelligent person shew them and their cause in a *true light*: I assure them with the utmost sincerity that I despise their wicked machinations, and pity the shocking depravity of their hearts. – Poor mistaken people! What pains they take to expose themselves.'

A notice in the same newspaper on 10 April announced that a letter had been received purporting to be from Caroline's uncle John Stewart, but that before publishing it the editor wished to satisfy himself that it was genuine by meeting the author in person. His doubts must have been allayed, because two days later another notice stated that 'the editor received back Mr. Stewart's letter last night at eight o'clock, which was too late an hour for inserting it in this day's paper; Mrs. Rudd may, however, depend upon its appearing in the *Morning Post* to-morrow.'

The letter, when it appeared, was addressed to Daniel Perreau and signed by 'John Stewart of Balimoran, County of Down Ireland, currently in London'.[25] Its tone was predominantly one of sputtering fury: 'Mrs. Rudd's tenderness and mercy to you and your brother, shall not deter me from publishing my sentiments of you, your family, advisers, and colleagues, and exposing the numerous arts you *jointly* and *separately* practised, to work upon her compassionate, feeling heart and affection for you.' Reciting the account of the capture according to Caroline's version of events, it again raised the question of a wife's legal responsibility: 'she (as a woman) being entirely ignorant of *such* matters and the consequences to herself of adopting your advice, also from affection and what she religiously believed her absolute duty as your wife, complied with your desires; for *your wife* she was in every moral sense, in the sight of man.' It followed that 'her mind must be on this and all occasions under the *same ascendency* as if the priest had joined your hands'.

The letter then slid more and more into something suspiciously like Caroline's own polemical style. It dilated on Daniel's 'unnatural, brutal conduct to your present offspring, those beautiful infants, whom you and your brother said might go to a workhouse, when Sir T. F——d asked how you would have them disposed of'. Of Henrietta Perreau's pretence at outrage over the fact that Caroline and Daniel were not married, it exclaimed, 'Fine affected madam! I suppose she derived those *high* sentiments from the *noble* descent of a West Indian parson's daughter, and the *elegant education* given her under the care and direction of the late Mrs. Perreaus, *Milliners*, in Tavistock-street. – Such little *gentry* are a *pest* to superior society, and a *burlesque* on the name of gentlewomen.'

The writer finished with an avuncular lament: 'My misery is inexpressible to see this child of my affection in her bloom of life and full perfection of sense crushed, sunk into the lowest abyss of misfortune.'

Claims that the letter was not genuine were soon received by the newspaper and Daniel Perreau later dismissed it out of hand, describing it as 'purporting to be written by her uncle Stewart, who so far from being in London, most certainly has not been in England for some years'.[26] Caroline angrily denied these accusations in a letter to the paper published on

29 May, but this did little to allay the sceptics' doubts, for she repeated many of John Stewart's points in strikingly similar terms.

In particular, she used the letter to relaunch a full-scale attack on Henrietta. Robert and Daniel had been moved to Newgate following a hearing on 29 April at which it had been agreed that their trial would be postponed until June. According to Caroline, Henrietta never once visited Robert in Newgate, nor did she give him any of the material help which was so vital to survive there. By contrast, Caroline described her own charitable behaviour towards Daniel: 'A matrass spread on the floor was all the bed he and his brother had between them, until I heard (from a lady Daniel wrote to) of their dreadful situation; upon which I contrived to send him a decent bed, with bedstead and furniture to it, enjoining the lady to say she gave it.' She added that in order to afford this, she had been obliged to 'part with one gown out of the only two I am mistress of'. She added that she would not have revealed these things had not Mrs Perreau's conduct been such as to make it impossible to ignore the matter. 'Destitute herself of sentiment and the amiable virtues which results from a feeling heart, her little mind prompts her to revile and misrepresent me, because heaven has indued me with both.'

Earlier in the same month, in the form of a thinly disguised 'X.Y.', she accused Dr Brooke of allowing Henrietta Perreau to talk him out of abandoning his prosecution against Daniel Perreau, as he had apparently been thinking of doing. X.Y. sneered at Henrietta's low birth and said of Robert, 'It's a pity Daniel did not desire him to hang his own wife. There would have been quite as much justice and propriety in the one as in the other, and it is not impossible more. I presume it is no treason to suppose that Mrs R.P. might be as well acquainted with, and concerned in her husband's affairs as Mrs. Rudd could be with Daniel's: I beg the latter's pardon, she has clearly proved that ever since they lived together he kept her in great ignorance of his affairs and transactions.'[27]

The X.Y. letter made an even more serious accusation, harking back to Caroline's suspicions of the lawyer whom Robert had been consulting prior to their escape attempt. 'Did not Mrs. R.P. on the Friday (previous to the parties going to Bow-street) with her husband, consult Mr. Henry D[agge] about fixing the forgery upon Mrs. Rudd?' It challenged Mrs Perreau to say whether the three of them had not been plotting against her, and talking about going to see the magistrate Sir John Fielding, when Caroline had come into the room and interrupted them – upon which Henrietta 'very artfully' changed the subject by saying, 'Aye, Sir John Molesworth, of Cornwall.'

Finally, there was another dig at Henrietta's apparent lack of concern for Robert's welfare. 'Has she since her husband's commitment shewn even a *decent* sorrow? has she not gone out as much as usual; sees company at home, and keeps two footmen to attend her; employs a great part of her time in getting scurrilous letters wrote abusing Mrs. Rudd?'

Caroline did have genuine supporters, and not all the letters in the papers taking her side could have been her own productions. Her plight moved some readers to paroxysms of gallantry. As someone signing herself 'A Friend to Suffering Merit' put it in a letter to the editor of the *Morning Post* on 17 May, 'Suffering merit, has in all ages been a subject much affected and descanted upon; accompanied with beauty and the *Graces* it becomes one of the most interesting subjects in Nature: the elegant, unfortunate Mrs. Rudd is a striking example.'

At around this time there appeared a poem described as a 'Pathetic Elegy', addressed to Daniel in Newgate and supposedly written by Caroline[28] – an unconvincing attribution, although it takes her part and was obviously composed by someone who had thoroughly digested her accusations against Daniel. It begins:

Unhappy partner of my widow'd breast,
    Once its dear pilot thro' life's stormy sea,
Tho' with unnumbered wrongs thou'st broke its rest,
    In spite of vengeance, still it beats for thee!

The poem continues in this vein for a considerable number of verses, claiming 'I never brand thee with a sable deed / Nor to thy charge impute a single woe!' When she looks at the children, Caroline sees Daniel's beloved face:

Eager I call my little young-ones round,
    And in each feature read thy manly charms:
A moment thus I tread enchanted ground,
    And clasp the husband in my children's arms!

Why, begs the poet, did Daniel not have the courage to do himself what he had planned? And why did he force Caroline to do it with threats to her life? She would gladly have committed the forgery for him if he had not treated her so harshly, and she would have died for his sake if she only knew that he loved her.

Oh! Hadst thou urg'd me to the fatal deed
    By softer means, thou hadst not been deny'd:
I ne'er had scrupled for my love to bleed,
    But for his sake, a willing death had dy'd.

Mine should have been the only guilt and shame;
    Dauntless I'd met the horrors of the tree,
Repaid, if spotless I preserv'd thy fame,
    And only got one pitying tear from thee.

*

Caroline's problems with Henrietta Perreau were as nothing compared to the battle that was now beginning with the man who was to become her worst enemy: Sir Thomas Frankland.

The repossession of the Harley Street house had been almost entirely his doing; the other creditors took a more relaxed view of the situation. This is understandable: Sir Thomas was owed almost £9000, far more than the others (Dr Brooke had given Daniel £1500, and the Drummonds were still owed £1400 on an earlier loan made to Robert). Brooke took £1000 worth of the assets found in the house, and the Drummonds received a similar sum – but Sir Thomas took the title deeds of the property itself, which the Drummonds had been holding as security. With less justification, he also combed through the house and claimed for himself any item of value that he could find, including much that did not belong to Daniel at all, but to Caroline. Rightly, she objected to this, for she was a free woman: no charges were being brought against her. She considered it nothing less than robbery, carried out by Sir Thomas with the connivance of Daniel and Robert, who had not only failed to oppose him but had even – she believed – actively co-operated. One of her letters complained that Daniel had 'left me at present to absolute beggary, and want of even the common necessaries of life; I have not a decent change of cloaths, nor what the meanest of my sex would think so'.[29]

Caroline was not the only one affected by Frankland's indiscriminate raid on the house. He took a ring belonging to a jeweller who had merely loaned it to Daniel. When the jeweller learned of the arrest, he went to see Daniel in prison, taking with him the well-known man about town William Hickey and Hickey's father. Daniel received the three visitors with his usual urbanity and said that he would gladly have returned the ring, but could not: Sir Thomas had seized it, despite being clearly told that it was someone else's property.

The Hickeys and the jeweller immediately went to call on Sir Thomas. He listened while the elder Hickey explained that the ring was not Daniel's and must therefore be returned immediately. As Hickey's son recorded in his memoirs, Sir Thomas heard him out and then answered, 'Humph! And that's your opinion, is it, Mr. Hickey? Then I must observe that I do not think your opinion worth two pence. I differ totally, and though no lawyer, Mr. Hickey, I am no fool, and, by God, I'll keep the ring, Mr. Hickey.'[30]

The Hickeys stormed out and the matter ended up in court – where Frankland lost the case in short order. According to Hickey, he did not manage to produce even one witness in his favour and his lawyers admitted that if they had understood the true facts they would never have agreed to act for Sir Thomas. The ring was restored, together with £200 in expenses.

Caroline was less immediately successful. However, she was determined that Frankland would not find her the pushover he expected. Writing to the editor of the *Morning Post*, she threw down the gauntlet: 'As Sir Thomas has no more right to my cloaths or any part of my property that he has than he has to yours, or any person's that he never heard of, I presume he thinks my poverty secures him from the power of the law; however he will soon find himself mistaken.'

An open letter from Caroline to Sir Thomas in the *Post* on 12 May began, 'Sir, I have so thorough a contempt for you, and for your character, that I should deem you beneath my notice, were I not informed you take advantage of my silence.' She accused him of taking £12,000 worth of goods when the debt to him was only £9000, and called it 'an act of savage brutality'. If he thought that his attempts to defame and ruin her were going to intimidate her into submission, or make her simply flee from the situation, he should think again. She fully intended to exercise her legal rights and fight for what was hers.

As in her attacks on Henrietta Perreau, Caroline also defended Daniel, asking why Sir Thomas had been trying so hard to persuade Brooke to go ahead with his prosecution. It was clearly a matter of greed: 'From what motives but to make yourself more secure of his property, have you daily

followed and urged Dr. B[rook]e to prosecute Daniel Perreau?' Sir Thomas's attitude towards Daniel was unpardon-
ably brutal: 'When that unfortunate man . . . sent to you for
a change of apparel, your answer was, "That he had
sufficient to last him to the session [when his trial would take
place], and you would then take care he should be hanged."
That horrid speech characterises you so strongly, as to
require no comment. Your falsehoods and abuse of me, have
the same ruffian-like mercenary motives for their source.' As
for his remark that her children could go to a workhouse,
that was the worst of all, and would never be forgotten or
forgiven.

She finished, 'You should reflect, Sir Thomas, when you
take impertinent freedoms with my name, that you are
speaking of a person greatly your superior; one who has the
mind, as well as the manners, of a gentlewoman, and would
think it a worse misfortune and reproach than any she has yet
experienced, to resemble you in either: consequently it best
becomes you to be silent, or to mention me with respect.'

Then, all of a sudden, a new enemy appeared on the
horizon. He announced himself with a letter signed 'Justice'
in the *Morning Post* on 15 May. Alluding to Caroline's
attack on Sir Thomas, Justice wrote, 'Madam, you have
wantonly attacked a gentleman of great honour and worth
for having done that which every man in his senses would
have done in his situation' – reimbursing himself for what
had been taken from him. Her claim that Frankland had
taken £12,000 worth to balance £9000 was nonsense: the
resale value of her precious property was probably £6000 or
less. As for her personal abuse, Justice would pass over that:
it was unnecessary to 'offend the delicacy of Sir Thomas
Frankland, by supposing it necessary to defend his reputation
against the rude unmannerly attack of a common slanderer
and a common ——'.

You talk of your nobleness of birth, your rank in life, your delicacy and the elegance of your manners; but your language, Mrs. Rudd, is surely more like the language of Billingsgate than that of a Gentlewoman . . . Who are you, Mrs Rudd? Of what noble family are you descended? Who are the Lords you honour by your alliance? Who is this man you call your uncle Stewart? Are not you and your uncle one and the same person? Till you answer these questions I shall look upon you as a common impostor, and forget the delicacy and respect due to your sex; but if you answer me with truth and candour, you shall hear again, in a milder manner, from: Justice.

The *Morning Post* published an angry reply, signed 'Fact', on Saturday 18 May.

You damn the cause you mean to defend; and raise the same you meant to traduce . . . Your whole letter is a compound of falsity and low-life'd abuse; with an affectation of being very smart, you are very stupid, glaringly ignorant and vulgar. You should [have] informed yourself who she was, before you insolently questioned the genteelity of her birth; and if your capacity would not allow you to distinguish the good sense, delicacy of sentiment; and polite language, conspicuous in all her writings, you should have taken the opinion of some person more intelligent than yourself, and prevented your ignorance.

Another letter also appeared on 18 May, this one signed 'No Puffer', demanding more information about Caroline's claims to aristocratic blood. 'The purport of this is to request to know *who was* your father, and to desire you openly to aver what family you are of; I am much interested in the noble family to whom you have the assurance to claim an alliance, therefore doubt your veracity that you ever belonged to the most distant branch of it.' No Puffer warned that if no adequate answer was received, that would only confirm his opinion: 'that you are sprung from obscurity'.

'Sir,' wrote Caroline to the editor of the *Morning Post* on Saturday 20 May, 'I have repeatedly publicly declared, that I will not condescend to answer anonymous letters, nor can any one, with common sense, expect I should. The notice I have taken of Justice (though not a full reply) answers in general both his and the one signed No Puffer, the author of which is one and the same person.' The following Monday an unsigned notice in the *Post* offered a reward of £300 to anyone who could identify Justice and No Puffer. It specified that the information should be sent to the publisher of the newspaper, and properly authenticated.

The next day a new letter jauntily announced:

Jack Spy presents his most respectful compliments to the sensible and tender-hearted Mrs. Rudd; and having seen her advertisement wherein she offers a reward of three hundred pounds for the discovery of the author of the letter signed JUSTICE, Jack Spy is ready to gratify Mrs. Rudd's curiosity, provided she will be so kind as to let him know where and by whom the money is to be paid, whether it is lodged in the hands of her relation Mr. Stewart; in which case she need but give notice who this Mr. Stewart is, and where he lives, that he may be applied to; for hitherto the public has taken him for a ghost raised up by a witch.[31]

'Mr. Editor,' replied Caroline on Wednesday,

Please to inform the anonymous defamer who writes under the several signatures of Justice, No Puffer, and Jack Spy, that the glaring falsities he has advanced refute themselves, and recoil on their author the scandal he aims at me; and that as I don't know who inserted or offers the reward Spy mentions, it is probably he or his party did it with some sinister malicious design or other, and to afford a new subject for their pens and fertile imaginations.

Poor creatures! they expose themselves sufficiently to save me the trouble of doing it; what they write, properly understood, is my panegyric. However, to ease them of their doubts about my knowing who Justice is, I condescend to tell them that I do know who he is, and he shall in good time be convinced I do; therefore I need not, nor my friends, offer any reward to discover him.

One would imagine Justice, No Puffer and Jack Spy to be pseudonyms of Sir Thomas Frankland, but Caroline believed, and later asserted in her 'Narrative',[32] that the letters were in fact written by a sleazy friend and former stock-jobbing confederate of Daniel's, Colonel George Kinder. This odious man had never liked her, she said, and now that Daniel was in trouble he was trying to save him by attacking Caroline with every weapon he could lay his hands on. And worse, according to her, was to come.

Caroline was still a free woman, but her situation was perilous. Her enemies were arrayed against her: Frankland, Henrietta, the two 'unfortunate Perreau brothers', as they were already being called, and now Colonel Kinder. On her side, she had only a few allies: her lawyer Bailey, the 'friends' who were supporting her financially but who otherwise kept safely out of the way, and the occasional kind gentleman who was moved by her elegant suffering to write to the papers.

Now, however, the date was set for the decisive event: the trial of the two brothers was to take place in the first few days of June. Caroline was going to testify against them; in return for this she would have her final, formal release from all culpability. Then she could turn her attention to legal proceedings against Sir Thomas. She could reclaim her possessions, move into a proper home, be reunited with her children and start a new life.

But Caroline was in for a very unpleasant shock.

CHAPTER
SIX
— ✦ —
THE PERREAUS ON TRIAL

Robert's trial was the first. It took place on 1 June 1775 at the Old Bailey, with Sir Richard Aston presiding over a panel of judges which also included Boswell's friend John Wilkes, currently Lord Mayor of London. The prosecutor was Sir James Mansfield and the defence team was headed by a highly regarded lawyer named John Dunning. With the twelve-man jury, the defendant's team, the large assembly of witnesses and a 'most amazing crowd',[1] the room was packed to capacity and quickly became airless and suffocating. Robert himself was the focus of all eyes as he was brought in and took his place quietly in the dock.

Foremost among the witnesses was Margaret Caroline Rudd, dressed in her best and ready to do her duty. However, before the trial got underway Sir Richard Aston made an unexpected announcement. Her evidence was to be dispensed with. He 'spoke with much warmth' on the impropriety of her having been promised immunity by the magistrates: they had no authority to do such a thing. Instead, the prosecution would proceed without her testimony. She would have no legal protection, and would forthwith be prosecuted by Sir Thomas Frankland for the forgeries conducted against him. And so – to Caroline's utter surprise and horror – Aston ordered that she be taken to Newgate and imprisoned pending Sir Thomas's charges.

Caroline was removed from the court without further ado and thrown into Newgate Prison, conveniently located right next door to the courthouse.

According to her later assessment of events, the prime mover behind this U-turn had been John Wilkes, who was motivated by an obscure grudge against her and had convinced his fellow judges to discard her immunity arrangement. If so, the cause of his vengefulness is a mystery. Caroline herself was far from uncertain about it, though. She believed it was because Colonel Kinder, who had become friends with Wilkes in the course of an (unsuccessful) attempt to court his daughter, had exerted his baleful influence over the Mayor.[2] Others, knowing nothing of Kinder, assumed that a sexual affair between Wilkes and Caroline had gone wrong and that it was a case of sour grapes – Hell having no fury like a womanizer scorned. The absence of evidence for such an affair did nothing to dispel the rumours. A more likely interpretation than either of these is perhaps that Wilkes simply did not like her, and wanted to see her take her chances on the same terms as the Perreaus.

And so the trial went ahead without Caroline. She sat fuming in a stone-walled cell while the drama went on next door, suffering agonies of suspense as to what might be happening and what effect it would have on her.

The jury and audience, still recovering from the thrill of Caroline's unexpected dismissal, listened as the formal indictments against Robert Perreau were read out. They were: 'falsely making, forging, and counterfeiting' a bond for £7500 with the intention of defrauding William Adair, doing the same with the intention of defrauding Robert and Henry Drummond, and 'feloniously uttering and publishing the same bond as true, well knowing it to be forged', with the intention of defrauding William Adair and the Drummonds respectively.[3]

The first witness to be called was Henry Drummond. The banker ascended the small spiral staircase that led into the witness box, and was invited by Mansfield, the prosecution lawyer, to tell the court his version of the events leading to Robert Perreau's arrest.

Mr Drummond said that he had known Robert socially and as an apothecary for some years, and had lent him £1400 for a short period in January 1775. The loan was only supposed to be for ten days, but Robert did not repay it or call at the bank again until 7 March, when he came in with the bond signed by William Adair and asked to borrow a further £5000, saying that he would repay the original loan out of that amount.

Henry then related how he and his brother Robert Drummond had examined the bond and voiced their doubts to Robert, who took the bond away with him for a few hours and returned with the letter purporting to be from William Adair. He described their request that Robert leave the bond with them overnight and their proposal the next day that they all visit William Adair together. At this point in the story the bond was produced in court. Henry looked at it and confirmed that it was the one Robert had brought to him.

He then recounted their reception at William Adair's house, Adair's failure to recognize Robert and his disowning of the bond, Caroline's arrival and confession, and the decision to allow her and the Perreaus to leave unhindered. After that, Henry had not seen Robert until three days later at the magistrates' office in Bow Street, when he was summoned to give evidence after the arrest.

The prosecution now handed Henry over to the defence lawyer, John Dunning, who began his cross-examination by asking him whether he had ever seen William Adair write. Henry replied that he thought he might have done, but it was so long ago that he couldn't be sure. Dunning then asked exactly what they had said to Robert to indicate their doubts about the bond. Henry said there had been a 'delicacy' to it;

he and his brother had not wished to accuse Robert outright of bringing them a forgery, but they nevertheless made their opinion clear.

'Did he take away the bond that time?'

'He did the first time, but not the second.'

'He readily left the bond?'

'Yes, without even a memorandum.'

'Without any hesitation?'

'Yes.'

'He did not offer any excuse not to leave it?'

'No.'

'He complied with your desire of leaving the bond, as the most innocent man would have done?'

'Yes, readily.'

Asked for more details concerning the trip to William Adair's house the following day, Henry testified that it was either his or his brother's decision, not Robert Perreau's, but that the latter had again 'most readily' consented to going. He added that if there had been any hesitation or reluctance, he would surely have spotted it, 'for being convinced in my own mind that it was a forged bond, I looked steadfastly on his countenance, and could not see him alter in the least'.

Dunning now turned to Caroline's confession. Had she acknowledged the whole of the responsibility? 'Yes,' said Drummond. She had said that 'nobody was meant to be injured; that it would all be paid; that she never meant to injure us or anybody'.

'Do you recollect her mentioning any circumstances how she came to be induced to do it, or how she carried it on?'

'I do not recollect: she took the whole from Robert Perreau, and said she was the guilty person.'

'Did she say under what circumstances she had written the name?'

'I do not recollect that she did.'

Pressed to continue, Henry described how Caroline had demonstrated her ability to write a masculine hand by reproducing the signature in front of them on a piece of paper, which his brother had immediately burned in accordance with his promise.

'And it was the same hand?'

'It did appear to us to be the same.'

'This was readily performed by her?'

'Yes.'

The court was now shown the letter which Robert Perreau had told the Drummonds was written by William Adair. Dunning asked Henry whether he thought it resembled the hand demonstrated by Caroline, and he replied that he did. 'I think the W in the letter here is pretty much in the same style, as the W to the *William Adair* that she wrote.'

Having made its point, the cross–examination concluded with a few character questions. Henry acknowledged that he had known the prisoner as a reliable and respectable apothecary for many years and that he had never heard anything against him. He was 'remarkably happy in his character'. The letter was presented for his scrutiny again – to imprint it on the jury's memory – and he repeated that the writing looked the same as Caroline's 'forging' hand. Then he was allowed to step down.

His brother, Robert Drummond, took the stand next and retold the same story in all the key points. Despite the defence's emphasis on Caroline's confession and – most importantly – her perfect reproduction of the signature, there was no escaping the other implications of the Drummonds' joint testimony: it was Robert who had brought the bond to them, not Caroline, and he had lied about knowing William Adair. Why would a man lie unless he had something important to conceal? The question was left to hang in the minds of the jury.

Sir Thomas Frankland was the next to testify, occupying the stand only briefly. He described Robert Perreau's good reputation as an apothecary and a gentleman, and said that during the fifteen or sixteen years that he and his family had been regular clients of Robert's they had always trusted him; indeed, his uncle had dubbed him 'Honest Perreau'. During the last few months, however, Robert had brought him several bonds and used them to borrow money, most of which had never been repaid. This was all Sir Thomas had to say and he was not cross-examined. His testimony was not directly relevant to the current case (and perhaps Caroline was right in alleging that he and Robert had made a deal concerning the other forgeries for which Robert might have been tried), but it served the prosecution by establishing a view of Robert as a superficially respectable man with a secret financial vice.

Richard Wilson, one of the scriveners, then deposed that he had drawn up the £7500 bond for Robert Perreau in late February or early March. He had had no dealings with anyone else in relation to the bond. Robert had called in person and had written his instructions on a piece of paper. He then asked Wilson to destroy this paper, but Wilson told him he could not do so because an important legal note relating to a different matter was written on the other side. So Robert waited until Wilson had copied the bond, then took the instructions and carefully crossed out the words, 'William Adair of Pall-Mall in the parish of St. James's, in the county of Middlesex, Esq. to Robert Perreau of Golden-square, in the county of Middlesex, aforesaid, Esq. the sum of £7500 to be paid on the 7th of July next.' Wilson still had the paper: it was produced and shown to the court. His testimony carried a strong suggestion that Robert knew there was something illegal about the bond.

Scroope Ogilvie, a clerk who had recently worked for William Adair, testified that he was familiar with Adair's writing and that the signature on the bond was definitely not his.

James Adair was the next to climb the few narrow steps to the witness box. He also stated that the writing was not

William's. Apart from that his style of giving evidence was laconic, to say the least.

In cross-examination, Dunning brought up the mysterious letter which was to appear in the newspaper many months later. Presumably hoping for an answer which would leave the jury with something more useful than puzzled incomprehension, he asked, 'Did you receive any letter from Mrs Rudd?'

Adair said, 'Yes.'

'Was she with you?' asked Dunning, alluding to Caroline's visit seeking help with William.

'Yes.'

'Had you any conversation with her?'

'Yes,' replied Adair for the third time.

'Who was present when Mrs Rudd had the conversation with you?'

'Nobody, only her and myself.'

'For what purpose did she come to you?'

'She knows a gentleman that I know in the north of Ireland,' he answered irrelevantly.

'That cannot be evidence,' interrupted one of the judges.

Dunning said, 'My lord, it has already been given in evidence, that Mrs Rudd took it upon herself, and declared the prisoner totally innocent.' He explained that he believed the letter received by James Adair might contain a similar confession, and thus help to prove that Robert Perreau was innocent.

'Can her letter be stronger evidence that her own personal declarations?' replied the judge. 'Both the Mr Drummonds declare, she took it upon herself; that she did it: that the whole was hers and he was innocent; that is certainly stronger than her writing it down upon a piece of paper.' Dunning had to drop the subject of the letter and James Adair stepped down, being pressed no further about his dealings with Caroline. The letter was not asked for or seen by the court.

Arthur Jones next testified that his name, which was signed on the bond as a witness, was not in his handwriting and that he knew nothing at all about it. Asked whether William Adair had a servant by the name of Thomas Hart or Start – the other witness whose name was signed on the bond – Jones said he had never heard of such a person.

The bond was read out in full to the court, followed by the letter which Robert Perreau had given to the Drummonds as being from William Adair, and which Henry Drummond had testified that he now believed to be in Caroline's 'forging' hand. And that concluded the prosecution's half of the trial.

The defence had done its best to undermine the prosecution's case, but it remained largely intact. According to their picture, Robert Perreau had commissioned a bond from Wilson, the scrivener, and then attempted to destroy the evidence of its having been made. He took the bond to the Drummonds, where he lied about visiting and receiving a letter from William Adair. James Adair and Scroope Ogilvie both stated unhesitatingly before the court that the writing on the bond was not William's, and Arthur Jones similarly disowned his own signature. Sir Thomas Frankland's fragment of testimony also suggested that Robert was someone whose trustworthy surface was not to be relied upon. It was a damning network of evidence.

It was now the turn of the defence to try to undo all this, and to paint an altogether different portrait of Robert in the jury's minds.

They began with a prepared statement read out by Robert himself. He spoke for an hour and twenty minutes, calmly and clearly, using a sheaf of notes which he held in his hand.[4] His speech was a well-crafted, eloquent piece of work, and there was later something of a tussle to claim authorship – no one pretended that it was written by Robert. It was generally thought to have been composed by a Hugh M'Aulay Boyd, but the playwright and diarist Richard Cumberland also laid claim to it in his *Memoirs*, where he proudly stated that it was 'to a word drawn up by me'.*[5]

Robert's statement was addressed to 'My Lord, and Gentlemen of the Jury', and began: 'If I had been wanting in that fortitude which is the result of innocence, or had felt any hesitation in submitting my proceedings to the strictest scrutiny, I need not at this day have stood before my country, nor set my life upon the issue of a legal trial.' He reminded the jurors that he had presented himself at the magistrates' office of his own free will, something he would never have done had he been guilty. 'I have forced that transaction into light, which might else have been suppressed.' Ever since, he had been 'ardently looking forward' to his hour in court as the one in which he could vindicate his character.

He alluded to his unblemished reputation as an apothecary and gentleman, known for his 'diligence, honesty, and punctuality' and devoted to his 'worthy wife, and three promising children', with whom he had enjoyed the fruits of 'affluence and innocence' until this unexpected affliction came upon them. 'I have followed no pleasures, nor launched into any expences; there is not a man living who can charge me with neglect, or dissipation.'

Next he flattered the jury by telling them that as good upright men themselves, they must be able to understand his predicament. 'Honest undesigning characters have at all times been the dupe of craft and subtilty.' He promised to tell them a story that 'will furnish strong instances, indeed, of credulity on one part, but which, at the same time, will exhibit a train of such consummate artifice on the other, as is scarce to be equalled in all the annals of iniquity, and which

---

* Cumberland added that over lunch the same day the great actor David Garrick had praised it to the skies and said that the man who wrote it had doubtless saved Perreau's life, 'and what would he not give to know who it was? I confess my vanity was strongly moved to tell him; but he shortly after found it out, and perhaps repented of his hyperboles, for it was not good policy in him to over-praise a writer for the stage.'

might have extorted belief and confidence from a much more cautious and sagacious person than I can claim to be'.

He launched into a vivid description of the machinations of Margaret Caroline Rudd, who had deceived and abused him every step of the way. 'Now that detection has broken the charm, [her contrivances] appear too glaring for imposition: but when they followed in the order of their conspiracy, prefaced as they were by every artifice that could engage my confidence, the facility with which the truth might have been discovered became with me the strongest reason for never suspecting that it could have been so daringly transgressed.' Moreover, he added, his critical faculties had been impaired by wishful thinking. 'What we ardently wish, we are well inclined to believe . . . Not only the prosperity of a brother, twin-born with myself, was displayed in my sight, but the welfare and advancement of my own family (the tenderest, and of course, the blindest, side, on which I could be attacked) was cunningly held forth.

'Many and recent instances have occurred of men of much more enlightened understanding than I can claim, who have been made the dupes of adventurers less able and less artful than she is to whom I fell a sacrifice; and yet, when I have either heard or read their stories, I have thought I should not have been trapanned into the same snares. They and the world in general may think the same of me; but they must recollect, that they are commenting on a plot after it is detected – they are reasoning upon the deception of a juggler, when the whole process of the trick is laid open.'

Like Daniel, Robert said that he had received a number of letters full of instructions and promises. He had been told that Adair wished to help him as well as Daniel, by setting both of them up in the banking business. Whenever Robert suggested meeting the Adairs in person, he was delicately put off and told that it could damage his and Daniel's prospects if they intruded too much. Entirely convincing reasons were given to explain why the Adairs needed money raised through bonds, and why Robert himself should put his good reputation to use in cashing them. He was further encouraged by the fact that when he handed the money over to Caroline, he saw it spent wisely, 'in the purchase of a house, and all the material ingredients of a solid establishment'.

Having set the scene and appealed to whatever fellow feeling might lurk in the jury box – it being likely that of any twelve gentlemen, at least one or two must have felt misused and outwitted by a woman at some time or another – Robert than narrated at length his version of the story of the bonds for which he had been caught.

He said that Caroline had persuaded him to cash them as usual, telling him that William Adair had requested it; when he raised objections to what seemed to him 'an unpleasant business', she convinced him that it was best to do as Adair wished. Robert therefore had the bond written up, and gave it to Caroline to take to Adair for his signature and those of the two witnesses. A couple of days later, after she had brought it back signed, Robert presented it to the Drummonds. He had had no doubt at all that the signature was Adair's, which was why he had not hesitated to tell the Drummonds that Adair had personally validated the bond when he had not.

In fact, he now said, it was not Adair but Caroline he had seen during that interlude between visits to the Drummonds. He had gone to tell her about the bankers' scepticism and on hearing of it she simply took the bond and went off with it. When she came back an hour or two later she told Robert that she had been to see Mr Adair, catching him just as he was about to go out riding, and Adair had said that it was certainly his hand, but that it might have changed since he was younger. This was the message that Robert faithfully passed back to the Drummonds – with the small, and according to him entirely innocent, alteration that *he* was the one who had visited Adair. Not doubting Caroline's honesty, he had seen no harm in this refinement. The idea of the bond's being a forgery never crossed his mind until the accusations at William Adair's house.

Robert concluded his statement by repeating his pleas for understanding and sympathy. He again reminded the jury that although the truth about the bond might seem obvious now, it had not been so at the time. He had cashed bonds of the same sort before, always at Caroline's instigation; no one had ever questioned them, and the handwriting had been the same on all the bonds and in all the letters received from 'William Adair'. They had made a convincing package. He fell for it – but who would not? Gullibility was not the same as guilt. And how could anyone who doubted his honesty explain his willingness to go with the Drummonds to see Mr Adair in person? No guilty man would have put himself in that situation; nor would he have left the bond with the bankers in the first place had he suspected that anything was wrong with it.

'In my defence, proofs rise upon proofs, and the least of them is incontrovertible,' he said. His conduct was 'absolutely irreconcileable with every idea of guilt'. Above all, he begged the jury to remember that he had voluntarily entrusted himself to the magistrates on that fateful day – such was his desire for honesty. Had he not done his best to clear his name, he could not with a clear conscience have gone 'through the remainder of my days in peace and serenity in the bosoms of my family and my friends (to whom I trust the justice of this Court will this night send me)'.

With these poignant words, Robert Perreau concluded his statement and sat down. The jury had only a few moments to digest what they had heard, for now the first of the defence witnesses climbed into the witness box. It was one of Caroline's greatest foes: the treacherous Colonel George Kinder.

Kinder stated that he was an intimate acquaintance of both Robert and Daniel Perreau, as well as of Mrs Rudd, whom he knew only as Mrs Perreau. He had frequently heard her talk of her kinship with James Adair; he had also heard her say that James had recommended her to his relation William Adair, and that the latter intended to set up both Perreau brothers in the banking business. He had seen letters sent to Robert purporting to be from William, and remembered mentioning to Robert that it would be a good idea to hold on to these letters as insurance if Mr Adair failed to keep his promise. Finally, Kinder asserted that he had believed all Caroline's stories himself, as did both the Perreau brothers, as far as he could observe.

The defence prompted him for general impressions: 'In the course of the time you was at Daniel Perreau's, you might be able, probably, to make an observation of the art of this woman?'

Kinder readily obliged. 'She seemed to be rather artful in the conduct of her business; and she wanted the Perreaus to consider that an obedience to her will would be the only means in which these favours were to show to them.'

Kinder remarked that Robert had visited Daniel's house three or four times daily during the period when these events were taking place. He described everything he had heard about the Adairs' plan to set the family up in business, buy them a house and give them a comfortable income, as well as their supposed intention of making Daniel a baronet and procuring for him a seat in parliament – 'and she has told me very often, so and so, when I am a lady, I shall do so and so'.

He remembered Caroline talking about James Adair's wife, with whom she also claimed to be friendly, but whom she considered miserly and dull. Caroline had related to him a conversation in which Mrs Adair had talked about the parliamentary seat which her husband was buying for Daniel. 'It will cost three thousand Newmarket pounds,' Caroline had apparently told Mrs Adair, using a slang phrase, and the latter had asked, 'What are Newmarket pounds?' – 'Guineas,' said Caroline. To this Mrs Adair had replied that pounds would serve very well and she would not give more –

a guinea being worth a shilling more than a pound. A day or two after this Caroline told Kinder that James's wife was rather mean in money matters, and so William had instead taken on the responsibility of arranging for Daniel's position in parliament.

Having delivered himself of these colourful stories, Kinder left the stand and was replaced by John Moody, who had been Daniel Perreau's footman from March 1773 to July 1774. Moody testified that he had seen Mrs Rudd writing letters which were then passed to Daniel.

'Do you know Mrs. Rudd's manner of writing?' he was asked by the defence lawyer, Dunning.

'Perfectly well.'

'Did she, in the letters she wrote to be conveyed to Daniel Perreau, write her ordinary, or a different kind of hand?'

'Quite different from her common hand; the R's in those letters represented a Z very much.'

Moody knew that the letters were supposed to be from William Adair. When Daniel was out, Caroline 'used to come down, and write in this particular character, and would say, When your master comes home, deliver this letter to him as left by Mr William Adair, and tell him, he has been an hour with me in the parlour'.

He confirmed that the signatures at the bottom of the bond and on the letters were in her special false handwriting. 'Sometimes, when I have gone up to her door, and she has been writing in this way, she has given me a short answer, and been angry with me. She had different pens: she used to send me for hard crow-quill and goose-quill pens, and I used to mend them, because she said, she could write better with pens of my mending.' He also brought her 'thick gilt-edged paper', different from the thin paper normally used by Daniel. She had indeed visited James Adair occasionally. 'I have seen her go to Mr James Adair two or three times,' said Moody. 'Once I remember her seeing Mr James Adair in Soho-Square; another time she went to Mr James Adair's, and was answered by the servant, to the best of my knowledge, that Mr James Adair was at his office in the city.' Asked whether he understood her to have a similar acquaintance with William Adair, however, he answered only that she had sometimes seemed to want Daniel to believe that she had seen William, when in fact she had not. 'She said to me, if your master finds out I have not been with Mr Adair, or that Mr Adair has not been here, he will never pardon me.'

Moody also described exactly how Caroline used to fool Daniel into thinking that a message had been delivered from William Adair. 'Mrs Rudd has frequently come down to the foot of the parlour stairs and called me up, and bid me go, when I had an opportunity, and give a double rap at the door, and then come up to the drawing-room to her, and say, a gentleman wanted to speak with her; then she would come down and write these notes ... and she has bid me carry those notes up as if they came from Mr William Adair.' She often slipped him half a crown for these services.*

Asked if he ever carried messages in the other direction, to either of the Adairs, he said, 'Yes, I was sent to Mr James Adair's with a present of some French pears.' He had also passed messages to James Adair's wife, with whom Caroline was apparently seeking to make friends at the time: 'I once carried a message, I believe it was a card inclosed, importing, that Mrs Perreau, as she was then called, intended to pay her a visit.' He thought he remembered Mrs Adair returning a card, and also visiting Caroline while the latter was pregnant.

'You had never seen Mr William Adair at the house?'

'No,' he said. 'Mrs Rudd once sent me to enquire if he was in town; I was told he was not.'

Robert Perreau's sister Susannah (usually called Sukey, but here appearing on more formal terms) next took the stand and confirmed that she had also heard Caroline talking about

---

* Commenting on this testimony in her 'Narrative', Caroline later explained these incidents by saying that they were conducted at Daniel's request, not hers, and that their purpose was to impress Daniel's business associate – George Kinder.

William Adair and promising that he would be 'a great friend' to the family. She had seen notes passed to Daniel, mentioning vast sums of money and signed by Mr Adair.

A servant of the Perreaus, Elizabeth Perkins, testified that she too had been asked to tell Daniel that letters had been left for him. On one occasion recently, she said, she had been given a letter by Mrs Rudd and told to bring it in a quarter of an hour later.

Next on the stand was Daniel Perreau himself. He began by confirming the previous witness's story, saying that a letter had been delivered to Caroline in this way a few days before the incidents for which Robert was being tried. Caroline read it and told him that the letter was from William Adair, and that it said Robert should procure £5000 upon bond. The two of them talked to Robert, and he, 'after a great unwillingness', eventually agreed to have the bond drawn up and bring it back to Caroline. Nothing more was said until Monday 6 March, when Daniel saw a paper lying on the bedside table. He asked Caroline what it was, and she said it was the bond, signed and ready for Robert to take to the Drummonds. The next day she gave it to Robert. Daniel heard her reminding him to approach the bank with 'the same privacy that he had done upon other occasions', as Mr Adair did not wish it to be known that he was raising money in this way. Robert 'showed a vast deal of reluctancy, and said it was a very unpleasant work'. Daniel agreed but, knowing that the Drummonds were acquainted with Mr Adair, could not see that his brother should have any problem cashing the bond.

'Did it appear to you, that your brother believed Mrs Rudd's representation of her connection with Adair?'

'Certainly he did.'

'I need hardly ask you if you believed the same?'

'I did to my misfortune.'

In the prosecution's cross-examination, Daniel was asked,

'Did you not say, when you was at Mr Adair's, that you was a perfect stranger to the bond?'

'I said, I had never seen the bond before,' answered Daniel carefully. 'I never had, upon my oath, a perfect knowledge of the bond before I saw it in Mr Adair's hand.'

'Did not you tell them, or convey the idea, that you was a perfect stranger to the whole transaction?'

'I did not.'

'Did you tell them the story you told now?'

'When I came into the room, and saw them in such a state of confusion, I hardly knew what I said. When Mr Drummond told me it was a forged bond, I was shocked and amazed, knowing it had been managed by Mrs Rudd. She said, make yourself quiet, your brother is clearly innocent. I told Mr Drummond, I knew Mrs Rudd had given a bond to my brother.'

'Did you tell Mr Drummond, that it was that bond?'

'Mr Drummond was in that degree of warmth, that I did not know how to speak to him.'

Daniel was allowed to step down. Robert's assistant David Cassady was then sworn in. He said that Caroline had come to take tea with Henrietta Perreau on Saturday 4 March, and when Robert came in he handed her 'something wrapped in a bit of whity brown paper', saying, 'Madam, there is your affair.' Cassady did not see what was in the paper, so the jury could only be left to assume that it was the bond, and to ponder the implications of the words 'there is *your* affair'. Cassady left the stand.

John Leigh, clerk to Sir John Fielding, now testified that Robert Perreau had come voluntarily into the magistrates' office on 11 March, reporting a forgery. As a consequence of his information, Mrs Rudd was taken into custody. Asked whether Caroline had said anything prior to the hearing of evidence to incriminate Robert Perreau, Leigh said he could not remember all the details of events before the hearing, but was sure she had said nothing like that on the first examination. Another clerk, Henry Partington, was also called on to testify concerning the same occasion; he could not remember what had been said either.

Henry Drummond was recalled and the prosecution asked him, 'Did Mr Daniel Perreau say at Mr Adair's, that Mrs Rudd had given a bond to his brother to carry to you?' Henry replied, 'I do not think that he did,' and added, 'In general terms he expressed great surprize at the affair.'

Robert Drummond contributed further impressions of Daniel's reaction. He had 'seemed greatly amazed, and shrugged up his shoulders, I do not believe he said ten words, while I was in the room'. In his passive, taciturn way Daniel had appeared 'totally ignorant of the matter'.

There followed a flurry of character witnesses for Robert Perreau, many of them clients and neighbours. Said William Watts, 'I always looked upon him in a very respectable light.' Mr Grindal: 'A very upright man; and if he had asked me to lend him the money the day before this affair broke out, I should have done it with the greatest readiness.' Mrs Tribe, the widow of the apothecary to whom Robert had been apprenticed, said that he was 'always very diligent'. Sir John Moore: 'He bears an exceeding good character.'

'Could you have imagined that he was a man likely to be guilty of such a charge?' Sir John was asked.

'He is one of the last men I should have thought of.'

Another twenty such witnesses appeared, all testifying to Robert's respectability and to their astonishment when they heard of his arrest. Dr Baker said, 'I never could in the least have suspected him guilty of this charge.' Dr Pennant agreed, saying, 'I should think him . . . incapable of committing any dishonest transaction.' Richard Broadhurst: 'He is a very honest man . . . a man that any body will do any thing for.' General Rebow: 'No man better.'

The judge then briefly summed up the evidence to the jury. The two sides had presented two different Roberts, between which the jurors would have to choose. The prosecution's

Robert was hypocritical, mendacious, and foolish enough to get caught red-handed in a greedy scheme. The defence's Robert, instead, was all too guileless and had been nothing more than a puppet in the hands of Margaret Caroline Rudd.

Having painted the outline of their picture, the prosecution felt able to sit back and relax, certain that the details of the case would simply speak for themselves. Robert had tried to pass off the bonds to the Drummonds: when challenged, he had lied about where he had obtained them and produced yet another forged document to try to shore up his case. The fact that he had been proved a liar seemed enough to negate the effect of any excuses or explanations.

The defence, on the other hand, had their own reasons for feeling confident. Their portrait of a Robert hoodwinked and manipulated by Caroline was not only well supported by testimony, but could be expected to appeal to the sympathies of an all-male jury. The jurors had even seen Caroline accused and hauled off to prison as a criminal before their own eyes. Yet the defence would also have been aware of the accompanying danger that this might inspire pity for her rather than disapproval. She was, after all, a popular figure – especially in the eyes of gentlemen. The result could go either way and would depend not so much on what the jury thought of Robert as on what they thought of Caroline.

The court did not have long to wait: the jury was out for just ten minutes. Short deliberations were the norm at the time, but this was brief enough to draw adverse comment later. The foreman got to his feet and delivered the decision. It was: 'Guilty, upon the third count, of uttering and publishing the bond, well knowing it to be forged.'

This was just one of the four counts and implied only that Robert knew what he was doing in cashing the bond, not that he had actually planned or executed the forging of it. Still, it was enough. The jury had condemned him. He was led out of the courtroom and taken back to Newgate, where he would be obliged to sit and wait for several days before learning his punishment – sentencing was not to take place until the end of sessions on 6 June.

As soon as Robert had gone, Daniel was brought forward to be charged with the forgery of the same bond. This was a mere formality: there was no evidence of his direct involvement in it and he was acquitted immediately. The following morning, however, he would be charged with a different crime, the real one: the forgery of the bonds presented to Dr Thomas Brooke, who had, in the end, been persuaded to press his prosecution.

Robert and Daniel each spent an agonizing night in Newgate. Robert did not yet know his sentence, but he could not fool himself – it was almost certain to be death. As for Daniel, he could only expect the worst from his coming trial. If Robert had been judged guilty, what hope could there be for him? He knew what the public thought of him, the jobless, footloose gambler, doubly bankrupted and living in sin with a woman who accused him of forcing her to commit forgery at knifepoint. If Robert's jury did not believe his story, Daniel's were hardly likely to be more sympathetic. His defence statement was every bit as long and eloquent as Robert's; it was beautifully written and full of feeling, and it told almost the whole story of his life, at least that part of it that had been blighted by Caroline. Now there seemed hardly any point in bothering to read it out.

While the two brothers endured their night of uncertainty, Caroline sat in her cell on the other side of Newgate, thinking hard. Whether or not she had heard the news of Robert's conviction, she would have been exercising all her mental powers in considering her own likely fate and figuring out ways of bringing it back under her control.

Daniel appeared in the dock at nine o'clock the next morning, Friday 2 June. He was indicted on four counts: 'feloniously forging and counterfeiting' a bond for £3100 with the intention of defrauding its guarantor William Adair, doing the same to defraud Dr Thomas Brooke, and 'feloni-ously uttering and publishing this bond as true, knowing it to be forged', with the intention of defrauding Adair and Brooke respectively.[6]

Both sides seemed keen to get the trial over with, and there was little cross-examination. Dr Brooke was the first to testify. He said that he and Daniel had been friends for some years. On 1 November 1774 Daniel had come asking to borrow money for a short period; Brooke had replied that he had none available. Daniel told him that something of the greatest importance was afoot and if he could only get hold of some money he could benefit from it, otherwise the opportunity would be lost. When Brooke repeated that he could not help because he did not have the cash, Daniel asked, 'Have you not got some Ayr bonds?' – referring to bonds issued by the Ayr Bank in Scotland, of which Brooke had bought a number as an investment. 'Let me have them', said Daniel, 'and I will give you as security a bond of Mr. William Adair's for £3100, and I will leave the Ayr bank bonds as a deposit, in Mr Drummond's bank.' Brooke agreed and took his roll of Ayr bonds from a drawer – there were 'about twenty-one' of them, each to the value of a hundred pounds. He asked Daniel how many he needed, and after a little hesitation Daniel said fifteen.

Brooke produced for the court a list of the bonds' numbers, which he'd noted down at the time, and a receipt for them from Daniel Perreau. Daniel had promised to return them within eight days, and had not done so. At first Brooke had not pressed the point, but in mid-December he warned Daniel that interest was owing because the money was overdue. Daniel said he would return the bonds as soon as he could. A few days later, however, he asked Brooke if he actually needed the money for anything or whether it was just a matter of interest accruing. Brooke said it was just the interest, and Daniel replied that in that case he would rather keep the bonds and let the debt pile up. Brooke agreed and nothing further happened until he heard that Daniel had been arrested.

The scrivener Richard Wilson next testified that he had filled out the bond in question. Daniel and Robert had both been present at the time, as they had also been on other occasions when bonds were filled out in the name of William Adair. However, Wilson could not remember which of the two brothers had actually asked him to do it – not an uncommon problem, the brothers being so alike. William Adair's clerk Scoope Ogilvie added his testimony as well, asserting that the writing on the bond was not Adair's.

That ended the prosecution case: short and simple. As usual, the defence began with a prepared statement – but the long narrative which Daniel had prepared was not heard. Like Robert's, it claimed that everything came down to Caroline's scheming and that both brothers had been her gullible victims. Taking this line had not helped Robert; if anything, his woeful tale and willingness to make a woman the scapegoat seemed to have turned the jury against him. Daniel did later publish the text as a long pamphlet describing his relationship with Caroline and the appearance in their lives of the Adairs and their bonds. In the preface he referred to it as

the narrative and defence I had prepared for my trial, but which however I did not use; my brother having entered so largely into the detail of that most horrid train of deception, whereby Mrs. Rudd has involved us both in irretrievable destruction. I had been taught to believe I should be first tried, but as it was ordered otherwise, perhaps unfortunately, and the Court were already possessed of the most essential particulars of this iniquitous affair . . . I conceived it would be intruding improperly on their time, to enter into a second narration.[7]

So Daniel instead contented himself with a very plain, brief statement indeed. It exudes limp hopelessness:

My Lord, I received the bond from Mrs. Rudd as a true bond of Mr. William Adair's. I did really believe it to be a genuine, authentic, and valid bond; and I solemnly protest, by all my hopes of happiness here and hereafter, so villainous an intention of defrauding any man of his property never entered my mind. I adjure the Almighty to assist me, in my present dangerous situation, as I speak here before you.

The defence now proceeded with their witnesses, whose testimony was also abbreviated compared with what had been heard in Robert's trial. They began by once again bringing forward Daniel's former servant John Moody. Again he described Caroline's giving him 'Adair' letters to pass to Daniel and telling him to say that William had been to visit when he had not. After he had performed these services, said Moody, Caroline would come to him 'as though she was going to put her hand upon my shoulder, though she never did, and used to say, that was well done of you to save your master from being angry with me'. Sometimes she would give him half a crown. Moody repeated his account of the special hand he had seen her write and again proudly alluded to his own skill in repairing her 'forging' pens. 'She said, she could write better with them after I had mended them than with any other pens.'

The maidservant Elizabeth Perkins next testified that Caroline had once had her tell Daniel that a letter had arrived for him; Caroline had also instructed her that if Daniel attempted to send any letters himself, she should try to get hold of them from the footman and bring them to her.

Next came a fresh witness, Hannah Dalboux, the servant who had been looking after two of Caroline's children. She said that about a month after Caroline had given birth to her youngest daughter, 'she came to me, and said, tell your master, for God's sake, that I am going out; that Mr Adair called for her'. In fact Daniel did not appear, so Mrs Dalboux did not pass on the message. 'She never mentioned Mr William Adair's name particularly to me, but has named it as her acquaintance: she sent me down to shew the children to a gentleman; who he was I don't know.'

After this there were only character witnesses, fewer than had spoken for Robert, and rather less gushing in their praise. George Forbes: 'I have had dealings with him in money-matters; he always paid me very honourably, and like a gentleman.' John Sullivan: 'I have trusted him with three thousand pounds, and he paid me very honestly.' A couple of his character witnesses didn't seem to know much about him: Peter Woolfe had met him in Guadeloupe but 'I have not known him since he has been in England'. Captain Charles Ellis: 'His acquaintance with me was through his brother; I never was acquainted much with his transactions in life . . . but I always looked upon him to be an honest worthy gentleman.'

Mr Justice Aston summed up the evidence to the jury, who withdrew to deliberate. This time they were gone for only 'a few minutes', an even shorter period than for Robert. They returned with the expected verdict: guilty of uttering and publishing the bond, knowing it to be forged.

The brothers now had to wait four days in Newgate before sentencing. Then, on 6 June, they and the other prisoners convicted of felonies during the same sessions were brought back into the Old Bailey. The prisoners waited all together in the dock, each stepping forward in turn to hear the judgement.

Daniel and Robert both received the same sentence. It appears as a single word in heavy Gothic type at the end of the published accounts of their trials: Death.

Another brief hearing took place in a different court on the same day. It determined that this time Margaret Caroline

MARGARET CAROLINE RUDD

Margaret Caroline Rudd at the height of her fame.

Margaret Caroline
Rudd, ready to be
tried at the Old Bailey.

Daniel Perreau.

Robert Perreau.

In Newgate Prison.

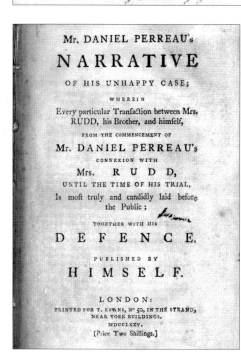

Mr. Dan: Perreau, with a drawn Knife, threatening to murder Mr.ˢ Rudd, unless she would sign ÿ Bond.

Caroline being bullied into committing a forgery, from her own description. Frontispiece to *Forgery unmasked*.

Admiral Sir Thomas Frankland

Mr. DANIEL PERREAU's

NARRATIVE

OF HIS UNHAPPY CASE;

WHEREIN

Every particular Transaction between Mrs. RUDD, his Brother, and himself,

FROM THE COMMENCEMENT OF

Mr. DANIEL PERREAU's

CONNEXION WITH

Mrs. RUDD,

UNTIL THE TIME OF HIS TRIAL,

Is most truly and candidly laid before the Public;

TOGETHER WITH HIS

DEFENCE.

PUBLISHED BY

HIMSELF.

LONDON:

PRINTED FOR T. EVANS, Nᵒ 50, IN THE STRAND, NEAR YORK BUILDINGS.
MDCCLXXV.
[Price Two Shillings.]

FORGERY UNMASKED;

OR,

GENUINE MEMOIRS

OF THE

Two UNFORTUNATE BROTHERS,
ROB. and DANIEL PERREAU,
And MRS. RUDD.

CONTAINING,

A Number of curious and interesting PARTI-
CULARS, and many ANECDOTES relative to the
FORGERIES of Messrs. PERREAUS; with suit-
able REMARKS, &c. &c.

TOGETHER WITH

A Full and Circumstantial ACCOUNT of their
EXAMINATIONS before Sir JOHN FIELDING,
and the other Magistrates; the DECLARA-
TIONS made by Mrs. RUDD; and her CASE,
as communicated by HERSELF.

Never before published.

Illustrated with a New and Beautiful Engraving of MR.
DAN. PERREAU in the Act of threatening to Murder
MRS. RUDD, unless she would Sign the Fatal BOND.

Nothing extenuate, nor set down aught in malice.
SHAKESPEARE.

LONDON:

Printed for A. GRANT, Bridges Street, Co-
vent-Garden; and sold by all the Booksellers
and News-carriers in Town and Country.
[Price One Shilling.]

Daniel's *Narrative of his unhappy case*, based on the defence statement prepared for his trial.

A typical example of the many pamphlets capitalizing on the public's hunger for details of the case.

Robert and Daniel Perreau
on trial at the Old Bailey.

Margaret Caroline Rudd
on trial at the Old Bailey.

Caroline in court.

THE LONDON TRAGEDY,

Or, the Widow and her Fatherless Children in Distress:

ing an Account how two Gentlemen, (twin Brothers,) were brought to an untimely End, by the A
fice of a base Woman, well known by the Name of Mrs. F——d, supposed Daughter of the PRETENDER.

In THREE PARTS.

The London tragedy, a contemporary song about the case.

A 1777 satire in which candidates compete to be elected Queen of Hell.
Caroline, a runner-up, stands fifth from the right.

Thomas Lyttleton, 2nd
Baron Lyttleton.

Francis Rawdon-Hastings,
1st Marquess of Hastings.

James Boswell in 1785.

Rudd would not be granted bail, but would have to wait out her time in prison pending her trial.[8]

The two Perreau brothers were taken back to Newgate and incarcerated in the 'Press Yard', which was the prison's Death Row. There, together with a crowd of other condemned men from their own and previous sessions, they were left to sit out the interminable system of appeals and petitions which always followed a capital sentence.

Death sentences at the time were almost mandatory for felonies, but what was much less certain was whether actual execution would result. The traditional 'benefit of clergy' loophole, according to which anyone who was literate was automatically exempted, had now been closed,* but many people still expected to escape the noose by other means – usually by having the sentence commuted to transportation. There were two reasons for the Perreaus to worry, however. First, forgery was treated with less indulgence than any other crime apart from murder: burglars and muggers were far more likely to be spared. Second, 1775 was a very bad year to be convicted because there was a sudden shortage of colonies to which convicts could be transported. The Americans were in the middle of a successful struggle to seize independence, and a side-effect of this was to terminate England's habit of dumping human detritus in their country. A few years later Australia's Botany Bay would replace the American convict colonies, but in the meantime the authorities had to choose whether to house the extra felons in the already overcrowded prisons and try to find something useful for them to do, or just hang them and be done with it. The latter often seemed a more attractive option.

* It was technically still in force, but had been democratically extended to all felons whether or not they could read. The result of this had been its effective abolition: felonies were divided into 'clergyable' and 'non-clergyable' types, and by the late eighteenth century almost all were non-clergyable.

It was now up to the Perreaus to convince the King and his functionaries that this should not happen to them. Their best chance was to seek to have their execution delayed until Caroline's trial took place. If she were found guilty, they could not expect a retrial, but at least it would make their defence arguments look a lot sounder and they might expect more merciful treatment.

Fortunately for Robert and Daniel, their class worked in their favour. As gentlemen, they were given more leeway than most condemned felons and were allowed to wait for Caroline's trial where others probably would not have been. (A letter to the *Morning Post* many months later specifically attributed this to their social status and claimed that any ordinary forger would long since have been hanged.)[9] Their gaolers also catered to their special circumstances by arranging some privacy for them, making their lives less of a torment than they might have been. The *Morning Post* reported that 'the unfortunate brothers now under sentence of death in Newgate, intreated of [the governor] Richard Akerman, that he would not let them be made a public spectacle during their confinement, as was generally the misfortune of most malefactors; he instantly assured them that they should not, and to his honour has punctually kept his word.'[10]

Still, their situation was grim. The Press Yard was filthy, congested, and pervaded by an almost tangible sense of hopelessness. The Perreaus were to spend over seven months there, occupying themselves with legal manoeuvres, newspaper propaganda and the effort to win friends and influence people. Daniel expanded and published his unspoken courtroom defence as the *Narrative of His Unhappy Case*; its detailed account of himself and Caroline was lapped up as entertainment by the public, alongside Caroline's 'Case' and 'Narrative' and a number of pamphlets picking through every scrap of evidence presented in Robert's trial.

Family and friends did their best to help, particularly

Robert's. Daniel barely saw any visitors, but Robert had constant attention from his wife and children as well as from former colleagues, neighbours and lawyers. Newspaper readers were moved by his plight and also (contrary to Caroline's libels against her) by the loyalty of his wife. It was reported in the *Morning Post* of 6 July that

> a gentleman who was present at the first interview between Mr R.P. and his wife in prison . . . declares he never beheld any thing half so moving; the wretched objects beheld each other with speechless anguish for several minutes, not being able to address each other till many floods of tears had fallen from both, and those gave them the power of utterance: the keeper himself acknowledged at the same time, that during the exercise of his office (which had been many years) he never beheld a scene so affecting.

Robert was generally considered an 'unfortunate man, who has fallen a sacrifice to *imprudence*, but not to *guilt*'.[11] A common analysis of his case was that he had been found guilty not because of proven involvement in the forgery, but simply because he had been caught in a lie. 'The jury have found him guilty of the *forgery*, for no other reason in the world, but because he was certainly guilty of a *falsehood*,' wrote the pseudonymous author 'Marcellus' in *A Letter to the Right Hon. Earl of Suffolk in Which the Innocence of Robert Perreau is Demonstrated*.[12] The lie to the Drummonds was easily explained, argued Marcellus, by the fact that Robert trusted Caroline so completely. It was the best way of getting the bond accepted without delay, and he lied 'not with a *bad design* of defrauding Mr. Drummond, but with a *good design* of serving his friend'. Like many others, Marcellus also felt that the jury had not taken sufficient care in their deliberations. 'Where the life of a citizen is at stake, it were to be wished that no jury should give their verdict without having at least a week to consider of it.' He suspected that the jury simply wanted to find *someone* guilty, knowing that a crime had taken place and having no one else to pin it on – Caroline not having been prosecuted for this particular forgery, although all set to be tried for another.

Not everyone was convinced. The *London Magazine*'s review of the *Letter ... in Which the Innocence of Robert Perreau is Demonstrated* remarked that it is 'a sensible, well penned letter, but falls far short of what is promised in the title'.[13] A detailed response to the *Letter* appeared in the form of a pamphlet called *Mrs. Marg. Car. Rudd's Case Considered, Respecting Robert Perreau*. It mocked Marcellus's efforts: 'From the uncommon pains that have been taken to save Mr. Robert Perreau, one would really think that the witnesses who appeared against him were men of no credit, the jury dead to all sense of feeling, and the judge out of his senses.'[14] Instead, it proclaimed that the testimony was clear, the witnesses reliable and the jury 'composed of a set of very upright, respectable, and humane gentlemen'. It dissected Marcellus's arguments one by one and concluded that Robert was every bit as guilty as the court had found him. His willingness to go to William Adair's proved nothing: he was obliged to behave thus, if he were not to be thought guilty and arrested on the spot. Besides, he was probably counting on Adair being out riding. The instructions written by Robert Perreau for Wilson the scrivener, which he had tried to have destroyed, were another damning piece of evidence. 'Would any innocent person have expressed that anxious concern for the burning the instructions given to Mr. Wilson, which Robert Perreau shewed? Surely not!'[15]

Meanwhile, except in his own sad *Narrative of His Unhappy Case*, Daniel was more or less forgotten. No one bothered to pick over the few brief pages that constituted the transcript of his hearing; no one disputed the testimony presented either for or against him. It was as if his wild and disorganized lifestyle rendered him such a sinful soul in general that his guilt or innocence of this crime in particular didn't really matter. Only one letter-writer, signing himself 'Nobody', exerted himself far enough to say of him that 'the conviction may very possibly be just, but, by the Lord, I cannot believe it legal.'[16] That was about all the attention Daniel ever got in the press. When the author of *Mrs. Marg. Car. Rudd's Case Considered* wrote that 'if either of them ought to have been saved, for aught that appears on their trials, Daniel is confessedly the least guilty',[17] it was merely a rhetorical flourish, implying that Robert was *so* undeniably guilty that even Daniel could not be thought more so.

And so, while Caroline waited on one side of Newgate Prison for her own ordeal in the courts, the two Perreau brothers waited on the other, preparing either for an ugly death or for a miraculous salvation – which, if it came, would very probably have to be paid for by substituting her death for theirs.

CHAPTER
SEVEN
◆

'HER PRESENT
DREADFUL SITUATION
AND MISFORTUNE'

Caroline now settled herself in for the resumption of hostilities. This time no quarter would be given: she was fighting for her life.

She found prison a generally unpleasant experience. 'Accustomed hitherto to delicacy and elegance,' she wrote, 'what must I feel from the miseries of a prison, and the horrors attendant upon it?'[1] Her health was also poor and she reported feeling 'too bad to admit my writing much, or long, at a time' – a moving claim, but one rather contradicted by the prolific output she actually managed during her incarceration.

Caroline's former servant Christian Hart was shocked at what she saw when she visited her: a scene of squalor and hardship.[2] But other accounts of her Newgate lifestyle present a different picture. As in most prisons of the time, if one had money it was possible to arrange a fairly decent life inside. Newgate was still a hideous dungeon; a replacement was being built, but was not finished until 1777. The old prison was dark and disease-ridden, and there was no getting away from the all-pervasive stench – visitors described having to air their clothes and notebooks after a few hours there. However, a modicum of cash could buy properly cooked food, a bed and freedom from manacles, while a good deal more of it could pave the way to a private cell away from the crowds, dinner of one's choice and the attention of servants.

Caroline was definitely in the privileged-prisoner category. Whether the money was her own or was given to her by friends and admirers is not certain, but somehow she managed to purchase a private room in which to receive her many visitors, among them lawyers, merchants and messengers. Mrs Hart mentioned that there had been a collection amongst Caroline's friends to which she had contributed as generously as she could, but there must have been other sources of cash as well. The most likely one was Lord Lyttelton, with whose name Caroline's was soon to be connected in the newspapers.

The days of making do with just the few gowns saved from Sir Thomas Frankland and Henrietta Perreau were gone. Every time Caroline appeared in court she was wearing a new and supremely dignified creation, the details of which were eagerly noted by the reporters. It was recorded that whilst in Newgate, Caroline managed to start a brand new fashion for 'polonaise' jackets, which were still being worn by society ladies some years later.[3] An anecdote retold by Horace Walpole in one of his letters also shows how thoroughly Caroline had regained her aplomb. One day she sent for the finest mercer in town and ordered him to bring brocaded silks to her cell for her to choose the one she wanted. She made her selection and asked him to cut off the quantity she required. By this time it had dawned on him who she was, and he realized that as she was very likely soon to be hanged he might never be paid. He muttered some excuse about having no scissors with him. Caroline perceived his anxiety at once and handed over a £20 banknote, saying in an amused tone, 'There is a pair of scissors.'[4]

When not occupied in choosing silks and consulting lawyers, Caroline wielded her pen, producing numerous letters to the papers and an extended sequel to her earlier

'Case', entitled 'A Narrative of Mrs Rudd, written by herself'. It carefully sifted the evidence given at the Perreau trials, arguing for the brothers' utter guilt and dishonesty. The *Morning Post* serialized it, beginning on 1 July.

At the same time Caroline objected strenuously to the production of similar works by her enemies. She asserted that it was unfair of the Perreaus and their cronies to publish such material in the run up to her trial, potentially influencing the minds of her jurors, even if it was to try to save their own lives. In particular, she complained about the two pamphlets whose imminent publication was announced in July: Marcellus's *Letter to the Earl of Suffolk* and the similar *Observations on the Trial of Mr. Robt. Perreau*. They were 'plainly calculated to influence the minds of the jury and the public at that very critical and awful moment, the hour of trial', she wrote, adding that it was 'much, very much to be lamented, that human nature should be fallen into such a state of degeneracy as to suffer private resentment to get the better of that justice and humanity which is ever due, even from one man to another, much more so to an unfortunate injured woman'.[5]

Marcellus himself noted in his preface that he would not have published the *Letter* before her trial were it not for the necessity that it should appear before the Perreaus' appeal for clemency, due to be conveyed to the King on the very day after the trial date. (Since the trial was later postponed, events did not in fact turn out this way.)[6] He also made dramatic capital out of the disagreement by ending his pamphlet with the abrupt note: 'The writer was proceeding, but was suddenly stopped by much complaint in the *Morning Post* . . . by which it appears that every word said in Mr Perreau's behalf is most injurious to Mrs Rudd' – and he added in brackets: 'very probably true'.[7]

Caroline presented herself as a person with an artless and simple mentality, whose only defence was to tell the truth and rely on the gallant nature of her contemporaries to save her.

'I rest my defence on stubborn facts, and plain-told truths,' she wrote on 12 June, 'and have no doubt but that will yet prevail over all the fallacies of a fine dress'd tale, and the power, perjury, and bribery which has been exerted to destroy my character, and take away my life.'[8] Her 'Narrative' was prefaced by the statement: 'Truth is my theme; my stile is as simple as my story; equally free from sophistical positions and logical arguments.' – 'I have not the invention of a Perreau . . . to decorate my defence.'[9]

In reality, she was more than a match for her opponents in both rhetoric and logic. She even managed to turn to her own advantage Henrietta Perreau's snootiness about her living with Daniel out of wedlock. Since Henrietta's relationship to Robert *was* blessed by the legal sanctity of marriage, she argued, one could presume that Henrietta must have known 'more of her husband's transactions, than I could of Daniel's', and was therefore more implicated in the Perreaus' crimes than she could ever be.[10]

She still had supporters: 'Mrs Rudd is requested to make herself as easy as possible under her present dreadful situation and misfortune,' wrote a *Morning Post* correspondent on 7 June. 'Likewise is informed that she has friends that are still persuaded of her innocence and merit, and will exert their utmost to extricate and redress her.' Another writer, 'Achates', remarked soothingly in an open letter addressed to her in July, 'I find the town, since my return from the country . . . very much in your favour.'[11] But Caroline knew that she was in no position to relax and rely on sentimental admirers. Only her own lithe and unscrupulous wits could save her now.

On 20 June a preliminary hearing was scheduled at the King's Bench court in Westminster Hall to discuss the charges on which Caroline would be tried and also to consider a new application for bail. The event was well publicized in advance and so, as usual, the area was 'extremely crouded by ladies and gentlemen whose curiosity induced them to attend in expectation of seeing Mrs. Rudd'.[12] To the crowd's disappointment, the hearing was postponed: Caroline was too ill to appear.

The hearing finally took place two weeks later, on Monday 3 July – and once again 'all the avenues leading to the Court of King's Bench were crouded early in the morning'.[13] Caroline arrived at eleven o'clock, dressed in an elegant black outfit and accompanied by the Keeper of Newgate. One of the two men who had offered to stand bail for her was running late, so she and her entourage waited in a room above a coffee house called Alice's, which had a special relationship with the court. The man finally turned up at around half-past twelve and Caroline was brought into the court, 'accompanied by a prodigious concourse of people, who waited for her coming from the Coffee-house'.[14] An observer remarked that, despite her recent illness, she 'seemed to be in no way impaired or dejected by confinement'.[15]

Presiding over the bench of judges was Sir James Mansfield, who already knew the case and its protagonists well, for he had been the prosecutor in Robert's trial. Whether this was a good omen for Caroline or a bad one was anyone's guess. One thing was for sure, though: Mansfield was not likely to waste time dithering over niceties. His gruffness and impatience were legendary. When travelling the country as a circuit judge, he was renowned for rising at five every morning to go out and kill something before breakfast, and he brought a similar trigger-happiness to his job at the King's Bench court. As soon as he took up the post of Lord Chief Justice he put a firm stop to the discursive, leisurely legal wrangling that had prevailed hitherto – and many thought he had gone way too far in the opposite direction. Cases these days tended to be open and shut regardless of their complexity.

Representing Caroline was a lawyer named Davenport; a Mr Wallace spoke for the Crown. The hearing began with the recital of Daniel and Robert Perreau's indictments and other legal documents, a process which took up a considerable time, to Mansfield's irritation.

When it was finished, Davenport stood up and stated the grounds on which Caroline sought bail, saying that at the first hearing at the magistrates' court she had made a voluntary declaration concerning the forgeries and had offered to testify against the Perreaus. In return for this, she had been led to believe that she could expect immunity. Under these circumstances she surely deserved bail whilst awaiting a trial which, in any case, all right-thinking people hoped would never take place.

Two affidavits were read out to support Caroline's position. The first was her own and repeated the arguments made by Davenport, as well as adding an angry complaint concerning Sir Thomas Frankland and the public attacks he had been making on her ever since the original arrest. Frankland's reason for pressing the prosecution against her was nothing but greed, she said: he was hoping that she would either die in prison or be hanged, so that he could keep all the possessions he had stolen from her.

The second affidavit was also aimed at undermining Sir Thomas. It came from a pawnbroker who said that he had originally offered to stand bail for Caroline, but that Frankland had talked him out of it. He had convinced him that the court would never accept less than £20,000, and that even if this colossal sum were somehow raised it would be lost at once because Caroline would abscond as soon as she had the chance.

Mansfield asked whether there was any transcript of what had taken place in the original hearing before the magistrates, so that they could all be sure exactly what they were discussing. Strangely, neither side seemed to have one.

Another of the judges, Mr Justice Aston, remarked that he understood the real reason for promising Caroline protection had been a 'point of delicacy' concerning the Drummonds:

namely, the fact that when she had confessed the forgery to them it was in private, and the all-important paper on which she had given them the proof of her handwriting had been destroyed. The magistrates had presumably felt that such a nebulous confession should not be used against her. Mansfield retorted that it was simply not possible to know what had gone on in the magistrates' hearing without a proper transcript. How could both parties have failed to equip themselves with such a crucial document?

The Crown presented its principal argument: Caroline was not entitled to the benefits normally due to an accomplice who confessed, because she was now denying any culpability and therefore could not be regarded as an accomplice. A claim to immunity implied a preparedness to plead guilty and tell all: she could not simultaneously plead innocence and claim the court's protection.

Davenport turned this on its head. There were two possibilities, he said. If Caroline was indeed deemed to be involved in the forgeries, then she *was* an accomplice and should be given the benefits due to one. But if her claim to innocence was given sufficient credence to rule out complicity in the crime, well then there was no justification for holding her at all: she should be immediately and unconditionally released.

The two sides charged into battle over these points and the arguments could have gone round and round for ever, but Mansfield soon called a halt. Caroline was allowed to speak, briefly. She simply stated that she had offered herself as a witness against the Perreaus for one reason only: she had thought she would be protected in return.

Mansfield now announced that they would pack up and continue the next day. He ordered the lawyers on both sides to use the time in between to find the records of the original hearing. Caroline was remanded back to prison for the night; the following morning she was taken again to Alice's Coffee House. Public interest was undiminished: 'In less than half an hour, the Court of King's Bench, and all the avenues leading to it, were more crouded than ever known in the memory of the oldest man living.'[16] The judges arrived at eleven o'clock and Caroline was brought into court.

Mansfield asked the lawyers whether they had found the documents he'd asked for. They fudged the issue, because they had not. Instead the prosecution offered a fresh affidavit which they had obtained from the three magistrates present at the original hearing, as well as a number of extra affidavits from Sir Thomas Frankland and others. Mansfield was not happy, but allowed the papers to be read out, taking up what little remained of the morning.

The magistrates' affidavit showed signs of backpedalling, probably because they had been shunted in that direction by the prosecution lawyers. They stated that Margaret Caroline Rudd had appeared before them on 15 March, and was offered the protection of the court on condition that she revealed not only what she knew of the matter immediately under consideration, but also whatever else she might know concerning any other felony in which the accused parties were involved. This was the only condition attached to it, they said, but their promise did not extend any further than her honesty in confessing what had taken place.

Wallace repeated the prosecution's point that this condition ruled out her claim to immunity, since she had not told everything she knew. Davenport countered rather weakly that they should not take up the court's time quibbling minutely over the interpretation of statutes. Instead, he ventured to affirm that he did not know of a single case in which protection had been denied unless there was reason to believe that justice was thereby defeated, or that the witness was building a claim on a false foundation in order to escape punishment. The question was not one of narrow legal definitions, but of what treatment Caroline was morally entitled to expect.

Mansfield had had enough. He declared that although the

magistrates' affidavit did imply that Caroline was an accomplice, she was now claiming to be innocent and this made any entitlement to protection invalid. If the magistrates had led her to believe otherwise, that was beside the point: it was not their business to make such promises. 'No authority is given to a Justice of the Peace to pardon an offender, and to tell him that he shall be a witness against others. The accomplice is not assured of his pardon . . . and it depends on the title he has from his behaviour, whether he shall be pardoned or executed.'[17] That was Mansfield's judgement: Caroline was denied bail and sent back to Newgate.

The *Morning Post* noted, 'A correspondent who sat close to Mrs Rudd the whole time that she was in the Court of King's Bench on Tuesday, assures us, that she never changed colour the whole time. She had a smelling-bottle in her hand, which she often applied to her nose; and when she retired, she made a very low curtesy to the Court, but did not appear in the least dismayed.'[18]

Mansfield's decision, and the disagreement between him and the magistrates, was to be greatly argued over in the newspapers. The *Morning Post* sympathized with the magistrates as well as with Caroline herself: it observed that the King's Bench justices simply didn't seem to like the former getting ideas above their station.[19] The paper later published an open letter from 'An Uninfluenced Individual' warning the chief magistrate Sir John Fielding that he should be wary of allowing his authority to be undermined. 'How an invasion on your prerogative could be critically advanced to crush an helpless woman, moves the wonder of the whole kingdom.' – 'The savages in the wilds of America strictly adhere to their compacts, and shall sacred ties, by far fetched quibbles, lugg'd from the dark recesses of law, be trampled in Britain and set at nought? – Oh! forbid it justice.'[20] This was of no help to Caroline, though.

The date for Caroline's trial was now set for Thursday 13

July, but it was put off: the defence lawyers objected to a last-minute change made by the prosecution to its planned course of evidence. At first it was only to be postponed until the following day, but Caroline herself delivered an impassioned speech to the Old Bailey judges asking that it should be put off a good deal longer – until the next sessions some months later.

'Supported as I am,' she said, 'even in this melancholy situation, with a consciousness of innocence, which I hope in God, will at length defeat the most wicked and unnatural conspiracy against me, I cannot expect a fair and impartial trial at the present sessions. Give me leave to assure your Lordship, that there are various things essential to my defence, which I have not had time to prepare myself for: and every hour teems with discoveries of the most abominable schemes against my innocence or my life.' She blamed these schemes predominantly on the Perreaus – 'the two unhappy persons who are now under sentence, and whose fate the public are told, waits the event of my trial' – but also hinted at skulduggery on Frankland's part. 'I am almost distracted with the reflection, that there is born a man, who can wish to tear their mother from three helpless, friendless children, who had already lost their father.'[21] The Perreaus had been allowed to delay *their* trial, she pointed out: almost three months had passed between the accusation and their appearance at the Old Bailey. 'I have had scarcely as many days as the two persons I have mentioned had months, to prepare for my trial,' she said, stretching a point.

Caroline then referred to the two pamphlets about which she had complained before, adducing them as reasons for postponement. She even hinted that perhaps the whole trial might be abandoned on their account: 'I do not doubt, your Lordship will shew a just indignation to so wicked an attempt to prejudice me with my jury, at the very moment of my trial. I have been informed, that a noble Judge refused to try the right to a foot-path through Richmond Park, merely because an improper publication upon the subject appeared just before the Assizes.'

'My life is now in your Lordships' hands,' she finished quietly. 'I know that it is safe *there*.' Whether because of legal deliberation or because their hearts were won over by this intimate expression of trust, the judges agreed that the trial should be postponed until the following sessions in September.

Meanwhile, the battle with Sir Thomas was still going on as before. In one sense the old admiral wasn't doing well. Now that Daniel had been convicted, the question of the rights to his property took on a new colouring. The law said that a convicted felon forfeited his property to the sheriffs of the City of London, and these officials duly put in a claim for the Perreaus' goods. Frankland opposed it, saying that Daniel's property had been signed over to him before the conviction and was therefore his.

This dilemma was debated at length in the papers: law students tried their newly honed legal wits on it. The question, wrote 'A Student' on Wednesday 26 July, was 'whether the forfeiture is made at the time of a felony being committed, or at the time of conviction'.[22] If the latter, Daniel had been free to sign it all over to Sir Thomas Frankland and it was now Sir Thomas's property. If the former, it should now belong to the state. The 'Student' believed that this was the case and that Sir Thomas had no claim.

The law appeared to agree with him. A notice in the *Gentleman's Magazine* dated 20 July stated that the arrangements made between Frankland and the Perreaus were invalid. 'Two executions in the house of Daniel Perreau, one by virtue of an assignment to Sir Thomas Frankland, the other at the instance of the upholsterer who furnished the goods, were withdrawn, by virtue of the sheriffs claim, who, on the conviction of capital offenders, are entitled to the goods and chattels, land and tenements, of the convicts, under the city's charter.'[23] Caroline's entitlement was also acknowledged: 'Mrs. Rudd has claimed an exemption of her goods in the same house, she not being the wife of Daniel Perreau, nor yet a convict.' The trouble was that Sir Thomas did not abide by this ruling. When the issue was raised again in court five and a half months later, he was still in possession of both Daniel's and Caroline's property.

By August another problem had developed and Caroline believed that it was not unrelated to the Frankland issue.

Her three children were now all living in different places. Susan was with Mrs Jacques, Stewart had been taken in by another family and the youngest daughter Caroline was still with the nurse Hannah Dalboux. Caroline had been continuing to pay for this during the summer, with money obtained from her mysterious sources. The arrangement had gone satisfactorily enough at first, but the fact that Mrs Dalboux had testified in Daniel's favour at his trial and told stories about Caroline's dealings with the Adairs did not endear her to her former mistress. And now a serious confrontation occurred: Caroline's payments having apparently dried up, the Dalbouxs responded by holding the child to ransom.

The Gazetteer reported on Saturday 5 August that 'Mrs Rudd on Wednesday summoned a woman before the Magistrates in Bow-street, in order to make her surrender her child, which she was entrusted with as a nurse'. Mrs Dalboux's lawyer asserted that the legal claim for the child had not been properly authorized by Caroline (who was not free to appear in person), and the hearing was therefoe abandoned. The following day Caroline's lawyer John Bailey showed the magistrates a letter addressed to the nurse and correctly signed 'M.C. Rudd'. The letter commanded Hannah Dalboux to give Bailey the child Elizabeth Caroline Perreau, together with all her baby paraphernalia – a sheet of Indian long cloth, clothes, a silver pan and a cradle. The letter was approved, and Bailey and an officer of the court set off to deliver it. However, when they arrived at Mrs Dalboux's address there was no sign of either child or nurse. Her

husband would give no information about his wife's where-
abouts, and the lawyer came away empty-handed. When
Caroline heard of this, she was in 'a state of mind bordering
upon distraction', and had Bailey send a spy to watch the
house constantly in case the nurse came back.

On Friday morning Hannah reappeared. Bailey's man
went to talk to her, and while he was doing so, 'Sir T——
F——s servant came to her on a message from his master' –
which was odd, thought Caroline. Sir Thomas was no longer
paying for the support of her children: there was no reason
why he should be there. He was obviously up to mischief.
Then Henrietta Perreau, too, became implicated in the
kidnapping of baby Caroline. A report in the *Gazetteer*
alleged that she had been meeting clandestinely with Dalboux
and concluded that 'this intelligence betwixt the Baronet [Sir
Thomas] and her, added to her frequent visits in Golden
Square, and Mrs Robert Perreau bringing her with her in a
coach several times lately to the Messrs. Perreaus, fully
explain from what cause and for what views this woman
refuses to deliver up the child to its mother; and it is hoped
this new and horrid injury offered to Mrs. Rudd, a matter
which so deeply wounds every tender maternal feeling, will
not escape the particular notice of the humane public.'

The *Morning Post* covered the same story, and on Tuesday
8 August noted that 'a Frenchman' – Dalboux – had been
arrested for kidnapping Mrs Rudd's child. He was also
accused of a physical assault on John Bailey, who had gone
back to have words following the discoveries made by his
spy. In the same issue the *Post* printed a denial from
Henrietta Perreau: 'There having appeared a paragraph in
your paper of Saturday last, setting forth that Mrs Robert
Perreau has frequently taken Hannah Dalboux with her in a
coach to visit the Mess. Perreaus in their present confinement,
you are hereby desired and authorized to contradict that
assertion: it being entirely false and groundless; Mrs Perreau
never having carried the said Hannah Dalboux to see the

Messrs. Perreau, or having any intercourse or conversation with her since the trial of the Messrs. Perreaus.'

The newspaper published a further letter the following Monday:

Mr Editor,
You may assure the public, that the advertisement in this paper of Monday last [sic], respecting the commitment of a Frenchman for detaining Mrs. Rudd's children [sic] is entirely misrepresented, the fact being as follows: Mr and Mrs. Dalboux did not assault Counsellor Bailey – They are willing to deliver Mrs. Rudd's children as soon as whatever is due to them is discharged. In regard to the assault with which Mr. Dalboux is charged, so far from being able to commit one, he could not lift his hand to his head, being confined to his bed these thirteen months with the gout. Indeed the poor old man was at one time provoked to say, that if he was younger he would act in such a manner as to make them remember it; but this was the mere peevishness of illness . . . However, it appeared sufficient provocation to his humane prosecutors to hurry him away to Newgate, where he might have still languished, if his good character in the neighbourhood had not soon procured him bail . . . Acting in this manner is not the way to interest the public in Mrs. Rudd's behalf. – If she means to solicit mercy and clemency, she should not begin herself with cruelty and injustice.

Hannah Dalboux.
No. 4, Orange-court, Swallow-street.[24]

The reply came back a few days later:

Mr Editor. Hannah Dalboux . . . has regularly received six shillings a week for the child; added to this, I promised to continue her wet nurse wages to her, which was twenty guineas a year, and accordingly have paid her three guineas towards it, and lent the remainder, which was tendered to her when my child was demanded. Anyone who knows anything of giving children out to nurse, knows, that this was much above the usual pay of nurses, but as the child was not weaned when my unfortunate children was turned out of their father's house by Sir Thomas Frankland, and I had no opportunity of situating them elsewhere than with this woman, and knowing her a most avaricious, mercenary creature, I gave her this extraordinary allowance, in hopes to induce her to take the greater care of my poor infants. However, she now pretends to think this infinitely too little, and has delivered a demand, as she calls it, of upwards of twenty pounds, besides, six shillings a week, for the nursing of the child four months: this, of course, I refused paying her, as it certainly is a most evident, vile extortion, as ever was attempted in this world.[25]

Caroline detailed the arrangement that had been made at first with Sir Thomas, and his agreement to pay for the children's keep since he was the one who had made them homeless. She described how his payments had dried up after the first month and quoted his callous remark about the workhouse. Hannah Dalboux had been happy to accept just five shillings a week from *him*, added Caroline, but now saw the opportunity to extort more and was shamelessly using her power over the mother's feelings.

The letter concluded:

I am sorry, Sir, to have intruded so much on your paper, but as this woman has carried her baseness so far as to say in the public papers, that she refuses my child till her demand is discharged, I thought it incumbent upon me to explain to the public WHAT HER DEMAND IS, and the true circumstances of the matter. As to her being frequently with the Messrs. Perreaus, and in Golden square, as set forth in a late paragraph in your paper, it is strictly and literally true, notwithstanding the contradiction Mrs. Robert Perreau has ventured to give the said paragraph.

I am, Sir, Your obedient Servant,
M.C. Rudd.

Immediately following this on the same page there appeared a letter addressed to Mrs Rudd from J. Wright, the messenger who had been entrusted with delivering the payments to Hannah Dalboux. He confirmed that:

I punctually paid the nurse twelve shillings per week when she had the two children; when the one was taken away I paid only for the other, which did not in my opinion seem pleasing to her, though she did not think proper to tell me so . . . She was paid punctually up by me till within about three weeks, since which time I have not heard of her, as I was informed you was about to take the child away. Her husband I have met repeatedly in the streets on his legs, without his being in a bed as she wants to make the public believe, as well lately as several months past. I could have wished in her account to the public, she had also informed them, that her husband, during the time of your affluence, received by your order six pound of meat every week . . . Signed, J. Wright. Charing Cross.

Eventually the situation was resolved, probably by a payment from Caroline, and the child was surrendered. Caroline then had the problem of finding someone else to look after her daughter and until alternative arrangements could be made she may have kept her with her in her cell – a common practice, but one that Caroline did not favour. With its stink and disease, Newgate was no place for a baby, even in a private room. She did eventually manage to find a nurse to take the child away, although details of these arrangements were not recorded.

Meanwhile, Sir Thomas Frankland continued to keep Caroline under pressure. A letter addressed to him in the *Morning Post* on 29 August referred to his 'extraordinary activity and indefatigable zeal in the prosecution of that defenceless woman'. It went on:

> Sir Thomas, the eyes of the whole kingdom are now upon you; hitherto it has been suggested, that interest engaged you in the quarrel; but as the Sheriffs have, to a critical nicety, proved that you have none to reap from the issue, it is earnestly hoped that prejudice will not influence your proceedings ... What man, Sir, possessed of common sensations, or in whose bosom dwells an atom of humanity, can behold a noble mind struggling with the grievous pressure of accumulated sorrows, and deny the tear of pity, or the fostering hand of succour?

Far from desisting, Sir Thomas continued to work for her complete undoing, and now concentrated his energies on demolishing her claim to noble descent. He wrote a letter of protest to the Lyon Record Office in Scotland, from which she had obtained a pedigree confirming her own version of her background back in 1773. As Caroline later joked to Boswell, he 'would not allow me to be a gentlewoman and said my pedigree was forged – as if one would forge a pedigree when certainly one cannot raise money upon it'.[26]

She was not the only one to feel affronted by Sir Thomas's claims. James Cummyng, Keeper of the Lyon Records, had taken a liking to Caroline and was annoyed by the tone of the letter. He therefore forwarded it to the *Morning Post*, saying that he wished to expose these ungallant efforts against her.[27]

Sir Thomas's epistolary style was most peculiar, mixing naïve grammar and spelling with a veneer of pretentious polysyllables and Latinisms. The letter began, 'Sir, Among Mr. Danill Perreaus effects in Harley Street house I found a pedigree and as £41,900 bonds have been forged by that triumvirate as also £22,000 notes of hand and draughts on bankers: Now *Quaere* why not the pedigree also?' Frankland quoted a portion of the pedigree, which referred to 'Margaret Caroline Youngson'. He remarked: '*Margaret* Youngson not Caroline was born in the north of Ireland, her father a poor mean surgeon and apothecary in Lurgan her father married a farmers daughter named Stewart at Ballymarron with no fortune. Her grandmother Youngson was as mean and low as you can conceive. And she in Febd 1762 married a Lieut. of the 62 Regt. of Foot – now alive in Dublin living on his half pay. I think its impossible she could so deceive the office besides our podegre is come from the male line. I shall be extreamly obliged to you If youl find out whether its a forged testimonial or not, and am in hopes of your answer and am Sir Your most humble servt, Thos. Frankland. Old Bond Street, 20st Sep. 1775.'

In his covering letter to the *Post*, Cummyng mocked Frankland's grammar, defended the Lyon Office's reliability and asserted that Caroline's pedigree must have been properly attested by documents held by the office or they would never have approved it. 'Since the receipt of Sir Thomas's letter, to which a proper answer has been given, I have delivered to Mrs. Rudd an authentic extract of her pedigree and arms, as it stands recorded in the Lyon Office, duly ratified, confirmed, and assigned to her; to the veracity of which, and of what I have published above, I hereunto subscribe my name. James Cummyng, Keeper of the Lyon Records. Oct. 1775.'

Besides his attempts to demolish her aristocratic pretensions, Sir Thomas also had another bee in his bonnet. Unearthing a minuscule scandal of the previous decade, he tried to prove that the lady at the centre of it had been Caroline, going by yet another false name. It was not until the following year that any allegations appeared in print, but Caroline was having Sir Thomas watched closely and probably knew what he was up to, although she did not seem too concerned about his 'discoveries'.

The story dated back to 1764, when a young lady named Caroline de Grosberg had answered an advertisement seeking a governess to work for an Earl of Northington in Scotland. Once she was installed in the household, it emerged that she not only lacked the linguistic and musical skills called for in the job description, but was also morally suspect – 'a person utterly unfit to be entrusted with the education of his daughters', in the words of the anonymous pamphlet of 1776.*[28] Miss de Grosberg was dismissed, and promptly took the Earl of Northington to court, claiming compensation and back pay. At the hearing she mentioned that she had been shown the advertisement by a Mrs Potter of Hackney, with whom she had been lodging at the time. On the basis of handwriting samples, Frankland believed not only that the Carolines Rudd and de Grosberg were one and the same, but even that this Mrs Potter was another of her alter egos.

The idea is intriguing, but not very convincing. For one thing, Caroline was still living in St Albans in 1764: her move to London was two years away. No other source mentions her ever lodging in Hackney. Moreover, Caroline de Grosberg was accused of having an illegitimate child and a lover nicknamed 'Rob. Crucifix', who wrote her steamy letters. This does not fit with what we know about Caroline's life: she was still freshly married to Valentine Rudd at the time, and they were childless. Sir Thomas's theory seems to have been based on very little other than the coincidence of first names, a perceived similarity in handwriting and the fact that both were 'excellent pen-women, quick at invention . . . [and] boasters of high descent'.[29] His amateur detective work was to come back to haunt him later, in the courtroom.

Caroline's trial was now rescheduled for 16 September.

* *She Is and She is Not.* It does not appear to be written by Sir Thomas himself, although it mentions him.

When that day dawned, the Old Bailey was once again completely packed by seven o'clock in the morning. There was even some comic relief, as a linen draper disguised as a lawyer tried to get into the gallery reserved for the gentlemen of the inns of court. He was discovered by a door-keeper and thrown out 'amidst a peal of universal laughter'.[30]

Caroline was brought to the bar just before nine o'clock. Her counsel immediately queried the legality of the trial. The prosecution argued that it should go ahead, the forgeries concerned were different from those on which she had offered evidence, and she had no right to immunity. Transcripts of her previous examinations were read out. The three judges on the bench decided that the issue was too difficult to settle amongst themselves and that the trial should wait while the question was put before the complete team of twelve Old Bailey justices.

'She made a genteel appearance,' wrote the *Morning Post* reporter of Caroline in the dock: 'had on a black satin gown, her hair dressed, without either hat or bonnet. During the arguments she behaved with great composure, and wrote several notes. She had in her hand when she came in a paper of her own writing, containing some notes, from which it is believed she intended to make a defence had the trial been proceeded upon.' He added that 'she was extremely pale, owing to long confinement, and natural anxiety', but whenever the discussion seemed to turn in her favour, 'her countenance became bright, and expressive of feelings beyond the power of description. At the idea of liberty and life she could not conceal emotions, which, at the apprehensions of death, she was superior to.'

The trial was deferred and Caroline was returned to Newgate. 'On retiring she saluted the whole assembly with modest dignity, and withdrew to her captivity, repugnant to the sentiments of every generous auditor.' The *Morning Post* writer was also inspired to remark that 'had the whole tenor of Mrs. Rudd's conduct through life been equal to her behaviour since the ungenerous attempt to sacrifice her, she would be an object of universal admiration'.

During the long delay which followed while the twelve judges slowly chewed over the problem, public debate over Caroline and the Perreaus went on as usual. Robert's supporters protested about the mental agony he was suffering in prison while waiting for the trial. Those who had no sympathy with the Perreaus at all made the same complaint, but for quite a different reason: why waste prison space on them? The trial for which the execution was being delayed might never take place at all – why not just get the execution over and done with? A letter signed 'Neitherside' to this effect appeared in the *Morning Post* and was immediately countered by one from 'Viator', who wrote that Neitherside should more accurately have signed himself 'Oneside', since he seemed so eager to see the Perreaus hang.[31] Viator's letter was in turn met with one from 'Humanity', who warned him to refrain from trying to prejudice the public against Caroline. 'Men are but men, and when they are on the jury, if their ears have been filled with bad stories against the prisoner, it may perhaps influence some.'[32] Viator replied the following day saying that he would publish nothing further concerning 'the female culprit of Newgate', unless she or her 'black emissaries' attempted any further impositions or lies. If they did, though, he would 'throw open the lid of Pandora's box, and make the character of the culprit, and of her black list of train-bands stink in the nostrils of every honest man and woman in the kingdom'.[33]

An altogether gentler and more poetic soul wrote in with 'Some thoughts in favour of Mrs. Rudd', on Wednesday 13 September. Signing himself only 'W.D.', he said that Caroline had been acting not of her own free will but under the 'witchcraft of love' for Daniel. She gave him her entire fortune, and 'how she came by these sums, is a question equally indelicate as needless, it is enough to know, that what

Mrs. Rudd gained by her *wisdom*, her *folly* squandered away!' In confessing at William Adair's house, she had bravely 'snatched the halter from the Perreaus necks, and twined it about her own'. No legal wife could have acted more nobly: 'Mrs. Rudd only wanted the sanction of a religious ceremony to have changed the halter to the most becoming ornament, and made it the envy of every virtuous matron in the three kingdoms.'[34]

And so the autumn dragged by, with no announcement from the judges. The newspapers continued to report on Caroline's difficulties, but other matters also contended for the public's attention. There were dramatic events in America, of course, but also regattas on the Thames, visiting musicians and their concerts to be advertised and praised, new fashions in dress to be scoffed at. Bets were flying concerning the true sex of the mysterious Chevalière d'Éon: on Saturday 11 November it was running at 7 to 4 in favour of the female.[35] Other famous trials besides the Perreaus' also had their turn in the limelight that year: there was the trial of the popular Jane Butterfield, a housekeeper who had poisoned her lecherous employer and was acquitted of the crime, and that of the bigamous Duchess of Kingston, currently delayed while arguments raged over the propriety of subjecting a lady to such extreme public disgrace in court.

Another high-profile case was that of Captain David Roche or Roach, who confessed to murdering one John Ferguson in September and who was sent to Newgate to await his day in court. His proximity there to Caroline, while they both kicked their heels awaiting much-postponed trials, inspired an amateur poet to dream up a 'Poetical Billet from Captain Roach to Mrs Rudd', which was published in the *Gentleman's Magazine* in September.[36] It proposed that Captain Roach was secretly wooing Caroline in Newgate, and imagined that they would make a splendid pair:

Yet dread not thou a vulgar swain's approach,
The man who courts thy hand is Captain Roach;
Both sought renown, yet different paths pursu'd
Fraud mark'd thy course, while mine was drench'd with
    blood;
Small diff'rence yet our wayward fates afford,
The crow-quill pen was dang'rous as the sword.

A wedding was envisaged, together with a banquet in the prison cell, at which the couple would celebrate their union while others hanged:

... when with felons the full cart is crown'd,
And the bell tolls its elevating sound,
When ropes and fetters strew the press room floor,
And parting drams confed'rate gin-shops pour.

A bitter counter-poem was published the following month in the *Gentleman's Magazine*: 'To the Author of the Poetical Billet from Captain Roche to Mrs Rudd'.[37]

Of all the subjects that invite the Muse,
Was there no other left for you to chuse?
Or is your spirit of such hellish mould,
The more you wound, the happier is your soul?

Caroline's defender reminded the poet that 'none are guilty till their trial's past', and chastised him in the sternest terms:

If 'tis your nature that your happiness
Is fed by mortals ling'ring in distress,
Indulge your feast unenvy'd and alone;
For company, I trust, you can have none.

The sufferings of Caroline Rudd certainly aroused strong feelings in the masculine breast. An anonymous letter in the *Morning Post* lamented that 'a woman well educated, of an elegant and engaging person, without art herself, and therefore not suspicious of it in others, has ever been an object for the licentious, dark-designing libertine'.[38] The very idea of such a guileless creature forging bonds was absurd. Surely these complicated transactions must be the work of men accustomed to financial trading, not of 'a woman, who, by their own accounts, employed herself more in the frippery of dress, than in a line of business'.

When another correspondent suggested in the same newspaper that 'the influence Mrs. Rudd gains over her acquaintance, is by no means owing to her beauty, of which she has a very small portion',[39] he triggered furious reactions. Yet his overall assessment was not entirely negative, if somewhat ungallant: 'She is of the middling size, and was always exceedingly thin, with a rather sallow complexion, a dark piercing eye and fine teeth. Her dress and tone of voice are very distinguishing and captivating, and such as would make her an object of attention in the politest circle: to these she adds an uncommon degree of understanding and presence of mind, which never forsake her on any exigency.'

A reply two days later says that the writer obviously did not see Caroline in the courtroom, where 'her cheeks availed themselves of a bloom that, with her whole deportment, diffused the gratefulness [sic] of her nature'. Or, if she did perhaps appear pale at times: 'it is difficult to determine whether the rose or lilly demanded the most admiration. The former excited admiration, the latter humanity.' – 'Her manner of address was beyond conception engaging. There wanted nothing more than an opportunity to plead, with her sweet voice, that innocence which her eyes, the most expressive, together with her whole deportment, figuratively and irresistibly depictured.'[40]

At last, in November, the twelve judges announced that they had made their decision on the question of Caroline's trial. She was due to be taken to the Old Bailey on Wednesday 6

December to hear their verdict. When the day dawned, however, she was so ill that it seemed that moving her might endanger her life, so the decision was given in her absence. She *was* to be tried after all, and the date of the trial would be just two days later. The reasons would be formally explained to her in full then.

Although two days seemed barely enough to recover from such a serious illness, by Friday morning Caroline was quite well and ready to face whatever was to come her way. Between Robert Perreau's trial and her own, almost exactly six months had passed. It had been six long months of waiting, planning and writing – and of shopping for the perfect trial outfit. And now it was all to be decided, one way or the other.

CHAPTER
EIGHT
◆
TRIAL

The trial of Margaret Caroline Rudd began at the Old Bailey on the morning of Friday 8 December, and attracted the largest audience yet. People were queueing before daylight to see this highly publicized, long-awaited performance. The public galleries opened early, and shortly after dawn they were already crowded.[1] By nine o'clock, when the three judges filed into the court and proceedings formally began, not an inch of space remained to be filled. The audience waited eagerly for Caroline's entrance, as hungry for entertainment and as willing to endure the discomfort as Covent Garden theatregoers. They had paid for their tickets; they expected to get their money's worth. For the overwhelming majority of them, Caroline was a beleaguered heroine: they wanted her to win.

The cast of the show was a large one. Presiding over the stage was the trio of judges: John Sawbridge, who had succeeded Wilkes as Lord Mayor of London, Sir Richard Aston of the King's Bench and Sir John Burland of the Court of Exchequer. Other high officials had also taken their places in the courtroom, most notably the Recorder, John Glynn. Then there were the two opposing legal teams. For the prosecution there were three lawyers: Howarth, Lucas and Murphy. The defence was led by William Davy, a brilliant, truculent, and supremely confident character, known as 'Bull Davy' for his aggressive style of cross-examination, but also renowned for his ready wit and repartee.* Accompanying him were Davenport – the lawyer who had defended Caroline in the earlier hearings – and another lawyer who had not previously been involved, by the name of Cowper. John Bailey did not form part of her team: he was not a barrister and in any case was excluded because he was going to appear as a witness.

More important than any of these were the twelve jurymen, holding Caroline's life in their hands. They sat to one side of the room and were a mixture of types. Some of the men were stolid and stern; in others' eyes a sympathetic twinkle might have been visible. But however hard the onlookers scrutinized their faces, there were no visible clues yet as to which way they would finally lean.

With the officials, the lawyers, the jurymen, the newspaper journalists and the audience all stuffed into the cramped and ill-ventilated courtroom, the temperature quickly began to climb. Outside it was winter, but the Old Bailey's interior became almost tropical as the long Friday wore on.[2] Clothes were surreptitiously loosened in the galleries; flushed faces were fanned with papers. Around the prisoner's dock and the judges' bench, bouquets of strong herbs had been strewn as usual – they were supposed to disinfect the diseased miasma which inmates generally brought with them from Newgate. The herbal scent occasionally wafted over the aroma of overheated bodies in the gallery, but did little to lighten the atmosphere. If any of the audience were expecting to be out in the cool streets again by mid-morning, as happened when ordinary people were being summarily tried for their lives, they would be disappointed: Caroline's life and death were to

---

* He was more than a match for the likes of James Mansfield. When Mansfield once snapped at him, 'If this be law, Sir, I must burn all my books,' Davy replied with perfect composure, 'Your Lordship had better read them first.'

be weighed in the balance for almost eleven hours – an extraordinarily long time.

And now the prisoner herself was brought in and led into the dock. She could not have looked more different from the bedraggled, cowed ruffians who normally occupied that small spike-walled box. Her dress was of perfect dignity and taste: she wore 'a black silk gown with a pelonese cloak, lined with white Persian around her shoulders', with her neatly powdered coiffure topped by 'a white gauze cap, ornamented with black snailing'.[3] Impossibly pale, almost spectral, she radiated a lofty composure which was to remain with her throughout the day; at no time did she display any hint of fear or weakness. Yet she was also alert and far from inactive. What astonished the spectators more than anything else was that throughout the trial she scribbled messages in a notebook, each time tearing out the sheet and passing it over to her lawyers. In the course of the day, she was seen to write at least fifty of these notes – sixty, according to Horace Walpole[4] – usually at critical points in the testimony. All who saw her agreed that she, not her lawyers, appeared to be managing the defence case.

With everyone installed and proceedings ready to begin, Sir Richard Aston opened by explaining why the trial was going ahead. There were two reasons why Caroline was to be denied the benefits owing to an accomplice, he said. First, she claimed to have acted under duress and to be innocent; so 'if the court looked no further than the prisoner's information . . . they could not have learned from thence that she had ever been considered as an accomplice at all'.[5] Second, she had not told the whole of what she knew, but had only given information relating to a quite different incident. Therefore she was to be tried as any other suspect, regardless of her offers of evidence against the Perreaus. Aston warned that these considerations should no more be held against her than in her favour: the jury should base their decision solely on what they heard in the courtroom. 'I hope and trust, the facts will be tried without the least attention to, or even a remembrance of, any one matter or thing whatever, which has either made its appearance in print, or been the subject of common conversation,' he cautioned them.

The charges were now read out. As with the Perreaus, there were four separate indictments. They were: 'feloniously forging and counterfeiting' a bond for £5300 with intent to defraud William Adair, 'feloniously uttering and publishing it' with intent to defraud the same, and respectively forging and uttering the same bond with intent to defraud Sir Thomas Frankland.

Next, the contents of the bond were recited in full:

Know all men by these presents, that I William Adair of Pall-mall, in the parish of St James, in the county of Middlesex, Esq; am held and firmly bound to Robert Perreau, of Golden Square, in the parish of St. James, and county of Middlesex aforesaid, Esq; in ten thousand and six hundred pounds of good and lawful money of Great Britain, to be paid to the said Robert Perreau, or his certain attorney, executors, and administrators, firmly by these presents, sealed with my seal, dated this twentieth day of December, in the fifteenth year of the reign of our sovereign lord George the Third, by the grace of God, of Great Britain, France and Ireland, King, defender of the faith, and so forth; and in the year of our Lord one thousand seven hundred and seventy four.

The condition of this obligation is such, that if the above bounden William Adair, his heirs, executors, or administrators, shall and do well and truly pay or cause to be paid unto the above-named Robert Perreau, his executors, administrators or assigns, the full sum of five thousand and three hundred pounds, with interest, of good and lawful money of Great Britain, on the twenty-third day of March next ensuing the date hereof, then this obligation to be void, or else to remain in full force.

William Adair.
Sealed and delivered (being first duly stamped) in the
presence of
Arthur Jones
Thomas Start.

This concluded the formalities and the first witness for the
prosecution was called: Henrietta Perreau. She took the
stand, but before the prosecution could begin the questioning
of their witness, the defence team interposed a line of
interrogation designed to show that her testimony should not
be admissible.

'I believe you are the wife of Mr Robert Perreau, now
under sentence of death?' Davy asked her.

'I am.'

'Is it not your opinion that the fate of your husband will
depend upon the conviction of Mrs Rudd?'

'I am not clear of that,' she replied.

'Do you not hope or expect that the conviction of Mrs
Rudd will be a means of obtaining your husband's pardon?'

'I have nothing but the truth to say.'

Davy persisted. 'I desire an answer to my question. Do you
not hope that the conviction of Mrs Rudd may be a means of
obtaining your husband's pardon?'

'I don't hope for the conviction of Mrs Rudd.'

'That is not an answer to my question.'

'I hope Mr Perreau's innocence will clearly appear.'

'But do you not apprehend that Mrs Rudd's conviction
will contribute to it?'

'If Mrs Rudd is found guilty, I suppose it will,' admitted
Henrietta. 'I hope it may be the means of procuring Mr
Perreau's pardon.'

Davy turned to the judges and said that he believed Mrs
Perreau could not be considered a competent witness because
she had an interest in the outcome. This, according to the
principles of the day, completely disqualified a witness from

giving evidence – indeed, it was the reason why defendants rarely testified on their own account, but merely delivered a prepared statement. Waivers could be signed, since otherwise many trials would have no witnesses at all, but this had not been done in Henrietta's case. Davy's colleague Cowper added that the crucial point was whether she *believed* her evidence could help Robert rather than whether it actually could. It was 'the very imagination' of the witness that was significant, since it could distort the testimony. He quoted precedents.

The prosecution countered that the principle should not be adhered to excessively or no case would ever produce a conviction. One had to draw the line somewhere. The judges agreed and ruled that although Henrietta's credibility might indeed be affected, it would be going too far to rule out her testimony altogether. After all, this trial did not even concern the same crime as that for which her husband had been convicted. The examination was to go ahead.

Davy sat down and the prosecution proceeded to question Henrietta about the morning of 24 December 1774 – the day on which Caroline had allegedly given Robert the forged document for which she was being tried. Henrietta answered that on that morning she had indeed seen Caroline pass him a bond at their house in Golden Square.

'How do you know it was a bond?' asked the prosecution lawyer.

'Mr Perreau laid it down upon the table; while he was brushing his coat I looked at it.'

'Can you tell what sum it was for, to whom it was made payable, and what name was signed to it?'

'It was for £5300 made payable to Robert Perreau, and signed William Adair; and the witnesses were Arthur Jones and Thomas Start, or Hart.'

'When did you see it again?'

She replied that it was the day after Robert's conviction. (This was also the day after Caroline's imprisonment, so the magistrates were starting to gather their evidence: Henrietta was clearly one of their first ports of call.) 'I was in my own room upon my bed: it was brought by Justice Wright; there was another justice with him, whose name I do not know. They brought two or three bonds to see if I knew the bond that was delivered upon the 24th of December: I took up this bond, and made a mark upon it.'

Henrietta then told the court that she had heard Caroline inform Robert that Mr Adair wanted him to raise £4000 in cash, using the bond as security. Caroline had told him she had got Arthur Jones and Thomas Start to witness it, although if James Adair had been in town he would have been the witness instead. Robert replied that he would try to borrow money from Sir Thomas Frankland upon the bond, but not until later in the day. Caroline left shortly afterwards, with Daniel.

That evening Caroline returned to Golden Square alone. She asked for Robert, but he was out seeing Sir Thomas. 'She seemed very impatient for Mr Perreau's return,' Henrietta remarked. To hurry him, Caroline asked Robert's assistant David Cassady to send for Robert at Sir Thomas's, saying that a patient wanted him and that he should call at home. This was done and Robert came back. He gave Caroline a cheque of Sir Thomas Frankland's for what Henrietta described as a sum slightly less than £4000. (Her memory was correct, for the sum was £3890 9s: Sir Thomas had deducted the difference for interest owed to him by Robert.)

'You say the sum was under £4000 – did you hear that, or did you see it upon the draught?'

'I saw it, and I observed there were two or three blots upon the draught.'

'What kind of a draught was it?'

'A banker's draught filled up.'

'Have you seen that since?'

'Yes; I saw it upon the same day I saw the bond.'

The cheque in question was produced in court and Henrietta identified it as the one she had seen.

She continued the story: Caroline had left with the draught, saying that she had to return to William Adair to tell him that Sir Thomas had lent them the money as he had wished. The following day was Christmas. Daniel and Caroline dined with them at their home, and some other friends were also present. After dinner, when the group had retired to the sitting room, Caroline sat next to Robert, while Daniel leaned on the back of the sofa behind them. Henrietta heard Robert ask Caroline about her visit to William. Caroline replied that she had seen him and he had told her to give the draught to Daniel to pay Mr Collins for the Harley Street house.

'Did Daniel Perreau say anything upon hearing this?'

Henrietta said he had complained that he needed the full £4000 to pay for the house and the costs of conveyancing. Frankland's cheque fell short of this by just under £110, and he did not have quite enough cash to pay the difference. Either Daniel or Caroline – Henrietta could not remember which – asked Robert to lend them some money to make up the sum they needed. Robert pulled out a £20 note and asked if that would do. They took it; Caroline said to Daniel, 'Dan, you have a £10 note in your pocket, give it to your brother in change.'*

'Was there any company in the room then besides you, your husband, Daniel Perreau, and Mrs Rudd?'

'Yes; Mrs Williamson, and Mr Barker, a clergyman from Wales. Mr Barker and Mrs Williamson were conversing

---

* Daniel apparently had little difficulty in making up the remaining deficit of nearly £100; it emerged later in the trial that he paid the full £4000 into his bank the following day. Indeed, his banker was to testify that there had already been plenty of money in Daniel's account anyway. It is not clear why he asked his brother for £10, unless it was sheer greed – an idea which both prosecution and defence could adapt to their own advantage.

together about Carmarthen. I sat next to Mr Perreau, and heard the conversation.'

The prosecution now handed the witness over for cross-examination. 'Bull' Davy immediately set out to cast doubts on every aspect of Henrietta's memory and powers of observation. First he queried how she could have observed so clearly what occurred between the Perreaus and Caroline on Christmas Day.

He briskly reviewed the scene: 'Mr Robert Perreau and Mrs Rudd were sitting upon this sopha, Daniel was leaning behind, you sat next the sopha, and these two visitors were upon the opposite side of the fireplace?'

'Yes,' said Henrietta.

'And they were engaged in a conversation touching Carmarthen?'

'Yes.'

'You are a well-bred woman, and therefore of course, you were attending to the conversation of your visitors, and you perfectly well remember their conversation: how came you, when you had not a thought that anything was wrong in the transaction, to attend to the particular conversation of your husband, Daniel Perreau, and Mrs Rudd?'

'I should not have attended had they not been engaged in conversation.'

'But you did attend to their conversation; in short you attended to the conversation of two sets of company?'

'I did attend to their conversation, as I sat next to them. I cannot say I attended particularly to Mr Barker's conversation, only I remember that they were talking about Carmarthen: Mrs Williamson was asking me after my sister-in-law,* who lived in Carmarthen.'

Davy then asked whether Mr Barker and Mrs Williamson could also have heard the exchange between Mrs Rudd and the Perreaus, and wondered why they had not been called as

* Hetty.

witnesses. Told that Mrs Williamson was in the West Indies, and Mr Barker in Wales, he queried whether Barker could not have easily been brought to London.

'I don't know that he attended to that conversation,' said Henrietta.

'But if he had been here we could have asked him whether he had ever been there or no?'

'He is not here.'

'Then it rests entirely upon your account,' said Davy.

He then turned to the events of the previous day, when Henrietta had peeked at the bond while her husband was brushing his coat.

'You say you did not in the least imagine that there was anything improper or extraordinary in the transaction?'

'Not at all.'

'And yet I observe you were very curious to look at this bond ... and also afterwards to make very particular observations upon the draught even to the blots that were upon it, and to the particulars of the bond, so as to be able to know it again at the distance of three months: how came you to be so particular in your observations upon a matter that did not strike you then to have anything material in it?'

'My husband never restrained me from looking into his papers; when he was brushing his coat I read it. I looked at the bond as a mere matter of curiosity.'

'There was nothing about it that should lead you to any particular attention to it?'

'No: I don't know that ever I saw a bond before, and I looked at it.'

'Then I am a little surprized that never having seen one before, you should be able to recognize every circumstance about it; to know the names of the witnesses, Arthur Jones and Thomas Start; to observe the name of William Adair, the obligor of the bond; and to observe to whom it was made payable: it is surprizing to me, never having seen it afterwards till the day of your husband's affliction, which was at the distance of five months, that you should be able to swear so positively to it?'

'Because it was similar to the very bond itself.'

'To the witnesses, the name of Mr Adair, the name Robert Perreau to whom it was made payable, and the sum . . . ?'

'Yes . . .'

'How happened it, that at the distance of five months you should be able to be so very particular to the exact similitude of all the circumstances of the bond, never having seen any bond before in your life, and not being led by any suspicions to make any particular remarks upon it?'

'I have the happiness to have a good memory.'

Whether or not his belligerent cross-questioning style was succeeding in breaking down Henrietta's testimony, Davy was certainly managing to upset her a great deal. Several times she came close to fainting from the stress of his interrogation. To some extent his questions did dent her credibility, but he also risked encouraging sympathy for her amongst the jurors. This, after all, was a woman who had seen her husband condemned to death and had been struggling to raise her family alone for most of the previous year. Davy decided it was time to bring the cross-examination to a close, and he finished with some questions designed to remind the jury in a general way of Caroline's generosity and Daniel's meanness.

'The draught for £3890 odd was delivered to Daniel Perreau?'

'Yes.'

'. . . Then the story supposes that she had given to Daniel the whole produce of this bond, to enable him to pay for the house, and had not applied one shilling to her own use?'

'Yes . . .'

Yet, asked Davy, Daniel was supposed to be so short of cash that he had to borrow £10 from Robert, to make up the money?

'Yes, he was.'

With that Henrietta Perreau was allowed to leave the stand, and a more formidable enemy of Caroline's now mounted the little staircase to the witness box: Sir Thomas Frankland.

'You are acquainted with Mr Robert Perreau?' asked the counsel for the prosecution.

'He was my apothecary for seventeen years,' replied Sir Thomas. 'He came to me the day before Christmas day 1774, between three and four o'clock, before I had dined; he brought to me a bond, which I thought was Mr William Adair's of Pall-mall.'

The first part of Sir Thomas's evidence was straightforward enough. He identified the bond exhibited to the court as the one which Robert had brought him, and said that he had given only £3890 9s on it rather than the full £4000, because he deducted a small amount of money as a 'discount' relating to the previous debt of £5000, which was still outstanding.

Having established all this, the prosecution handed him over to the other side. This time it was Davenport who conducted the cross-examination rather than Davy. He was less ferocious in manner than his colleague, but every bit as tenacious.

'I believe you know the prisoner at the bar?'

'I don't believe I sat down above once in her company in my life,' replied Sir Thomas.

'I don't ask you the position,' said Davenport. 'I ask you only whether you know her?'

'I mistook you. I never saw the prisoner in my life till I saw her at Guildhall, Westminster.'

'Then this money was lent upon the credit of Robert Perreau only.'

'All upon the faith I had of his being an honest man.'

'Perhaps, though you may not know the prisoner, you may know something about her substance and her personality?' suggested Davenport.

The prosecution apparently objected to this question, but

Sir Thomas said, 'I have no objections to answer. As to her property, everything I have is sold to me by the two Perreaus by a bill of sale, and what there is I hardly know.'

One of the judges put in: 'Everything you have was in Harley Street?'

'Yes.'

'Then I will ask you', continued Davenport, 'whether any part of it consists of jewels or ornaments of a woman's person, and of a woman's apparel?'

'I fancy there are gowns, petticoats; jewels there were none in the house.'

'Then you have no jewels under the bill of sale from the Perreaus or from her?'

'I don't say so.'

'I wish you would answer me.'

'I have jewels sold to me by Daniel and Robert Perreau, and the poor jeweller is not paid to this hour.'

'The jewels being unpaid, do you retain and keep the jewels as your property?'

'The jeweller sold them in fact.'

'And notwithstanding the poor jeweller is unpaid, you retain these jewels as your property; be so good as to answer me another question, what is the value of them?'

'I am no judge.'

'Have you not had them valued?'

'Yes.'

'Then you are a judge of the appraisement. What are they valued at?'

'£2800.'

Davenport asked Sir Thomas whether he did or did not know that these were jewels which had been worn by Caroline Rudd. 'I know nothing of them,' he said.

'Nor have any reason to believe that?'

'Reason?' repeated Sir Thomas.

'Aye, reason to believe that these were worn or used by the prisoner?'

'I don't know whether she has got holes in her ears to hang them or no,' answered Sir Thomas rudely.

The question was asked again. Did he have any reason at all to believe that the jewels had been worn and used by Caroline?

'I have not reason enough to understand your question,' he retorted.

'You have reason enough to understand the discount upon £5000,' said Davenport.

The question was repeated word for word, and then rephrased. 'Did you ever hear that she used them?'

'I never heard of her, or saw her till I saw her at Guildhall, Wesminster.'

Davenport plugged on. 'As you knew the Perreaus very well, did you not know that she lived at the Perreaus'?'

'I knew nothing of Daniel Perreau: I did not know that he had a house in Harley-street; I had no connection with him.'

The question about the jewels was asked yet again. Did he believe them to have been used by Caroline? 'I suppose if women have jewels they wear them,' came the grudging reply this time.

'Now, do you suppose she is the woman who did wear them?' asked Davenport, probably feeling that he was getting somewhere at last.

But Sir Thomas reverted to his former line. 'I know nothing of it.'

A judge intervened. 'Sir Thomas, the question is not whether you knew it at that time, but whether you know it at this time?'

He gave in. 'Yes.'

Davenport took a deep breath. 'Now,' he said, 'upon your oath, did not you understand that question when I put it five minutes ago?'

'No,' said Sir Thomas.

'Upon your oath you did not?'

'No, I hardly understand your question now.'

The judge spoke up again. 'Now you have heard what passed between these Perreaus, and this Mrs Rudd, you now believe that she did wear them?'

'Certainly.'

'When I first asked you that question, did you believe it, or have you got that belief within these five minutes?' asked Davenport.

'I did not understand it.'

'You will pardon me, Sir Thomas; the manner of giving evidence is sometimes as strong as the evidence itself; I ask you, whether five minutes ago, when I first put the question, your belief was the same as it is now?'

No answer is recorded.

'By whom did you suppose the gowns and petticoats and other womens apparel were worn?' asked Davenport. 'By the two Perreaus, or by whom?'

'They might go in masquerade.' Whatever laughter this notion earned from the audience is not described in the trial transcript.

'As this man was your apothecary for seventeen years,' said Davenport, 'and you and he were acquaintances, you best know his manner of dressing; therefore, you suppose he might go to the masquerade in these cloaths?'

Sir Thomas was defeated. 'I suppose as these were womens cloathes she wore them,' he said.

'Do you believe now that they are hers?'

The witness changed tack. 'They are sold to me, as I said before, by a bill of sale.'

'Is the prisoner a party to that bill of sale?'

'No, I fancy not.'

Davenport wondered aloud about the validity of this bill of sale.

'Upon my word,' said Sir Thomas, 'I believe that affair must come into a court of law, and then it will be proper to decide that question.'

'I have as great an affection for a court of law as you have,' said Davenport. 'But as we are in a court of law at present, I would wish to have this question answered, whether these goods of hers that you claim, you claim under a bill of sale to which she is no party?'

'Whether they had a right to sell them, I am no judge,' replied Sir Thomas, 'But that will be settled I suppose in a court of law.'

'But I ask you now, whether you don't believe that these are her property?'

'Her husband has sent over a power of attorney from Ireland to claim them.'*

'I ask you, whether they have ever been demanded of you by the prisoner?' continued Davenport.

'She has demanded all the household furniture and everything in the world that was paid for with my money,' retorted Sir Thomas.

'Has she demanded these cloaths and jewels of you by her agent?'

'Yes; the tables and chairs, and the jewels, and all the things that are marked in the house of Daniel Perreau; but that is to be litigated in a court, and I hope what I say will not be made evidence.'

Sir Thomas did not win many friends in the courtroom, and although he was an exasperating creature for the defence examiner to deal with, he was doing their side nothing but good in the jury's eyes. He obstructed every single question, no matter how insignificant. Asked if he had lent Robert Perreau £5000 as well as the amount slightly under £4000, he replied, 'I did not: my banker lent it to him.' When the question came back, 'It was your money, was it not?' he had to admit, 'Yes, my money, in the banker's hand.'

* This is a surprising statement, since there had been no other mention of Valentine Rudd at this time, and by the following year Caroline was telling Boswell that she had vaguely heard of a man in Ireland 'pretending' to be her husband. Assuming that Rudd was not in fact trying to make a comeback, Caroline was probably just using his name to scare Frankland off.

A few more questions were asked about his transactions with Robert Perreau, seeking to establish that Robert knew in advance when the bond was to arrive, and therefore was likely to have known of the whole fraudulent plan. Then the cross-examination veered off in an altogether different direction. Sir Thomas answered every bit as amiably and helpfully as before.

'Do you know a Mrs Porter or Potter of Hackney?' Davenport asked. Mrs Potter was, of course, the landlady who had referred the mysterious 'Caroline de Grosberg' to her job as governess in 1764. Sir Thomas was thus to be quizzed about his pet theory concerning Caroline's past.

'I know no such body,' he replied.

'Have you ever sent or enquired whether the prisoner was that Mrs Porter or Potter of Hackney?'

'Certainly I have.'

'I ask you to whom you have mentioned your idea of this Mrs Porter or Mrs Potter at Hackney?'

'I wrote to the Earl of Northington about it.'

'Are you the prosecutor of this indictment?' asked Davenport.

'Yes; I was bound over to prosecute.'

'. . . Then I ask you, whether you have prosecuted this woman as, and believing her to be a Mrs Porter or Potter of Hackney?'

'I know nothing at all about that: I don't know that she is, but I believe that she is.'

'Do you know one Jane Williams?'

'I do not know that I do.'

The judge put in, 'Take time and consider.'

'I saw several people at Hackney,' said Sir Thomas. 'She might be one of them.'

'Have you enquired of one George Downe, whether this prisoner was that Mrs Porter or Potter that had lived in Hackney?'

'I did.'

'Did you enquire of any woman?'

'I believe there were two women.'

'Of Mrs Elizabeth Pendellow?'

'I know nothing of her.'

'Of Catharine Peake?'

'Catharine Peake called at my house one afternoon, and I did not speak two words to her.'

'But they might be very significant words,' said Davenport, not to be so easily thrown. 'Were they concerning Mrs Potter of Hackney?'

'They were.'

'. . . That Mrs Rudd might be this Mrs Potter; was that the subject of your enquiry with her?'

'She came to my house; I asked if Mrs Rudd was not the same woman that was at Hackney?'

'How came Mrs Peake at your house, for the purpose of discovering of Mrs Potter or Porter? Did you not send for her?'

'No.'

'How came she then?'

'Perhaps somebody sent her; I never sent for her, nor know nothing of her.'

'Do you know who sent her?'

'No.'

'How could Catharine Peake come to your house to be asked questions by you?' persisted Davenport. 'Did she tell you anything, or did you interrogate her? Did you speak to her first, or she to you?'

'She spoke to me first.'

'What introduced your conversation?'

Replied Sir Thomas, in complete seriousness, 'She said, "I heard you wanted to speak to me."'

'Now,' went on Davenport, 'who was your agent? To whom did you give the authority to make this enquiry?'

'I don't know that I did,' came the old refrain.

'To whom did you give authority?'

'Nobody that I know of.'

'Then, though you had given no authority to any one to enquire whether Mrs Rudd was Mrs Porter of Hackney, yet this woman found out your house, and came to you, and knew all the business without being told; now what answer did you make?'

'I told her I thought Mrs Rudd was Mrs Porter of Hackney.'

'Why did you believe so? . . .'

'I had seen Madam Groseburgh's writing.'

'Was that the same woman you believed to be Mrs Rudd and Mrs Potter?'

'Yes.'

'How came you to see Mrs Groseburgh's writing, to know that her writing and Mrs Rudd's were alike?'

'Because a Mrs Fellows, who hired Mrs Potter to send her down to the Earl of Northington to be a governess to his children, gave me a note which is like her handwriting.'

Sir Thomas was then asked to confirm that he recognized the bond exhibited to the court as the one he had received from Robert as security for the £5000 loan. He did so, and with that the cross-examination finished. The purpose of the long inquisition concerning the Caroline de Grosberg allegations seemed to have been to try to expose Sir Thomas as a man motivated by a personal grudge against the defendant – a grudge that bordered on obsession. What the jury made of this would have been hard to tell at this stage; they were probably more bemused than anything. In general, though, Sir Thomas had not made a good impression on them. Caroline was satisfied with Davenport's performance; she now prepared herself for the next stage, listening attentively and continuing to write frequent notes to her team.

Her prosecution opponents now set out to strengthen their case concerning the illegality of the bond and the benefits she received from its use. Two witnesses confirmed that the bond was definitely false: the clerk Scroope Ogilvie said the handwriting on it was not that of his former employer William Adair, and then a friend of the supposed signatory Arthur Jones testified that that signature was not Jones's.

Next on the stand was David Cassady, Robert's assistant, who had already been seen at Robert's trial stating that his former employer had given Caroline a paper on 4 March 1775. This time he merely confirmed Henrietta's assertion that Daniel and Caroline had been at her house on 24 and 25 December 1774. Cassady had seen them there and added that on Christmas Eve Caroline had been very eager for Robert to be called home. That was all he knew.

Mr Davenport now announced (perhaps prompted by extra notes from Caroline) that he wished to examine Sir Thomas Frankland further. Sir Thomas returned to the witness box, and Davenport asked him a couple of questions designed to show that Robert was both accustomed to borrowing money and given to gambling – thereby seeking to imply his probable guilt in all the forgeries. He asked Sir Thomas about Robert's earlier loans from him, and enquired whether he knew that Robert was in the habit of stock-jobbery and dealings in the Alley. 'I hope you have a better opinion of me than to suppose I would lend money for such a purpose,' replied the witness haughtily.

Davenport, expecting such difficulties, was quick to bridle. 'I don't ask you whether you knew it when you lent your money,' he said. 'I am asking you whether you don't know now that Robert Perreau had great dealings in the stocks?'

Sir Thomas answered inconsequentially, mentioning some papers of Daniel's – not Robert's – that he had seen in the Harley Street house.

'... Then why did you think Robert Perreau, who had never borrowed money for seventeen years, should want £9000 in May 1774?' (Actually Robert only asked Sir Thomas for £5000 that May, although further loans came later.)

'There were £13,000 in the whole,' replied Sir Thomas.

'For what purpose was the money wanted if there were no losses to settle?'

'Robert Perreau always told me that his brother Daniel had married a woman intimately connected with Mr Adair, and that he was paying her fortune by instalments.'

'I am asking you for what purpose it was that Robert Perreau wanted such sums of money?'

'That was best known to himself.'

'Then I am to understand you, that, upon your oath, you have never searched the books for Robert Perreau's dealings in the stocks?'

'I never have, I declare upon my oath.'

'Then I am misinformed,' muttered Davenport. 'I had heard so.'

This inconclusive line of questioning implies that Sir Thomas may have set himself to gather some dirt on Robert, but had later abandoned it for reasons unknown. (If true, this would support Caroline's theory that Robert had come to a deal with him.) Whatever he had or had not discovered about Robert before calling off the search, however, he was not going to reveal it to the court now and Davenport could not force him to do so. It was perhaps a mistake to have tried, although it did at least give the jury a nebulous impression that Robert Perreau might have had reasons to mastermind the forgery himself.

So Frankland was let off the hook again, and the prosecution now produced the first two of a trio of witnesses whose combined testimony was to prove that the money procured by Robert had gone not to himself but to Daniel – and therefore probably to Caroline as well, or so the prosecution hoped the jury would think. The first of these witnesses was Sir Thomas's banker, William Hoggard, who said that he had paid the draught on 26 December to a Mr Thomas Alexander, owner of the Union Coffee House. When Alexander appeared a few witnesses later he corroborated this, saying that he had received the draught and cashed it for

Daniel. Elias Isaac, who lived with the bankers Biddulph and Cocks, followed Hoggard and testified that Daniel Perreau had paid in the full sum of £4000 to his own account at the bank on 26 December. The counsel asked Isaac whether the bank had paid any money to Thomas Collins, the builder from whom Daniel Perreau had bought the Harley Street house. He confirmed that the bank had paid Collins £4000 on 31 December. The prosecution thus succeeded in making its point that it apeared to be Daniel and Caroline who had benefited from the fraud, rather than Robert. In cross-examination, the defence tried to claw back some advantage by implying that Daniel's behaviour in claiming to need money from Robert was greedy and dishonourable: they asked Isaac the balance of Daniel's account before the £4000 was paid in. It was £595 5s 6d; Isaac was asked, rhetorically, whether this would be enough to cover a conveyancers' bill of, say, £20. He replied that it certainly would. One could only deduce from this that Daniel's motive in borrowing the small sum of £10 from his brother had been petty greed, since he clearly did not need the money. And blackening Daniel's character in the jury's eyes should help Caroline's case – or so the defence had to hope.

Next to testify was Daniel's former servant John Moody, who had already appeared at the trials of both Perreau brothers. He told essentially the same story, saying that he had seen Caroline writing Adair's letters in a different hand from her usual one. When the prosecution showed him the bond, he asserted that it was in her 'special' handwriting. His evidence was brief but damning, since he claimed to be an actual eye-witness to her forgeries. The cross-examiners quizzed him closely on his powers of observation.

'Did you lean over her shoulder?'

'No.'

'Did you examine what she wrote?'

'No.'

'I want to know then how you could distinguish the feigned hand from the real hand?'

'Not to read it while she was writing it.'

'My question is, how you could distinguish that you did not examine, or read, from what you called a feigned hand?'

'When she has wrote papers containing directions for me to get in errands, that I might not forget, that was her common hand.'

'Did that bear the least resemblance in the world to the name of William Adair to the bond you have looked at?'

'No.'

'Nothing I suppose could be more unlike the two names?'

'No.'

The defence then turned to the motivation and character of Moody himself. 'When you left the family I suppose you was dismissed in the usual way?'

'I left them to better myself,' he said.

'Had you disclosed to your master before you left the family the circumstances of the imposition that you had practised upon him?'

'No, I never did.'

He was asked whether he had seen Daniel Perreau between that time and the time of his hearing before the magistrates. Moody said yes, in Clerkenwell Prison a few weeks after his arrest.

'Did you then disclose it to him?'

'Never.'

Asked more about the meeting, Moody explained that Daniel had summoned him from prison because he remembered Moody giving him some letters supposed to be from William Adair.

'Had you not, before that, heard that they were all committed to prison?'

'Yes, I had.'

'It was all over the town, therefore I suppose you heard it the day after?'

'I don't know that I did so soon as that; I had heard it.'

Moody was asked to relate what had taken place between him and Daniel Perreau in Clerkenwell.

'The first word he mentioned was, "Moody, you see the unhappy situation I am in." – I said I was sorry to see it.' Daniel then asked whether he recollected giving him letters as coming from William Adair, and Moody said yes. 'Did you make any observation of the date?' asked Daniel; Moody did not. 'Do you remember the handwriting?' Moody told Daniel he did remember it.

'He said hardly any more to me on that subject,' continued Moody, 'but begged me to go to his brother's house in Golden-square, where there would be his attorney, or Mr Cassady, or some of them, who would examine me, and he desired I would disclose all I knew of the matter.'

'This was in substance all that passed, was it?'

'Yes, it was.'

'Then at this time, when you was sent for by Daniel Perreau, and asked about the delivery of those letters, you did not say a word to him about Mrs Rudd's having imposed upon him, and your having delivered letters to him as from Mr Adair that were wrote by Mrs Rudd?'

'I told you,' said Moody, 'Daniel asked me whether I remembered giving letters to him that came from Mr Adair; I told him I did.'

The defence allowed him to leave the stand, hoping that the jury would consider Moody's failure to tell Daniel what he knew a sign of either disloyalty or mendacity, or both. Caroline continued to scribble: the pile of notes in front of her lawyers grew and grew.

Thomas Alexander, proprietor of the Union Coffee House in Cornhill, now briefly occupied the hot seat to confirm the testimony of the banker William Hoggard, saying that he had received a draught of Sir Thomas Frankland's from Daniel Perreau in December and had gone to cash it for him at Hoggard's while Daniel waited, then had given Daniel the money. The triple testimony of Alexander, Hoggard, and Elias Isaac added up to proof that Daniel had definitely received the money borrowed by Robert – plus a little extra – and had used it to pay for his house.

Now came what was to be the strangest testimony of all. The stand was taken by Caroline's former servant, Mrs Christian Hart.

'How long have you known Mrs Rudd?' the prosecution asked her.

'I lived with her as a servant; I went in December 1770, and then left her in March 1771.'

'In what capacity?'

'House-maid; she was the best mistress I ever lived with.'

'Did you at any time since her confinement go to Newgate to visit her?'

Mrs Hart, probably suffering from nerves, appeared to have rehearsed her answer: 'I was almost distracted when I heard of this unhappy accident, but most so for my mistress; I heard that my mistress was in Newgate; I went to see her there.'

'Do you remember when it was?'

The answer came out in a torrent: 'It was in June or July last: I was there twice, the first time was on a Tuesday; she asked me whether I was in lodgings, or kept a house? I told her I kept a house and let lodgings: she asked me if I could let a gentleman and a lady come there without being discovered by the neighbours? I said nothing was more easy.' Assuming that Caroline meant she needed a place to stay herself if she fled or was released, Mrs Hart 'put my hands together, and said, "My dearest madam, if you ever expect to get out of this place, come to my house, and I will never part with you till I get you to Ireland or Scotland."

'She wanted my husband to go on some message for her, I told her he was unfit, but I was at her service; she said it was necessary to go to Robert Perreau to find the house-maid Betty, and to know if Robert Perreau's wife was in town: I told her I would go immediately; I was to enquire for one Molly that was at the Magdalen Hospital, and also to enquire for the coachman; I begged of her to write down what she would have me do, and I would go immediately; she wrote it down upon a little bit of paper.'

'When did you go again to see Mrs Rudd?'

'The next day, which was Wednesday, I told her I had delivered all the messages she sent me with, and that it was impossible to know whether Mrs Perreau was in town, because the maid came to the door and answered me very pertly. Mrs Rudd said it would be a great means of saving her life if I would say that Mrs Perreau had lodgings at my house.' It was thus revealed that it was not for herself that Caroline wanted to know whether Mrs Hart let lodgings: she was concocting a story concerning Henrietta Perreau.

'I offered Mrs Rudd two guineas. She said, "I don't want money, but I want a sincere friend that will be true to me." She took up some papers after she had given my little girl a guinea, and said, "What I am going to say is as true as God is in Heaven, but I cannot find out where it happened." She then asked me if I knew Sir Thomas Frankland?' Mrs Hart answered that she did not. Caroline told her that 'it was necessary that I should see Mrs Robert Perreau. I asked her how I should get to see her? She said "Let me consider of that." After considering a little, she said, "Mrs Perreau is a fair-haired lady, with blue eyes something like me, but clumsier;" and if a black-eyed lady came, I might be sure that was not Mrs Perreau, but another. I said, "Well, what must I say when I see Mrs Perreau?" She said I must say I was satisfied. I said, "Madam, that is a very odd answer, she will take me before a justice of peace, and make me explain my words."'

Caroline did not deny this. She instructed Mrs Hart that if questioned, she should not give her own name but any Scottish-sounding name that came to her mind, and she should say that she lived in Westminster – 'but I was neither to go home afterwards, nor to go to Newgate to see her: and then she said I must see Sir Thomas Frankland. She described him. She said he was a little old man with grey hair, and that I might easily know him again. I told her, though I loved her as my life, I was afraid to meddle with such rich people, and I never was before a justice in all my life. She took up paper and said, what she was going to tell me was as true as God was in Heaven, and I was only to say it happened at my house. She said a great many had offered their service to her, but one in particular.'

'Did she name any person?'

'No, but she said she could not put that confidence in them that she could in me. She promised to give me a sum of money; but I cannot be positive whether she mentioned £200 or £100 but I believe it was £200.'

'For what?'

'As a reward for the lie I was to make about the papers. I said, I begged leave to know what was the contents of the papers, and that she read them.'

'Should you know the papers again, if you were to see them?'

'I wrote my name upon the papers. These are them.' Mrs Hart pointed at the papers, which were exhibited to the court. 'Here is my name upon them,' she said. 'They were delivered to me by Mrs Rudd on the Wednesday.'

'Do you know whose handwriting it is?' asked one of the judges.

'No,' said Mrs Hart.

'What did she desire you to do with the papers?'

'That I could never get out of her. I made many objections to it. I asked what a bond was? She said, it was a piece of paper; and she described what it was. She said the first thing the Jury would ask me would be, what a bond was? She said, she had provided a counsellor and solicitor, and witnesses to back me, and my life was as precious to her as her own; and my saying that, and that only, would save her life. She gave me the papers to show her husband, and I was to bring them back to Newgate at four o'clock that afternoon.'

'What was you to do with the papers in the meantime?'

'I was to consult with my husband about the papers. I told her my husband was an honest man. She said, if he would agree to it, and £200 would not do, it should be ten times more. – After I had consulted my husband, I was to bring the papers back; but I never went back.'

'Was anybody present at this conversation?'

'Nobody but herself and me.'

'If your husband had agreed to the papers, what were you to do with them?'

'Whether he had agreed or not, I was to return them again at four o'clock.'

'. . . You have mentioned something about a jury that were to ask you questions; what was that about?'

'She said I was to go to her trial, and to take particular notice of Sir Thomas Frankland's person, and she said if I agreed to this I should get £200.'

'Agreed to what?'

Mrs Hart did not know. 'I understood her I was to be at some trial.'

The prosecution lawyer asked again what it was exactly that her husband was supposed to be agreeing to.

'I was to swear all she had wrote down in these papers.'

'Then you left Mrs Rudd, and took the papers with you?'

'Yes; I did.'

'Are these the very identical papers?'

'They are.'

The papers were produced and the text read to the court. It ran as follows:

Christian Hart saith, That Mrs Robert Perreau used to come often to her house, during the last summer, and part of the winter, till January, with Mr Williamson of Frith-street, Soho, whom she, Christian Hart, hears is gone since to the East-Indies; and she did imagine it was a private intrigue, and had the curiosity to listen and observe them in private. That she often saw them writing letters and papers; that once in particular she was ordered to bring in some pens, and that when she came to the table to lay them down, Mrs Perreau had a paper like a bond (and which Christian Hart believes was one), and she, Mrs Perreau, was writing a name to one on the left side of the bond, where it is witnessed, and one name was wrote; the second was partly wrote when Christian Hart came to lay the pens down, and Mrs Perreau then stopped to look at the pens; and this was in or near November. That she often heard them mention the names of Adair, Jones and Start while they were writing; and that Mr Williamson once swore a great oath, and said he must have a thousand out of the next money; and Mrs Perreau answered and said, that she was afraid her husband would not give him so much.

The implication of the paper was clear, and it must have caused quite a stir in the courtroom. If Mrs Hart was telling the truth, then Caroline had tried to frame not only Robert but also Henrietta Perreau for the forgeries – together with the conveniently absent Mr Williamson. And there was more to come.

The paper continued: 'That in January the lodging was discharged by Williamson, and that Christian Hart saw nothing more of Mrs Perreau till about the 6th or 7th of last month, June, when she came and asked Christian Hart, if she could spare her a room to meet some people on business, that she did not chuse to see at home, as everybody there was on the watch.' Henrietta Perreau had then turned up with an unidentified 'tallish gentleman, young and pitted with the smallpox, and wore his own hair, and she called him brother'. Then:

an elderly gentleman came, whom Christian Hart knew to be Sir Thomas Frankland; and ... the other gentleman then left Mrs Perreau and him, Sir Thomas, together; and she thinking it was very odd, listened, and heard them agree, that Mrs Perreau should swear against Mrs Rudd about forging and giving to the Mr Perreaus some bond or bonds that Sir Thomas had; that he promised to reward her for doing so, and to make interest with the King to pardon her husband. She [Mrs Perreau] said she would do any thing on earth to hang Mrs Rudd, but must be careful not to say what would hurt herself. That they must stick by each other, for Mrs Rudd was keen, and would, if they did not take great care, find him out. A great deal more discourse passed, all to the same purpose. Mrs Perreau has met Sir Thomas Frankland several times since, and all their discourse has been, how to contrive to swear Mrs Rudd's life away, and screen themselves.

So Sir Thomas and Henrietta were to be stitched up in a neat little package together: two of Caroline's greatest enemies caught in conspiracy against her. According to this package, first Henrietta had masterminded the forgeries, and then she and Sir Thomas had jointly engineered the prosecution of Caroline as fall guy.

The paper concluded, 'Mrs Hart would fain have made this discovery sooner, but her husband was timorous to meddle with such rich folks, because too Sir Thomas Frankland swore he would hang Mrs Rudd, if it cost him all his fortune; and Mrs Perreau said she and all her family was resolved to do so too; but when my husband and I heard, that Mrs Perreau had made a false oath, whereby Mrs Rudd's life was likely to be taken away, we could not rest in our beds till we discovered and told all the truth, to save innocent blood from being spilt by such wicked people.'

This, then, was the statement that Christian Hart was supposed to have made. Instead of signing it, however, she had appended to it the following damning words: 'I received this paper from Mrs Rudd the 5th July, 1775. Christian Hart.' These few words changed the whole nature of the document. Christian Hart had chosen to betray Caroline instead of colluding with her.

To make matters clear, the prosecution asked her, 'Do you know Sir Thomas Frankland's person?'

'No.'

'Did you ever see him in your life?'

'No.'

'Did you ever see Mrs Perreau?'

'No, I never saw her.'

'This paper your husband took from you?'

'Yes.'

'How long after you received it did he take it?'

'The same day, and it was taken to a Justice of Peace.'

The prosecution stood down and William Davy stepped forward to dismantle her testimony as best he could.

'When did you write your name to these papers?' he asked Christian Hart.

'That very day,' she replied.

'When did you first mention this to your husband, and consult him?' Mrs Hart was unnerved by Davy's manner of firing questions and her answer came out in a garbled rush. 'As I came down stairs, we went to a public house, my child dropped a guinea, my husband asked what that was, I told him it was a guinea my wicked mistress gave the child. My husband asked for the papers; I said, my mistress wanted to hang you and me and all the world; but I said she never shall be brought into trouble for me and my husband was in a great passion at the Horseshoe and Magpie; he struck me and abused me much, and said he would go to Newgate and know what Mrs Rudd meant; and he insisted upon having the papers.'

'Did you give him the papers?'

'He insisted upon having the papers; and said, if Mrs Rudd

drew me in, he would appear against me, and hang us both; this frightened me a good deal, and I read the papers to him.'

Davy asked how she came to be before the Justice of the Peace. 'He took me there,' she said, 'and I made oath before the Justice.'

'You had been in Mrs Rudd's service two months, and she had behaved so well to you, that you had a great liking to her?'

'I had.'

Davy went back to the conversation she had had with Caroline in Newgate. He asked whether he was right in getting the impression that Mrs Hart had objected to the plan only because she did not want to be found out in telling lies, rather than because she was morally opposed to lying in itself. 'I was afraid,' she replied.

'At last you agreed to do all this, but you must consult your husband first?'

'I did not intend to go to her again; I intended to have wrote a polite letter, and sent the papers back.'

'. . . Then your resolution was not to say a word to your husband?'

'No.'

Davy repeated her testimony, as if reviewing it in his own mind. 'The moment you saw your husband he was angry with you for staying so long, and by and by the child dropt a guinea, and your husband asking what that was, you said it was a guinea, your wicked mistress had given the child?'

'Yes.'

'. . . Your husband asked you what you had it for?'

'No; he asked me what I meant by that; I told him it was given me to hang him and myself and all the world. He wanted to know what I said that for.'

'As you represent it, Mrs Rudd said it was a true transaction, which she would have you fix to have happened in your house?'

'Yes.'

'I observe a very remarkable expression you used. "I was afraid to meddle with such rich people."'

'Yes.'

'Because I observe that very expression is in the written paper.' Davy sprang into attack. 'Was the paper produced to you in the manner in which you have represented it?' he demanded. 'Or was it an offer that *you* made to this Mrs Rudd, and asked to have what you said you would swear taken down in writing?'

'It was ready wrote when I came into the room,' protested Mrs Hart.

'. . . Then you did not offer your service in the lying way?'

'No!'

'There was nothing said from you about giving evidence, or telling any lies?'

'No.'

'. . . Before she began to read she told you she wanted you to tell a lie for her?'

'Yes; and she said what she had wrote was as true as God was in heaven.'

'. . . And she told you what answers to make when you was cross-examined?'

'She did.'

'And after you had been with your husband you read over these papers?'

'I did, twenty times.'

This was a gift to Davy. 'It is necessary one should read a paper very often in order to be able to swear to it?' he asked, encouragingly.

'I was to remember the last word always . . .' said Mrs Hart.

Davy let this sink into the minds of the jury. 'Tho' you resolved from the moment you left Newgate never to do this wicked trick,' he said.

'I did.'

'Then why did you take the papers with you?'

'I was afraid to leave them behind,' she said.

'When did the Justice take the papers from you?'

'About four o'clock on the same day, that I came from Newgate.'

'When was the twenty times that you read these papers after you left Newgate?'

'While I was deliberating what to do with the papers for an hour. I read them over a great many times.'

Davy finished by asking once again whether there had been any witnesses to her conversation with Mrs Rudd in Newgate. She said that she had only seen Caroline's lawyer there. Davy pointed out Mr Bailey and asked if he was the man she had seen. Mrs Hart said she thought it was a taller gentleman, and that he was wearing a gown. 'Had you no conversation in his presence?' Davy asked. 'No,' she said.

And Mrs Hart was allowed to step down.

Her evidence was now corroborated by a woman named Mary Wilkinson, who took the stand briefly and was asked whether she had ever seen Mrs Rudd write. She said that she had.

'Are you acquainted with her handwriting?'

'She can write more than one hand.'

She was shown Christian Hart's text. 'What do you think of these papers? Are they not in her hand?'

'I positively believe that they are,' said Mary Wilkinson and with that was allowed to go.

John Hart, Christian's husband, was sworn in. He described the events of the Tuesday when his wife had gone to visit Caroline and said that he had followed her to Newgate.

'I sent up my name, and desired to speak to her: I went up. Mrs Rudd and my wife were together. Mrs Rudd asked me to sit down, which I did. Mrs Rudd said, she desired I would not be angry with her sending for my wife: she said she intended to send her children with her. I looked at my wife, and thought it very hard to be troubled with other people's children. Mrs Rudd said, I need not think that her children should be a burthen to me: that I might call next day, at 9 o'clock, and her counsellor and solicitor would be there, and settle her children with me. She asked me what part of my house was to let, she said if the parlour was to let, that she would have the parlour for her children. My wife replied, the parlour and first floor were let to a gentleman.'

'Where do you live?'

'At No. 1, in Coombes Court, Well Street, Oxford Road. I said the second floor was to let, and that was more airy for children. She desired me to get iron-rails for the windows, to prevent the children falling out, which I did intend to do. We came home, and the next morning my wife and I went, at nine o'clock, to Newgate, and sent up our names. She sent for my wife up, and desired me to wait in the tap-room. I waited there from nine o'clock, I think, till near twelve. About twelve I sent up the man to desire my wife to come down: she came down soon after, and I was in a very great passion. I asked her where the children were? She said there were no children. I asked her what was the reason? She gave me little or no answer; and I saw that she was all in a tremble. I said again to her, "Where are the children?"; she prayed me, for God's sake to hold my tongue: she said, "If you don't hold your tongue we shall both be taken up;" which put me in a great confusion. I saw some papers in her hand: we went to the Horseshoe and Magpie, and there I saw these papers.'

Mr Davenport cross-examined Hart only briefly.

'Did not Mrs Rudd desire you come?' he asked.

'Yes, with her own mouth.'

'Yet you was not called up?'

'No, not allowed to go up.'

'Did you see anybody else go to or from Mrs Rudd on Wednesday?'

'I cannot tell; I saw none that I know of but my wife.'

There followed a very short piece of character testimony by one Alexander Allen, who said that he had known and been the employer of John Hart since the previous May, and that so far as he knew he was an honest man.

And that was the conclusion of the prosecution's case. They had produced a carefully structured edifice of testimony, ranging from evidence that Caroline had written the forged signatures to proof that it was Daniel's household rather than Robert's that had benefited thereby. The construction had been set alarmingly a-wobble by Davy's and Davenport's clever cross-questioning, and some of their key witnesses had been made to look foolish or unreliable – but the scaffolding held. And now they had finished with a piece of real drama. Although inarticulate and easily overawed, Christian Hart was the star of the prosecution's show. It was now the defence's task to try to upstage her.

The defence opened with a prepared statement addressed to the jury by Caroline – who was capable of outshining anyone. It began with a direct appeal to their better feelings: 'Gentlemen of the Jury, I have now no other reliance but on you.' She then swept briefly through the prosecution's case, priming the jury for the idea that none of it was as conclusive as it might seem, and concentrating on trying to discredit each and every one of the witnesses:

> The bias upon Mrs Robert Perreau's mind is manifest: I am confident her testimony will not weigh with you; she swears to save the life of her husband. – Sir Thomas Frankland has behaved in a way sufficiently disgraceful to himself. – Moody, from his own account, must have been a very bad man; the only evidence to prove the forgery is upon this man's belief that the letters directed in his presence were like the name signed to the bond; this is too loose and vague a testimony to take away any one's life upon. – I have lost my property. – I have suffered a dreadful imprisonment; and now my life is to be taken away to save the Perreaus.

The witness Christian Hart is of a most infamous character: who has prevailed upon her to tell this story, I can't say; but can you believe I mean to trust my life to the testimony of one wretched ignorant woman? – I was to give her £200, or ten times more? – At that moment, gentlemen, I had been stripped of all I had in the world, and it was as possible for me to raise a million as £200.

She finished with an expression of guileless trust: 'Gentlemen, you are honest men, and I doubt not but I am safe in your hands.'

The defence's goal was to undo all the prosecution witnesses on grounds of bias, unreliability or plain bad character. However, it was only in Caroline's statement that most of the prosecution testimony was actually addressed. In the remainder of the defence case, the lawyers trusted the jury to make up their own minds, and confined themselves to attacking the one really dangerous, maverick witness: Christian Hart. If Mrs Hart's testimony were believed, effort expended on anything else would be wasted, and so they trained their entire armoury on her – a tactic very possibly dictated by another of Caroline's notes.

The first witness to appear for the defence was Caroline's original attorney, John Bailey. He was sworn in on the stand and examined by the defence lawyer, Mr Cowper.

Cowper asked him about his frequent visits to his client in Newgate and then pointed to Christian Hart. 'Do you recollect seeing that woman there?'

'I did,' said Bailey.

'When did you see her there?'

'The beginning of July.'

'Was there anyone present besides Mrs Rudd, Christian Hart and yourself?'

'No.'

'Please to tell us what passed between Mrs Rudd and Christian Hart?'

'I am oblig'd to go back a bit to tell you in what manner Christian Hart came there. When Mrs Rudd and I were sitting together she received a pressing note from somebody to come up; Mrs Rudd read it, and then threw it across the table to me; it was signed "Yours Christian Hart, till death," and that made Mrs Rudd smile. The answer she gave to the person who brought up the note was, that she knew no business she had with her, and that she did not desire such visitors; the person belonging to Newgate who had brought up the note, I can't recollect now; whoever it was said the woman had been there often in order to be admitted.'

'Was Christian Hart introduced?'

'Not then; she came two or three days afterwards. Captain Wright and I were going into Mrs Rudd's apartment, and met Christian Hart coming out; Mrs Rudd told me that was the woman who had sent up the note which made us both laugh.'

'Was the person that left Mrs Rudd the person you just now saw giving evidence?'

'Yes.'

'When did you at any time afterwards see that woman with Mrs Rudd?'

'I believe the very next day. Mrs Rudd told me that Mrs Hart had been with her, and told her a very strange incredible story, and she repeated what the woman had told her. I said I could not think there was any probability in such a scheme, and advised her to pay no kind of attention to it. Mrs Rudd coincided with my opinion, and she said Christian Hart had appointed to be there the next morning, and Mrs Rudd said she should be glad if I would be there or Mr Denton her solicitor. I accordingly went the next day, Christian Hart came about twelve or one, I believe; I did not see Mr Denton . . .'

'What passed then?'

'She sat down with Mrs Rudd at the table at the lower end of the room. Mrs Rudd asked her to tell me the story that she had told yesterday; upon which Mrs Hart said, I should be glad, Madam, if you would take it down in writing, for my husband and I are so scrupulously conscientious, that we would not for all the world say anything but what was really true, and therefore I should be glad to shew it to my husband, to know whether everything in that writing is not precisely the fact; accordingly Mrs Rudd did take down what she mentioned.' This, casually slipped into his account, was Bailey's neat explanation of why the paper was in Caroline's handwriting.

'Do you mean that Christian Hart then dictated to Mrs Rudd what Mrs Rudd then wrote down?' asked Cowper.

'Yes, she wrote nothing but what Christian Hart told her: after Mrs Rudd had wrote what Mrs Hart dictated to her, Mrs Hart desired to have what Mrs Rudd had wrote: Mrs Rudd refused that, but said she would give her a copy of it, and she did give her a copy.'

'Pray what became of the original?'

'The original remained in Mrs Rudd's hands.'

'Be so good as to look at that paper; is the signature John Bailey to that your handwriting?'

'This is my handwriting; this is the paper that Mrs Rudd wrote from the dictation of Christian Hart.'

'How long might this business be about?'

'Above an hour.'

'You perfectly well remember this woman?'

'Perfectly well.'

'You was present when all this passed?' (Christian Hart had said that no one else was there.) 'Yes, I certainly was,' replied Bailey, 'and upon a consultation that was had the next evening at Mr Davenport's chambers I shewed that paper, and said I did not place any reliance upon it, only I thought it my duty to point out everything.'

There now began a carefully orchestrated duet between examiner and witness, designed to establish that the tale of Mrs Hart's approach to Caroline was not just an *ad hoc* story created to explain away the woman's accusations: the whole defence team had known of it at the time it happened. Cowper asked, 'Do you recollect coming the morning after to Guildhall, and shewing it to me?'

'Perfectly well,' said Bailey.

'And telling me the same story?'

'Yes.'

'And my sentiments were the same as yours, that it was a very wild matter?'

'Certainly it was.'

'I observe the paper is numbered?' continued Cowper.

'Yes, I numbered it,' said Bailey. 'I numbered all the papers.'

'Do you know what day in July you delivered it at Mr Davenport's chambers?'

'I know it was a day or two after she was with Mrs Rudd.'

'I observe you have wrote upon the paper, that "Christian Hart came upon Wednesday, July 5th, 1775, to give Mrs Rudd and Counsellor Bailey this information."'

'That was the day.'

'Friday the 7th of course was the adjournment day in London; that was the day then you shewed to me at Guildhall?'

'I believe it was.'

'. . . And you say you mentioned the circumstances at that time?'

'I did not read the paper in Mr Davenport's chambers; but I mentioned my opinion of it then as a strange improbable romance, and the counsel were of the same opinion.'

With the defence's point made, the witness was now handed over to Mr Lucas of the prosecution for cross-examination.

'Pray do you recollect when it was that you first saw this woman?' Lucas asked.

'The first time I ever saw Mrs Hart, was coming out of Mrs Rudd's room,' replied Bailey.

'What time of the day was that?'

'Between five and six in the afternoon.'

'Was any body with her?'

'Yes, a child in her arms, which I took for Mrs Rudd's child; and not having seen her before, I took her to be Mrs Rudd's servant.'

'What time was you there on Wednesday?'

'At twelve o'clock.'

'You are sure it was twelve o'clock?'

'I think it was near that time,' said Bailey. 'Mrs Rudd always dined at two o'clock, and she did not dine till an hour after this conversation.'

'Hart desired it might be put down in writing?'

'She did; and Mrs Rudd wrote it from her dictation.'

'How long did Mrs Hart stay?'

'I imagine about an hour.'

'When was she to return?'

'At five in the afternoon; and the reason why she appointed that time was, because her husband would then have done work.'

'Did she return at five o'clock?'

'No; she did not.'

'Do you know where Mrs Hart lives?'

'Yes.'

A new story now emerged, which none of the witnesses had yet mentioned. Lucas asked, 'Was you ever at her house?'

'Yes,' said Bailey, 'that evening.'

'Did you see her?'

'No; I saw her husband at the street door smoking his pipe; I asked him if he was master of the house? he said he was. I asked to see his wife? he said she was out. I asked why she did not come again to Mrs Rudd. He swore violently that his wife should never go to Mrs Rudd more.'

'What time was that?'

'Near eight o'clock in the evening.'

'Did you ask him for the paper?'

'No, never.'

'How came you to be so anxious about a story which nobody gave credit to, and want her to go again to Newgate?'

'She might want something else to speak to her about,' answered Bailey vaguely.

One of the judges asked, 'Had you heard upon Wednesday before you called upon Christian Hart, that there had been any thing divulged of this story by Christian Hart, or her husband to the Justice of the Peace?'

'Not a syllable,' replied Bailey. 'I thought her a good-natured poor ignorant creature' – meaning that he would not have believed her capable of such a convoluted piece of treachery.

The judge asked, 'Had you carried the original to Mr Davenport's before you called upon Hart?'

'No,' Bailey admitted. 'It was the day afterwards.' So much for the defence's painstaking attempt to show that the paper had been Mrs Hart's doing and that, having been made aware of her offer from the start, they had all sat around laughing it off. Instead, it now appeared to the jury that Bailey had only shared the information with his colleagues *after* doing his utmost to make the Harts co-operate and discovering to his alarm that they would not. In short, the fact that the other lawyers had been shown the paper now looked like a mere damage-limitation exercise.

Seeking to push the point further, however, the judge next asked Bailey whether he had known, at the time of showing the paper to Cowper and Davenport, that the Harts had in fact taken their copy to the Justice of the Peace. He replied, 'Upon my oath I had never heard that any matter had passed.' The judge thus inadvertently helped Bailey to fudge the issue. It would have been enough for the prosecution to show that Bailey knew the Harts wanted no part of the plan, without trying – and failing – to prove that he knew they had gone to the magistrates.

'You say this story was all told by Christian Hart to Mrs Rudd?' continued the judge.

'Yes,' said Bailey.

'And Mrs Rudd told you, she had told the same story to her the day before?'

'She did.'

'How came it that Christian Hart should want a copy of this?'

'For the reasons I have assigned,' he said, referring to his statement that she and her husband were 'conscientious'.

'Could she not as well have told the story to her husband without a copy, as have repeated it over to Mrs Rudd; I want to know why she should want a copy?'

'That I cannot say; she wanted it to show her husband.'

As was their right, the prosecution cross-examiners now interrupted proceedings to consult Christian Hart again on this point. Questioned about the paper, Mrs Hart repeated that it had been prepared before she arrived in Caroline's cell on the Wednesday and had been lying on the bed ready written when she got there.

John Hart was then asked whether he remembered Mr Bailey's visit on that Wednesday evening. 'Yes,' he said, 'that very day we were at Newgate; he came in the evening between eight and nine o'clock. He asked me if Mrs Hart was within? I told him she was not. Said he, "Do you know where she is?" I said, "No. What do you want with her?" – "I want her to go down to her mistress immediately." I said, "She shall not go out of my door; I would sooner break both her legs." He asked me, what was the matter? I said, "Why her cursed mistress has given her papers to hang herself and all the world," and I was in a great passion; I told him, the papers were taken care of. The sweat ran down Mr Bailey's face very much. He asked me to go into the back yard with him, which I did. He took me by a button of my waistcoat,

and said, "Pray, Mr Hart, do not be in a passion; if you come
to the bar, speak the truth, and nothing but the truth about
these papers."'

'Did any body apply to you for the papers?'

'Nobody applied to me for them. I told my wife, when I
went from dinner to work, that if she was drawn into it, I
would certainly swear against her. She said, she was ready to
do as I pleased.'

'Were the papers given up at that time?'

'The papers were given up to the magistrate three hours
before Mr Bailey came.'

'Was any thing said about being given up to Mr Bailey?'

'I told him I had taken care of them.'

The judge asked, 'Did you tell him you had carried them to
a Justice?'

'No.'

'He said to you, do not be in a passion, and desired you,
when it came to the trial to speak the truth and nothing but
the truth; what did you understand him to mean?'

'I did not know what he meant by it; he took me by the
button.'

'Speak the truth? About what?'

'About the papers.'

'When what came to the trial?'

'The papers came to the trial.'

The defence lawyer Mr Cowper asked, 'Which came first;
did he tell you to speak the truth before or after you told him
you had taken care of the papers?'

'After I had told him that, he said, "When you come to the
trial speak the truth, and nothing but the truth"; and I told
him I would.'

The judge asked again, 'Had you carried the papers at this
time to the justice?'

'Yes,' said Hart. 'Three hours before.'

Lucas asked a good question from the prosecution side.
'When you said the cursed woman wanted to hang your wife

and you, and all the world, did Mr Bailey then tell you that your wife had dictated the paper?'

According to the record, the answer to this question came not from Hart but from Mr Bailey himself. He said, 'I did not.'

The prosecution could have made more of this point, but let it go, and the defence lawyer Cowper was now allowed to question Bailey further concerning Hart's evidence. He began by asking him whether he had heard what Hart had been saying.

'I have,' said Bailey.

'Is there any truth in it?'

'He was very violent about his wife; I never asked him about the papers.'

'Did he tell you at that time, that his wife had got a paper to hang him and all the world, or to that effect?'

'He blustered a great deal about the papers; I cannot tell whether he did say these words or no.'

'He was very indignant about the papers?'

'He was angry to the last degree.'

Perhaps foolishly, Cowper repeated the prosecution's question, 'Did you say anything to him at that time of his wife having dictated the papers?'

'No, never,' replied Bailey calmly, making no attempt to explain why he should have omitted such an obvious point in his argument with the Harts.

One of the judges cut in: 'Did he, during the conversation, call it a cursed paper, or give it any epithet that imported he was very angry at her having such a paper?'

'No,' said Bailey, 'he said, he was very angry at her going to Mrs Rudd, and she should never go to her again.'

'Did he say the papers were taken care of?'

'Yes. "I have taken care of the papers."'

'When you desired Hart, if it should come to a trial, that he would speak the truth about these papers, what did you mean by saying that to him?'

'I thought it a very extraordinary transaction,' said Bailey, and added that he had suspected that the Harts were 'persons sent to Mrs Rudd, in order to get out of her as much as they could to turn against herself'.

Bailey left this portentous answer hanging, apparently waiting for Cowper to ask him the obvious question: if the Harts were 'persons sent', who sent them? Instead, Cowper chose not to delve further for the moment. He simply let the suggestion of there being a conspiracy against Caroline float gently into the minds of the jury. To make wild accusations against Frankland (presumably the person Bailey meant) or anyone else would be dangerous for the defence since they had no hard evidence to back them up. But it did no harm to let the jury's imaginations play with the idea. Cowper confined himself to asking, 'But Hart had not told you at that time that Mrs Rudd had given any paper to his wife?'

'No,' replied Bailey, and again he said, 'I then had suspicions and doubts.'

Cowper gave him an opening. 'What doubt could you have about it, if you was present and heard the woman deliver all that story to Mrs Rudd?'

'I doubted very much that she had so much friendship to Mrs Rudd as she professed,' said Bailey. 'I thought rather she was a person sent with an intent to hurt her.'

'Did you impart these doubts to the counsel at the consultation?'

'No, I did not.'

Bailey's conspiracy theories were again left dangling, and one of the judges now changed the subject by asking him to explain what he had understood by Hart's statement that he had 'taken care of the paper'.

'I did not know what he meant,' came the simple reply.

Bailey was then left to enjoy a brief rest from the complex series of examinations he had been enduring from both sides. The defence turned to the next of its witnesses: Mrs Arabella Wright, the wife of a Newgate turnkey. Mrs Wright testified that Christian Hart had visited Newgate and had repeatedly tried to get in to see Caroline, but that these attempts were rarely successful. This was an important point for the defence, for it implied that it was not Caroline who had been seeking a favour from Christian Hart but the latter who had been trying to offer her services to Caroline. On one occasion, said Mrs Wright, Christian Hart doubted that a verbal message she'd sent up to Caroline had been delivered correctly, and therefore wrote a note on a piece of paper to be carried to the cell. As far as Mrs Wright knew, however, Caroline still refused to see Mrs Hart that day, putting her off with vague promises. Christian Hart had not liked this: 'Mrs Hart thought Mrs Rudd must have made a mistake, or she would have seen her, for she said, she was an old servant.' The next time Mrs Hart called, she was allowed in.

'When she was admitted, do you or not remember seeing Mr Bailey and Christian Hart in the room together?'

'Yes, I can remember they were both together one day a little while: I did not stay at all in the room; my business was to carry messages backwards and forwards.' Since Christian Hart had said that she had never been in the room together with Bailey, this directly contradicted her testimony – a useful step for the defence. If she had lied about that, could she not have lied about everything else?

After Mrs Wright stepped down, Bailey produced his copy of the paper at issue and read it aloud. It was similar to the version read earlier, but had numerous slight differences in wording: there was no mention of Mr Williamson's having gone to the East Indies, and the phrase which had caught the defence's attention about not wanting to 'meddle with such rich folks' was put differently. Almost every sentence was slightly altered, and – significantly – the whole text was shorter.

Also, of course, the endorsement at the bottom was crucially different from that of the other copy. Instead of saying simply, 'I received this paper from Mrs Rudd the 5th

July, 1775. Christian Hart,' Bailey's version had the note: 'This account was taken down in writing, in the presence of counsellor John Bailey, from Christian Hart's own words and dictating, who voluntary came upon Wednesday morning, July 5, 1775, to give Mrs Rudd and Counsellor Bailey the said information, and promised to return at five o'clock in the evening to make oath of it, if required. [Signed] John Bailey.' Similar though the papers were, these notes changed their meaning entirely.

One of the judges at once remarked, 'It is plainly a paper wrote from recollection; but it is no more like a copy than if a person was to endeavour to write again upon the same subject, and transposing some in one part, and some in another, and omitting some.' Bailey had said that the longer version read earlier was the copy, as given to Christian Hart by Caroline, while the original paper was this briefer one signed by Mr Bailey. But in fact the lengths were precisely the opposite of what one would expect if Bailey's story were the truth. It did not look good for him.

Having done all they could – with limited effectiveness – to demolish Mrs Hart's accusations, the defence finished with a strange witness who, they hoped, would provide an alternative explanation for the large sums of money shown by the prosecution to have been coming to Caroline and Daniel over the last few years. Unfortunately, the effect was rather to confuse the jury than to enlighten them.

The witness was named Mary Nightingale, and she described herself as an old friend of Caroline's: they had known one another for eight years.* Caroline had been in distressed circumstances when her husband first deserted her, said Mary, but 'a gentleman' had then provided support, enabling Caroline to live comfortably. He had given her

---

* *Authentic Anecdotes* describes Mary Nightingale as 'a lady long versed in all the hacknied ways of vice', and says that this name was a false one, the real one being coyly half-supplied as 'P–l–y [Polly?] H–s–m'.

£16,000 in total. 'In October 1770, she received £4,000 in my presence; in March 1770, she received £3,000 and some hundreds: I cannot charge my memory exactly, I believe about £700.'

'Was that before her connection with Mr Perreau, or since?'

'Since her connection with Mr Perreau.'

'This was part of the £16,000?'

'Yes.'

'Was it given her by will?' asked a member of the jury.

'No: it was left in a trustee's hand . . .'

'How do you know that these are parts of the £16,000?'

'Because I was present when the money was paid; it was left in the hands of a very near relation of mine that was the trustee . . .'

Asked more about how she knew all this, Mary replied, 'I know perfectly well the gentleman who left it her.'

Mr Murphy cross-examined her for the prosecution. He asked, 'I must beg the favour of knowing who this person was?'

'I will not tell,' she said.

'Was the money left by will?'

'No, it was not.'

'Was there any writing about it?'

'It was left in the hands of a trustee.'

'Then you can tell us the trustee perhaps?' suggested Murphy.

'I don't chuse that.'

'Then we are not to know the trustee, nor the donor, nor when it was paid; in whose presence was it paid?'

'In my presence.'

'Where was it paid?'

'In Mr Perreau's house in Pall Mall. In October 1770, she received £4000.'

'Who paid the money?'

'The trustee.'

'In what manner?'

'He paid her £4000 down.'

'Was a receipt given?'

'Yes.'

'Who drew the receipt?'

'The person who paid the money.'

'Was there any witness to it?'

'Yes, I was a witness.'

'It is no evidence, in my apprehension, unless you tell us who the trustee is.'

The judge put in, 'There can be no imputation upon the trustee, if you would tell us who the man is, that is trustee?' But Mary Nightingale would not divulge this information. In the end all her questioners gave up and she was allowed to stand down.

The defence announced that it had concluded its case, and so the presiding judge Sir Richard Aston now gave his closing address to the jury.

As far as 'the general weight and tendency of the evidence' were concerned, he said, he was satisfied that the jury had been paying close attention and were masters of all the facts, so he would leave that to them.[6] Instead, he proposed merely to guide them on the general principles according to which they should draw their conclusions. There were only two circumstances they should consider: first, 'to decide whether the evidence has been sufficient to satisfy that it was the prisoner forged the name "William Adair", to the bond, with which the prisoner now stands immediately charged', and second, to ascertain 'whether she has been proved guilty of the publication of the same bond'.

He summarized the evidence on these two questions in reverse order. On the second point, Henrietta Perreau's testimony meant that there could be 'little doubt that the proof of the publication is complete'. Crucially, however, it was still open to the jury to decide whether Mrs Perreau's reliability was damaged by her personal bias. If they believed it was, they could discard her evidence altogether. If, on the other hand, they accepted it, her testimony could be considered corroborated in its basics by David Cassady's statement concerning the presence of Daniel and Caroline at Christmas. But his testimony was not strong enough by itself. In short, there were two possibilities. 'If, therefore, you shall think the testimony of Mrs Perreau, strengthened by the circumstances deposed by Cassady, amount to a publication, then you will find the prisoner guilty, because the publication of a forged bond, knowing it to be forged, is equally criminal with the forging of it. On the other hand, if you think that Mrs Perreau's evidence, considering the relation she now stands in, does not deserve credit, and that the circumstances sworn by Cassady to support it, do not, taken together, amount to a publication, you will acquit her.'

As to the forgery charge itself, that relied on just one unsupported witness: John Moody, who had identified the handwriting on the document with her 'feigned' hand. Whether his solitary opinion was enough was for the jury to decide. 'If you are satisfied that this is a sufficient proof of the forgery, you will likewise find her guilty on that count.

'The prisoner has produced no evidence of any kind whatever, but what observations she made herself on the characters of the persons who have appeared against her,' he continued, accurately describing the defence's technique. 'Mrs Perreau, as to her credit [i.e. credibility]; Sir Thomas Frankland on the disgraceful evidence he has given; and Moody, from his contradiction, and the infamy of his character: all this, gentlemen, you will weigh in your own minds; and judge how far such a defence ought to determine you in your verdict. As to Christian Hart's evidence, and that of her husband, I must confess it is of a most extraordinary nature: it is flatly contradicted by Mr Bailey and Mrs Wright. Though it does not immediately affect either of the questions now stated, if the truth could be attained, it would go a great way in establishing or overthrowing everything that has been sworn here this day; but that from its nature being imposs-ible, you must adhere solely to the points before alluded to, and decide accordingly.' In other words, Aston instructed that since the truth of Christian Hart's testimony was undecidable the jury must simply exclude it from consideration.

'All I have to add', he finished, 'is that if any doubt should arise relative to the credit of one part of the evidence, or the sufficiency of the other, is to recommend to you to lean to the side of *mercy*.'

The jury retired from the room and deliberated for half an hour – considerably longer than the Perreaus' jury had taken. Finally, at a quarter to eight in the evening, they came back, and the foreman delivered their verdict.

'According to the evidence before us,' he said, 'not guilty.'

The courtroom erupted in cheers and applause.

A member of the public, who was sitting very close to Caroline, reported that he had guessed the outcome as soon as the jury had filed back in to the room: 'As the jury returned, the prisoner fixed her fascinating eyes upon the jury-box, when the conduct of the foreman ... did not escape observation; for by a smile, which he significantly glanced towards her, many anticipated the verdict.'[7]

The 'not guilty' verdict was a popular one. 'The whole Court shouted with applause,'[8] wrote Horace Walpole, and the *Annual Register* reported that 'there was the loudest applause on this acquittal almost ever known in the court of justice'.[9] Caroline herself 'appeared confounded with joy at her discharge'.

Her friends lost no time in spiriting her away. 'The moment she quitted the court, she stepped into a coach, which convey'd her from the dreary cells of Newgate, to the house of a friend, at the west end of the town.' The crowd was left to shuffle out of the stale, overheated courtroom and disperse into the welcome chill of the December evening, retelling and arguing over the extraordinary stories they had heard, and marvelling again and again at Caroline's escape.

CHAPTER
NINE
—◆—
UNHAPPY FATE

Why was Caroline Rudd acquitted, and why were the Perreaus condemned? At the outset of Caroline's trial there seemed to be a formidable array of witnesses against her and very few prepared to speak in her favour. The only significant testimony for the defence was that of her own lawyer – a fact hardly likely to impress the jury. The accusations against her were well supported: there was hard evidence, there were eye-witness accounts, and there was even her own original confession to the other forgery, although this had no formal relevance. The prosecution seemed to have everything it could want. How did they let her slip out of their hands?

One reason for her acquittal was simply that her lawyers were good – better than the Perreaus'. It was true that they presented little in the way of a systematic defence argument, either because – as Caroline later wrote[1] – they thought it more 'honourable' for her to be acquitted without one, or because they did not want to expose too many of their own witnesses to attack by the prosecution. (The main defence witness, John Bailey, did not stand up particularly well.) But whatever they lacked in a case of their own, they amply made up for in the total destruction of the enemy's. Davy and Davenport were both masters of the not-so-gentle art of cross-examination. Their information was good, too: they identified the prosecution witnesses' weakest points and went for them mercilessly. It is not hard to guess where they got their penetrating insight, for Caroline had a perfect grasp of the failings and weaknesses of Henrietta Perreau, Sir Thomas Frankland and John Moody. Not only did she brief her lawyers in advance, but the fifty or sixty notes she passed them during the day must have been full of *ad hoc* cross-examination ideas. Indeed, these notes may have completely dominated the defence's tactics. Walpole quipped that when Bailey had asked Caroline to explain the brief to him, she had replied, 'And do you imagine that I will trust you, or any attorney in England, with the truth of my story? Take your brief; meet me in the Old Bailey, and I will ask you the necessary questions.'[2]

Caroline's contribution went even further than that, for her victory also owed a great deal to the preparatory war she had fought in the papers during the summer. Because of it, both Sir Thomas and Henrietta were compromised in the public arena before the trial even began. Of course the jury were not supposed to be taking account of this, but it would have been hard for them to keep its subtle influence out of their minds. Procedures for insulating jurors from preconceptions were not as strict as they are today and at least some of the jury must have been reading the newspapers that year.

Indeed, according to one account Caroline's glamorous reputation had everything to do with the verdict – and all because of one single jury member, a man named James Walsh. The clergyman John Trusler recalled in his memoirs:

Among those who tried the famous, or rather the *infamous* Mrs. Rudd . . . was a Mr. Walsh, who had been a valet to the late Lord Chesterfield, and to whom she owed her acquittal . . . He once interrupted the judge whilst summing up the evidence, with 'I beg pardon, my Lord, either *your* notes are wrong, or *mine*, for I have no such matter in evidence as your Lordship has advanced.' The judge contested the point, and it was referred to Joseph Gurney, the short-hand writer, appointed to take down the trials at the Old Bailey, who admitted that Mr. Walsh was correct and his Lordship not. By this conduct, he was looked up to by his brother-jurymen, and he told me, that when they retired to consider of their verdict, that the whole of them, except himself, were for convicting the prisoner; that he went through the evidence again, and by his arguments brought them all over to his way of thinking, and she was acquitted.[3]

Trusler maintained that 'had it not been for Mr. Walsh, who was pleased to see things in a more favorable light, she would have suffered'. He also believed Walsh's boast that the judge had said to him, 'I wish every juryman acted as you have done, with the same attention and intelligence,' and had then added to Caroline, 'You certainly owe your life to this very lenient jury.'

Walsh might have been exaggerating when regaling Trusler with his memories of the trial: he would have had to argue very powerfully to reverse eleven men's firmly held opinions in half an hour. But if the other eleven had had no firm inclination either way, or if they were evenly divided, then Walsh's passionate liking for Caroline might well have clinched matters in her favour.

In this as in other respects, Caroline had one great advantage over the Perreaus: she was a woman. Whatever her contemporaries may have thought of feminine devious-ness, they found her claim that she had been acting under the brothers' duress more plausible than the Perreaus' story of having been fooled by her. Even those who believed the Perreaus' tale had little sympathy for them: what sort of a man allowed a woman to make such a nincompoop of him? As a letter in the *Morning Post* said of Robert, 'I own he appeared to me in a despicable light, when he asserted in his defence, that he had been deceived by Mrs Rudd.'[4] Caroline, on the other hand, could only benefit from being thought naïve and impressionable.

As for the apparent strength of the prosecution case, that was undermined by the way in which most of their witnesses managed to damn themselves without any help from the defence at all. Henrietta Perreau's husband was on death row: that made her a sympathetic figure but not necessarily a credible one, and the jury must have decided to disregard her evidence for this reason. Sir Thomas was neither convincing nor likeable. His desire to hold on to Caroline's property was clear, and although he was the immediate victim of the fraud he seemed altogether more sinning than sinned against. Indeed, Caroline laughingly told Boswell a few months later that she had been planning a lawsuit against Sir Thomas, but now thought that she would do better to thank him, since he had helped to save her life.[5]

John Moody could have been a damaging witness, as he stated unambiguously that he had seen Caroline forging letters from William Adair and that she had made him lie to Daniel. But Davy had found it easy to reconstruct him in the jury's minds as a shifty, untrustworthy ex-servant who had left the household in unspecified circumstances and who, after the arrests, had not even bothered to tell his former master what he knew about Caroline.

Only Christian Hart remained, and she could have destroyed Caroline if she had been believed. However, the judge specifically instructed the jurors to take no account of her story, and so the question of its veracity was ruled out of consideration.

Was Christian Hart telling the truth? We are not under the same constraint as the jurors and can speculate as freely as we please. If she were lying, that would mean that Caroline was probably right in accusing Sir Thomas Frankland of planning the whole thing as a fiendish plot – for there is no reason why Mrs Hart should have dreamed it up by herself.

Even if she is imagined to have been motivated by resentment or personal hatred, she does not come across as a woman given to sophisticated scheming – and in any case she could have achieved the same effect more easily just by testifying that she had seen Caroline in the act of forgery.

What of Sir Thomas? He had the motive: he hated Caroline; and he was certainly given to sneaky techniques. His attempts to undermine her genealogical claims make a good example, and he had operated in a similarly underhand way against his rival in Antigua many years before. Yet his machinations were usually simple, and the semi-literacy of his correspondence and the gruffness of his testimony in court hardly suggest a Byzantine intellect. Besides, the same argument applies: there would have been more straightfor-ward ways of using a false witness to destroy Caroline. Doing it this way would involve co-opting Mrs Hart, impressing on her an artificial story of great complexity, and then hoping against the odds that the jury would believe it. As a conspiracy theory, it seems excessively elaborate.

If, instead, we suppose that it was Christian Hart who was telling the truth and Caroline who was lying, everything falls neatly into place. According to this picture, Caroline called Mrs Hart to Newgate, gave her the paper and asked her to lie on her behalf – but Mrs Hart decided not to do it and instead turned against her. This at once makes sense of John Bailey's desperate trip to the Harts' house to try to bully them into co-operating and, once he discovered that they would not, his attempts to retrieve the paper and his hurried visit to his own colleagues to set up a cover story. It also explains the differences in phrasing between the two copies of the paper. In Caroline's version of events, Mrs Hart dictated the contents of the paper; Caroline kept the original, and wrote out a second copy for Mrs Hart to take away with her. But this would be odd, because the one in Mrs Hart's possession differed from the other – and it was the longer and more detailed of the two. It is more likely not only that it was written at a different time rather than being a direct transcript, but also that it was the first of the two papers to be composed, with the other copy being a later attempt to remember and reconstruct its contents – a situation which agrees perfectly with Mrs Hart's story.

The most probable sequence of events, then, is that Mrs Hart went to see Caroline after hearing of her arrest and offered to help in any way she could. Caroline took her at her word and cooked up a monstrous plot involving all her enemies, the description of which she laid out in a paper to be given to Mrs Hart. If Mrs Hart really wanted to help her, she said, she must swear in court that its contents were true and thereby save Caroline's life. Mrs Hart took the paper away, but made no promises and was visibly uneasy about it. Caroline therefore sent Bailey to her house to check up on her and to see how her husband had reacted. When the Harts refused either to co-operate or to return the paper, it became obvious to Bailey that Caroline was in serious difficulties. Together they pondered the disaster and decided that the only solution was damage-limitation. So Caroline wrote out a second copy of the letter as best she could remember it. Bailey gave it a number to establish the date and also appended the note stating that it was Christian Hart who had brought the paper to them rather than the other way round. He showed it to his colleagues and registered it with his office, hoping that no one would spot the fact that all this was done just *after* the Harts had turned in their copy of the paper to the magistrates.

Unlike Caroline's, Mrs Hart's version of the story is structurally simple and has everyone acting in character. It does not call for any networks of mismatched conspirators or fiendish schemes engineered by brains that otherwise seem positively oafish. It merely requires Caroline to be in a state of desperation, willing to try anything that might save her life, and operating in her distinctive style – mixing high deviousness with bold recklessness.

It was certainly not the best idea Caroline ever had. She came very close to being exposed for the Machiavellian creature she was and losing all credibility in the eyes of the jury and everyone else – a potentially fatal loss. The original scheme was not a success: Christian Hart turned against Caroline and the allegations against Sir Thomas and Henrietta Perreau were ignored. And yet ultimately she did not fail. As usual, her wits whisked her out of trouble just as quickly as they had precipitated her into it.

Caroline must have endured some terrifying moments in the Old Bailey on 8 December, listening to the Harts' evidence – but she did, after all, walk away from the courtroom a free woman.

Like everyone else in this story, Christian Hart had her own tale to tell, and she published a book after the trial. It may have been written with help, but if so the ghostwriter was careful to maintain verisimilitude, introducing the work with the proviso: 'However unable I am for the task of writing; yet, as truth is my guide, the grammatical errors that may occur, I hope, will be overlooked by the public.'[6] The book acknowledges Mrs Hart's narrative awkwardness in court and explains it by saying that she had been trying to tell the truth in plain terms, but was confused by all the people shouting at her and found herself unable to give coherent answers. 'The browbeating of the counsel also confounded my husband, who is an innocent man, and was not the least prepared for them.'[7]

Mrs Hart's account then goes through the story of her meetings with Caroline in prison and of the conversation in which Caroline gave her the paper and asked her to lie. (According to Mrs Hart, Caroline's words were, 'My dear Christy, there is no sin in telling a lie to save an innocent life, which if it is saved, you shall never want for a friend.')[8] Her relation of the main events generally follows what she and her husband said in court.

However, she also describes a great deal of further harassment which she suffered during Caroline's attempts to retrieve the paper and which had not been fully revealed at the trial. On the morning after Bailey's first visit, she states, a messenger arrived and started belabouring her with questions. Mrs Hart begged him to ask her nothing further, as the papers had already been passed on to the authorities and 'what was done could not be undone'.[9] – 'The next person that came was old A. W. the P.' – Caroline's old friend Andrew White, the pimp – 'who christened you lady Caroline Gore, and confirmed your assertions of your being the Pretender's daughter'. He said that 'he had been the making of you, as he had been of so many others; for when you came to London, he said, you was but bare in cloaths, till he introduced you to gentlemen who had weighty purses to throw away for particular purposes'.

After White came two other cronies of Caroline's: 'a gay lady and gentlemen' who pretended that they wanted to rent the Harts' first-floor lodgings. The lady said she had been given a recommendation by a mutual acquaintance, and when Mrs Hart asked who that might be, the lady replied, 'Mrs Perreau, of Golden Square.' – 'I told her, I never saw that lady.' But the visitor said she was sure she must know Mrs Perreau: for she had suggested employing Mrs Hart's husband, 'who, she said, was a very industrious man, and worked for Mrs. P—— and Sir T—— F——.' Mrs Hart told her she was quite mistaken. The lady then turned nasty. 'When she perceived her arts did not prevail, she then began to shew her character in its true light; seemed a little angry, and said, if I appeared against you, I should not escape punishment. That after you was tried, her husband would spend two hundred pounds to punish me.' Mrs Hart replied that it was out of her control, for John Hart had been bound over for £50 to ensure her appearance in court. The Harts had 'better lose that than be ruined', warned the lady, 'for did they think to hurt Mrs. Rudd, poor fools, they were only throwing away money'. Mrs Hart said she could not help that. 'If you was the King's daughter, I had not fifty pounds to lose' (an ironic remark, considering that she did believe Caroline to be the daughter of the Pretender to the British crown). The lady's companion said 'that he knew one that would pay that, and give me fifty besides, if I would get out of the way. I answered, that my character was dearer to me than gold, and I would not do it: they replied with threats, and after some more expostulations to no effect, they went away.' But they were not the last: 'several like them came afterwards'.

If Caroline was really using intimidation tactics such as these, it is easy to see why Christian Hart underwent such a dramatic change from adoring Caroline to hating her. 'Thou art *Belzebub*'s darling child,' she wrote bitterly to her former employer. '*Jezebel* was your mother, and the witch of *Babylon* your nurse, for all that knows you, are infatuated by your spells and love you, and all who love you, you bring to destruction as fast as possible.'

A full transcript of the trial was published quickly, to take advantage of the intense public interest. It was popular enough to be reproduced in several different editions, but once the initial euphoria had worn off a more guarded reaction to Caroline's acquittal became evident. The general feeling was that it was a relief to see a lady of refinement and education saved from the indignity of the scaffold, but that there was far, far more to the story than had come out in the courtroom. Horace Walpole wrote, 'A fair one . . . has just foiled the law; although nobody questions her guilt.'[10] The *Prudence* author remarked that her escape from conviction 'may be considered as one of the mysteries in divine providence, which will not be cleared up till the general resurrection takes place, and the secrets of all hearts are laid open'.[11] Elsewhere in the same volume there appeared an even more emphatic condemnation: 'She has slipped through the hangman's fingers, and being again let loose upon the public, going about like the devil, seeing who she can devour, it is necessary that the unwary be cautioned to be on their guard against the hellish machinations of such a monster of iniquity, for whom no name can be too severe, nor any species of punishment too great.'[12]

The author of the *Newgate Calendar* account hoped that the truth would emerge a good deal sooner than Judgement Day. 'There is a mystery in the story of the brothers Perreau, and Mrs Rudd, that no person but the latter can clear up,' he wrote three and a half years after the trial, adding that 'a declaration of the fact, if she *was* guilty, could not now affect her, as she was acquitted by the laws of the country'.[13] Despite his hints, no confession was ever forthcoming.

Daniel and Robert were now in the worst possible position. Had they confessed their own guilt and said that they were all in it together, Caroline might well have been convicted. But they had not been able to do that and could not do so even now, for they were still maintaining their innocence and desperately hoping for a pardon. The chances of getting one after Caroline's glorious acquittal did not look good at all.

The equation had never been a balanced one between Caroline and the Perreaus, even though each side had been struggling equally hard to blame the other. If Caroline had been found guilty, that would not necessarily have meant that the Perreaus were innocent, for they still could have been co-conspirators. The brothers' claim that they had been completely duped would not be the only possible interpretation of such a verdict – or even the most likely. But at least they could have argued that they should be given the benefit of the doubt. Instead, Caroline's acquittal meant that there was no doubt to have the benefit of. It implied the guilt of the Perreaus, for the only theory that made any sense of her supposed innocence was that one or both of the brothers had forced her into compliance, just as she claimed. Whatever people actually thought of the verdict, its implications were unequivocal so far as the law was concerned. The forgeries had certainly taken place: someone had to be guilty of them.

The two men had now been languishing on death row in Newgate for six months, submitting appeals and waiting to see what happened to Caroline. Their friends had done everything they could to help. At least, Robert's had. Daniel didn't really have any friends, and he just had to hope that if Robert were saved he might be pardoned as an afterthought. Some of Robert's supporters even argued that the sacrifice of Daniel would be enough for both of them – if Daniel were left to die he could atone for both of their sins.

The process of appeals ran its course throughout the remainder of December, the first aim being to try to get the sentences commuted when they were reported to George III by the Recorder on 5 January 1776. Fourteen death sentences were presented altogether in the Recorder's report, and the King's judgements were announced the following day.[14] Exactly half of the appellants were granted mercy. That left seven who were still condemned to die. Their names were listed in the newspapers: George Lee, Richard Baker, John Radcliffe, Saunders Alexander, Lyon Abrahams – and Robert and Daniel Perreau. The execution date was also announced: it would be Wednesday 17 January 1776.

On Sunday 7 January Henrietta personally presented a petition to the Queen, begging for her intercession with the King to save Robert. The weather was suitably bleak and cold that day, with 'the greatest fall of snow that has been known in England in the memory of man'.[15] A high wind blew it into deep drifts. Henrietta's carriage had to force its way through the snow to the palace; she was dressed in deep mourning and accompanied by her three children Susannah, Robert and Charles, now into their teens and more than old enough to understand their father's plight.

The petition was eloquent: 'The most unfortunate and most miserable woman that ever felt the hand of affliction, now approaches your Majesty and, in agonies of mind little short of distraction, throws herself at your Royal feet.'[16] Henrietta accepted that the King had made his decision and she submitted to it, but felt sure that the Queen's feminine nature could not fail to be moved: 'Nature will cry out; and to the voice of Nature your Majesty will not be deaf.'

> Your petitioner has nothing but her misery to recommend her; she does not controvert the justice of the sentence; she only presumes to deprecate the blow. A wife implores your Majesty in behalf of her husband, whom she has every reason to regard with sincere affection: a mother sends up her prayers and tears for her children. Your Majesty knows these tender relations; and the virtue of a heart like your Majesty's will be the best advocate for the wretched.

The *Gentleman's Magazine* described it as 'a picture of distress which surpassed imagination', and noted that the Queen 'seemed much affected'[17] – but perhaps she was not affected enough, for nothing was done. A diarist of the royal court, Charlotte Papendiek, later claimed that the Queen had in fact done her best to plead Mrs Perreau's case to the King,[18] but in any case the result was the same: there was to be no mercy for Robert.

On Friday 12 January Henrietta presented a second petition, this one directly to George III himself:

> The execution of Robert Perreau will, in its consequences, involve an innocent family in ruin: the agonies of his afflicted wife must shortly end her days, and his children must be left without a parent; shame and sorrow must be at best their portion . . . Your petitioner therefore flies to your Majesty's commiseration, presuming to hope that by changing the sentence of the law to transportation, the ends of justice would be answered. Justice has never been so rigorous in this country, as not to hear the cries of

humanity: for the sake of the innocent, guilt has often been spared . . . Your petitioner therefore, with resignation, but not without hope, commits her case to your Majesty's royal goodness.[19]

On the same day the *Morning Post* carried an open letter to the King from someone signed 'A.E.', pleading for Robert's life. 'The fate of an unhappy convict, whom your justice has most deservedly condemned, emboldens me, in the name of thousands, to approach the foot of your throne, not to extenuate his crimes, or arraign the sentence so justly passed upon him; but humbly to expose such considerations, as may move your royal breast to clemency in favour of a man whom folly, more than vice, has reduced to so dreadful a situation.'[20] A.E. reminded the king of a similar case some years previously in which he had exercised clemency because the condemned man had once saved the lives of shipwreck victims off the coast of Ireland. Could not the same be said for an apothecary? 'By his skill in his profession has he not perhaps saved thousands?'

The days slipped by, without further word from the King, and the date of execution drew closer. On Monday 15 January, with just two days to go, George III received yet another petition for Robert's life, this one signed by seventy-eight bankers and merchants of London. It urged mercy for the more reputable brother, while accepting that the other one might as well be left to his fate. Robert Perreau's actions were rash, admitted the petitioners, but he had never benefited from the forgeries himself – which could not be said of Daniel. Above all, 'the hand that actually forged the bonds is well known to the world from the evidence of Robert and Henry Drummond'.[21]

On the same day, too, the *Morning Post* noted, 'It is a maxim in humanity, if not in law, that it is better to spare ten guilty persons than to execute one innocent man,' and then went on to argue that it would be sufficient to kill Daniel alone. If the main reason for executing people was as a deterrent to others, then 'surely the fatal exit of one of the brothers . . . will answer all the ends of public justice'.[22]

Alongside this in the same issue appeared a letter from Daniel himself. Instead of pleading for his own life, he generously argued Robert's case. 'In hopes that the world may no longer be misinformed concerning the innocence of my unhappy brother, who at this time with myself is under the dreadful sentence of death . . . I solemnly declare, that he with myself was no more than the innocent instrument in the hands of Mrs. Rudd to perpetrate this wicked transaction.' Daniel admitted that, having put his faith in her, he had encouraged Robert to do the same. 'I therefore think it my duty, before I know the issue of my fate, to exculpate him from any imputation whatever, by declaring he did never detain any part of the money raised on Mr. Adair's security, or was in any respect whatever privy to any deception or knowledge of the forgeries; and that my unhappy infatuation, and the confidence which he had in my supposed marriage with Mrs. Rudd, has been the sole cause of this present dreadful affliction, he having all along understood her to be my wife.'[23]

During these final agonizing days Robert wrote a long and affecting letter to his former employer, Mrs Tribe; it was later reprinted in *Prudence Triumphing over Vanity and Dissipation*.

My dear Mrs Tribe,
Though it is painful to me at this solemn hour to bid a farewell to my friends, yet to you my heart feels too great a duty of gratitude and affection to deny itself that satisfaction and comfort . . . Remember my grateful thanks to my good friends. I know not how their good opinion is inclined toward me since my misfortunes, but am sure their hearts are too good not to feel something for my troubles . . . I am sensible of the propriety of the verdict against me,

for an innocent lie, and I must give the law its revenge; but I must however do myself the justice to assert my innocence of any guilt or knowledge of the forgery whatever. I say an innocent lie, because I neither knew of, nor had the least intention of defrauding Messrs. Drummonds, but was the unhappy deluded tool of others, and acted upon by the most premeditated artful wickedness that can be devised . . . For the sake of my poor unhappy wife and children, I hope an opportunity will one day or another happen to convince the world, that I die an innocent, injured and deluded man, for such I do, I call God in my last moments to witness . . .

Permit me, my dear Mrs. Tribe, to repeat my kind thanks and obligations to you, and to recommend the favour of your kind friendship to my dear unhappy wife, who I know has a sincere esteem for you, as well as myself, and that we may both meet in that world where no sorrow nor affliction dwells, is the sincere prayer of,

Dear Madam,
Your obliged and affectionate Friend,
Robert Perreau.
Jan. 13, 1776.[24]

Meanwhile Caroline, too, had something to say on the subject. Her contribution to the appeal process was dated 15 January – two days before the execution date – and was addressed to Viscount Weymouth, the Secretary of State responsible for constructing the final submission to the King proposing pardon. His judgement on the matter was usually crucial in influencing the King's response. While Weymouth was in the final stages of deliberation, and despite having nothing to lose should the Perreaus be spared, she picked up her sharpest quill and wrote:

My Lord,
It is not from a principle of tenderness for a man, whose

conduct to me has obliterated every sentiment of that nature in my breast, that I now take the liberty of addressing your lordship; the more unbiased motive, a regard for impartiality, influences me to state a few facts for your lordship's consideration ... The endeavours to save Mr Robert Perreau, your lordship well knows, are very numerous. I do not wish to prevent their obtaining that success, which, if we may credit public report, they are likely to be attended with; but, my Lord, the advocates of this unhappy man take such unjustifiable methods to gain their point, as ought for the sake of common justice to be exposed.[25]

Robert's supporters portrayed him as respectable, well-heeled, and motivated only by fraternal affection, she went on – but the truth was quite different. For many years he had gambled just as recklessly as his brother, and although many of their Exchange Alley transactions were conducted in Daniel's name alone, the two had been equally involved and had both suffered severe losses – which were initially covered by raiding her fortune. When that ran out, the brothers resorted to other means. Nor had Robert been content to lose money in partnership with Daniel; he had also gambled separately and had lost a great deal in his own right. He therefore had at least as great a motive to swindle money as Daniel, and had applied at least as much of the money to his own use. Moreover, she knew two brokers who could have testified to Robert's gambling losses over the previous few years, but who never appeared in the trials – 'the Court intimating that there was no occasion for farther evidence, and my counsel thinking it most honourable for me to be acquitted upon the case of the prosecution – to which I chearfully consented, as I wished not to expose the Perreaus more than was absolutely requisite for my own vindication'.

As for Robert's claim that he had always believed her and Daniel to be married, that was an outright lie: Daniel himself (before changing his mind and proclaiming the opposite) had admitted in his published *Narrative* that Robert knew all about it. 'What induced Daniel to contradict this assertion made in so solemn and public a manner I cannot pretend to say; unless it proceeds from that unaccountable influence which Robert has continually exercised over him ever since I knew them.'

She finished, 'In full confidence that your Lordship will allow the facts, I have presumed to state their due weight, and make such use of them, as you, in your superior wisdom and goodness, shall see proper. I remain, with the highest respect, My Lord, Your Lordship's most obedient and most humble servant, M.C.R.'

George III was scrupulous about minor tasks of kingship such as this one. He studied the final appeals of condemned convicts with care, anxious not to neglect any genuine argument for clemency. However, he was also less inclined to be lenient in forgery cases than in any others – and, most importantly, he did not like to go against the Secretary of State's recommendation unless there was a very strong reason to do so.

As always, Viscount Weymouth considered the records of the case together with petitions and any other material that was submitted to him. Most of these, especially the petitions from Robert's wife and friends, argued passionately for mercy for Robert at least, if not for Daniel. Only one document urged him not to hesitate over the execution of either: Caroline's long and articulate letter. Weighing everything up, Weymouth came to his decision. He passed on no recommendation of mercy for either of the Perreaus. The King accordingly rejected the final appeal and the twins' execution was ordered to go ahead on 17 January as planned.

Robert's wife and children came to Newgate on Tuesday 16 January and he spent the whole of his last day with them. In the evening they said their final farewells and departed, but a couple of hours later Henrietta came back, unexpectedly, to be alone with her husband for a few extra hours.[26]

On Wednesday morning Londoners woke to bitterly cold weather. The city was muffled in thick snow and a frosty mist hung in the air. Spectators assembled outside the entrance to Newgate Prison long before it was light, each person staking out a good spot and everyone wrapped in their warmest clothes. Similar crowds soon assembled all along Holborn and Oxford Street, the traditional route between Newgate and the execution site. At the end of this route, at Tyburn Cross, where Marble Arch now stands, the gallows were made ready. To the permanent scaffold at the crossroads was added another, temporary one; it collapsed during construction, slightly injuring a few bystanders, and had to be rebuilt.[27] As always, there were wooden stands near the execution site on which seats could be rented for the day; but on this occasion even more stands were built than usual – and they were all filled to capacity by the early morning.

As it got closer to the appointed time, there were traffic jams as carriages and people struggled past each other in the snow-clogged streets, all searching for a place along the way with a good view. The *Morning Post* reported other injuries during the day: a soldier standing on the wheel of a coach slipped and broke his leg, another man was nearly crushed to death between two coaches – 'and we fear many other accidents happened upon the melancholy occasion'.[28]

Executions were always popular events, but this promised to be one of the best ever seen. The brothers made a refreshing change from the usual scruffy thugs and thieves. Not only were they gentlemen; they were celebrities. So physically alike they could barely be told apart, one with his veneer of respectability and one without, both protesting their innocence to the end – Daniel and Robert Perreau were extraordinary figures. And many people hoped for a glimpse of the even more legendary Caroline. Perhaps she might hide somewhere to watch and gloat over her victims, or even throw herself at their feet and make a dramatic last-minute confession to save their lives. Anything could happen.

Christian Hart claimed that Caroline did in fact go to see them die: 'Their day of their execution you must go to Snow-Hill to see them pass by; nor did that give you sufficient satisfaction, but you with rapture asked your confederate, if it would be safe for you to go to see them in their last moments under the fatal tree.'[29] In truth she was probably still enjoying a quiet holiday in Bath at the time, having travelled there earlier that month to recuperate from her trial. With thousands of eyes looking out for her in London, there were no other reported sightings.

Early in the morning, Robert and Daniel dressed in mourning clothes and were taken from their rooms to the prison chapel, where they were allowed to pray. After a short time there they were taken on to a dayroom within the Press Yard of the prison, where they were left to wait for the hangman together with a number of friends, lawyers and officials. The prison keeper, Richard Akerman, and his assistants stood at the gate, keeping the crowds of eager onlookers at bay.

'Daniel came in first from chapel, bowed to the company, and went to the fire, where he warmed himself with the greatest composure,' says the report in the *Annual Register*.[30] Robert followed shortly afterwards, 'and looking at his brother for a moment, wiped off a falling tear, which he seemed anxious to hide: he then turned to a little table, where lay the ropes with which they were to be bound; his emotions were then so strongly painted in his countenance, that the surrounding spectators gave vent to their sympathy in loud lamentations'. The hangman arrived; Daniel and Robert shook his hand and gave him the customary present to ensure a quick and merciful execution: a guinea each. Having performed this ceremony, the brothers prepared themselves to be tied with the rope for their journey. Daniel 'assisted in putting the rope properly round himself with decent firmness;

but when he saw the man do the same office for his brother, it quite unmanned him; he sighed and wept'.

With their wrists bound, the brothers were then taken across the courtyard, following the sheriff towards the gate. At last, the crowd got the view they had been waiting for. There was an uproar and a great surge as they jostled to see.

The brothers looked handsome and dignified. 'Both appeared in new suits of deep mourning, their hair dressed and powdered, but without any hats,' reported the *Annual Register*. They politely took their leave of the prison keeper, said the *Morning Post*, 'and thanked him for the very humane and friendly treatment they had received during their confinement under his care'.[31] Then they stepped into their coach, where they were joined by the Ordinary (or chaplain) of Newgate, John Villette. It was his job to accompany and console* the condemned men in their final hours – and then to write up the case in suitably moral terms for the *Annals of Newgate*.

It took some time to assemble the long procession of carriages and carts. When at last all was ready, at around nine o'clock, the convoy moved slowly away from the prison gates and started towards Holborn.

First in line were the two City marshals on horseback, bearing their staves of office. After them rode the under sheriff, followed by a party of officers and constables. The two sheriffs in their coach followed next.

Then came an open cart swathed in black cloth: on it were three of the condemned men. Two, Saunders Alexander and

---

* Opinions differed about how much consolation the Ordinary actually offered: the idiosyncratic political theorist and former Newgate prisoner Edward Gibbon Wakefield wrote that 'the main business of the Ordinary is to break the spirits of capital convicts, so that they make no physical resistance to the hangman'. Villette in particular had a reputation for toughness: he viewed executions as important moral lessons for the public and therefore thought them worthwhile even in cases where the guilt of the condemned was in doubt. Even so, he displayed a marked sympathy for the Perreaus in his published account.

Lyon Abrahams, were burglars. The other was a cocky and good-looking teenager named George Lee. This trip marked the end of his very short career as a highwayman, for he had been caught in his first-ever attempt to rob a coach – or at least that was his story. It had been a naïve and impulsive act: having got a job on a ship sailing to the West Indies, he had been given money by some friends to buy clothes and provisions for the trip, but instead had squandered it on a single evening with an expensive prostitute. He had committed the robbery as a desperate measure to try to replace the money before his friends found out what he'd done.[32]

Lee wore a bright crimson coat and a ruffled shirt and played to the crowd throughout the journey, putting on 'an air of vulgar heroism, exceedingly improper for so dreadful a situation'.[33] As they passed a hackney coach in which a pretty young woman was sitting, he doffed his gold-laced hat to her with a great show of gallantry. The rowdy onlookers at once goggled into the coach to look at her, laughing and shouting obscene jests. The girl burst into tears, before the coach mercifully took her off in the other direction.[34]

Following the cart more slow horses plodded along, this time drawing a hurdle, a rough wooden sledge which bumped and scraped its way over the frozen mud of the road. On this uncomfortable vehicle sat two wretched-looking men who had been caught forging coins, Richard Baker and John Radcliffe. A more dramatic contrast with Lee could not be imagined. Inadequately dressed, they shivered pathetically in the icy air. Coining was considered a low form of fraud and they were unsophisticated men: they were granted no privileges.

After them came the Perreaus. Being gentlemen, they had been allowed to travel in an enclosed mourning coach. It gave them some protection from the crowd, although they were still visible through the windows. The two brothers were seen to be deep in prayer, their heads bowed, sometimes talking to each other or to Villette, who was later to recollect parts of their conversation during the long coach journey. Robert remarked that he fervently hoped that Caroline would not be in the crowd, but that he should not wonder if she were. Daniel replied that he did not believe she would attend. In any case, they both told Villette that they forgave her and prayed that she would return to a virtuous way of life.

It was a painful, chilly journey, taking two and half hours and covering a little under three miles, gradually leaving the urban scenery of Oxford Street and coming out into bedraggled countryside near Tyburn Cross. The slow dignity of the procession itself formed an eerie contrast with the raucousness of the crowd. They were a typical execution mob: shouting, jostling, fighting, running alongside the carriages, knocking each other over and deriving fun from the freezing conditions by hurling snowballs at each other and at the condemned men.

By the time the line of coaches and carts reached its destination, it was half-past eleven. The crowd waiting at Tyburn itself was the largest of all. Many had been there since the early morning and they were now joined by a tidal wave of others who had been following the procession. The *Gentleman's Magazine* estimated that there were 30,000 people there.[35]

The convoy slowly approached the two scaffolds isolated at the crossroads. The cart bearing Alexander and Abrahams stopped by the smaller, temporary one: as Jews they were to be hanged separately from the others. A rabbi climbed up and began speaking quietly with them, while George Lee was taken off their cart and put on to another one together with Baker and Radcliffe. As he climbed up the steps he hit his leg hard, 'which seemed to pain him very much'.[36] The cart was then driven under the crossbeam of the other, larger scaffold.

The manoeuvring of carts and swapping around of prisoners took about fifteen minutes, and the Perreaus were allowed to wait in their coach with Villette while it went on. Then the door was opened and they stepped out, carrying books in their bound hands. They were led to a third cart under the same scaffold as Lee, Baker and Radcliffe. First Daniel and then Robert climbed up on to the wooden floor of the cart and were told to go to the very end of it, where the ropes were already dangling. The other men also stood at the rear brink of their cart, each one beside a noose.[37] The sheriffs got out of their coach and came to take their formal leave of all the condemned men; the Perreaus thanked them for their kindness towards them during their imprisonment.

The ropes were now removed from the brothers' wrists and the executioner approached. He loosened the scarf which Daniel was wearing so that the noose could be slipped around his neck. Then he did the same for Robert.

Villette stepped on to the first of the carts and spoke quietly to the men one by one, spending a few minutes with each. After this long, hushed conversation, he asked them – as was usual – to acknowledge the justice of their sentence. When it was their turn, the two Perreaus instead gave him pieces of folded paper and said that every word written in them was true. Daniel placed his hand over his heart and solemnly swore that he was innocent. Then Robert did the same.

Having received the papers, Villette took his leave from them. Robert and Daniel bowed in return. Villette stepped off the cart and the two brothers kissed each other on the cheek. They 'embraced and saluted each other in a most tender and affectionate manner'.

The hangman came and lowered hoods over their eyes, then moved from one cart to the other, doing the same to each man. When all was ready, there was a brief pause, and then Daniel and Robert reached out and clasped each other by both hands. This was their signal to the hangman: it meant that they were ready. The hangman motioned for the carts to be driven forwards. Daniel and Robert's cart jerked out from under their feet: they fell from it and dropped to the full length of their ropes. There was a great shout from the crowd. The cart where Alexander and Abrahams had been standing moved at exactly the same moment, and after a few seconds' delay the cart with the other three condemned men followed.

The hands of the Perreaus were seen to be linked for some time, remaining 'clinched together about half a minute after the cart was driven away'. Then the swinging of their bodies separated them and their hands parted. 'They appeared to die without pain,' said the account published in the *Newgate Calendar*[38] – a piece of wishful thinking, unfortunately, for death by hanging was never painless.*

The spectators were profoundly impressed by the nobility and courage shown by the Perreaus. 'Not the least fear of death was discernable in either of their countenances,' wrote the reporter for the *Annual Register*, and 'they both behaved with a firmness and resolution rarely to be met with in men at the hour of death'. The obvious closeness between the brothers was also found moving – and many were struck by the poignancy of their twinning in death as in life. 'Thus two brothers, in the same moment quitted that world which they had entered together.'[39]

After the hanging was over, it was some time before the mob dispersed. Many of them had been given the day off work, as was the custom on hanging days, and they milled around the area. The hanged men were cut down. There were no special arrangements for the other corpses, but hearses were waiting to pick up the brothers' bodies and take them to Robert's house in Golden Square, where they were kept until the funeral four days later.

Robert and Daniel were buried together on Sunday 21

---

* Before the invention of trapdoors, which produced an abrupt fall and dislocation of the vertebrae, death was usually by slow asphyxiation. The ever-diligent Boswell had enquired into the matter in 1774 and been told that 'for some time after a man is thrown over he is sensible and is conscious that he is *hanging*'.

January, in Robert's family vault in the church of St Martin-in-the-Fields – a vault which already contained four of Robert's children.* Public interest had by no means diminished during the days since the execution. Indeed, word had been spreading of the Perreaus' courage and their quiet refusal to admit guilt, and they had become heroic figures. Their funeral was attended by a tremendous crowd of people.

The first arrivals stationed themselves outside the door of Robert's house in the early hours of the morning. They behaved initially 'with the utmost decency, order and decorum, lamenting his and his brother's unhappy fate',[40] but became more impatient and rowdier as time wore on, until finally, at half-past nine, the two coffins were brought out of the house and put into two separate hearses. The caskets were covered with black cloth; there was a black plate on each, showing the brothers' names, the date of their death, and their age: forty-two.

The two hearses moved off, followed by mourning coaches with Robert's wife, children and friends. The funeral cortège travelled the short distance from Golden Square to St Martin-in-the-Fields without any lights or ceremony, these having been deliberately avoided so as to attract as little attention as possible. Even so, the procession was followed all the way by a throng of people. There were more waiting at the church and by this time the crowd was getting out of control. Again to avoid attention, the church bell was not tolled, but an unmanageable quantity of people had heard about the funeral and turned up anyway, clogging the entrance and craning their necks for a view of the coffins and of Robert's family.

The coffins were taken out of the hearse and carried towards the door, covered with plain velvet palls and followed by the mourners and by liveried servants. There was an awkward pause at the entrance because the church wardens who were supposed to be waiting to meet them had

*The Perreau tomb was removed from the church in the 1850s.

not arrived. The mourners were forced to wait for about twenty minutes, 'the people beating loudly the whole time at the church doors'.[41] When the doors were finally opened, the pressure of people was such that the pallbearers could hardly extricate themselves. 'At the entrance into the church the crowd was so great and rude, that it was with great difficulty the bodies and mourners could get entrance, and one of the mob, unawed by this dreadful example and the sacredness of the place, snatched with violence from one of the mourners the hat-band out of his hat, and would have carried it off if not immediately detected and recovered; but the villain, from the immensity of the crowd, escaped for this time the hands of justice.'

Once the procession had finally made it inside the church, the onlookers who had managed to follow them quietened down somewhat. The funeral service was conducted 'with the usual solemnity', although still physically hampered by the vast numbers who continued to press upon the coffins and mourners. Robert's two sons Robert and Charles, in particular, attracted a great deal of attention and sympathy, with people audibly lamenting their sorry fate. The two boys impressed observers by conducting themselves at the funeral with the same 'becoming decency and dignity' that their father had shown at his execution.

After the service, the bodies were carried down into the vault. Very few people were admitted, although the rest were only 'with great difficulty prevented' from pushing their way in. A second service was performed and then the two coffins were placed near to the Perreau vault. Afterwards the mourners waited for some time in the vestry, where they were 'refreshed with wine' while the wardens did their best to disperse the mob so that they could leave in peace.

At last things quietened down sufficiently for the mourners to be escorted back to their coaches. They were driven back to Robert's house – where, once again, they found a horde of people waiting to get a look at them.

The register of St Martin-in-the-Fields describes the Per-reaus' deaths as 'sudden'; it says that they were forty-two years of age, and that the burial fees were £6 14s 8d for Robert and £6 7s 2d for Daniel. The difference in cost was because Robert had a few extras: he had prayers, candles and six men to carry the coffin. Daniel just had the basic service.[42]

The Perreaus received more public sympathy after their deaths than they ever did in life. The glamour of Caroline's trial had worn off during the intervening weeks and the brothers' brave conduct on the day of execution upstaged it completely. John Villette's account in the *Annals of Newgate* included transcripts of the letters they had handed to him from the scaffold, and these were also printed in the *Morning Post*. The letters once more affirmed the brothers' innocence in simple and dignified terms. This weighed heavily in the Perreaus' favour, for to have lied at the very end would have been a grave risk: it would have endangered their souls. Many people now became sure that they had been telling the truth all along and that Caroline was the villain after all. Yet there were still doubts: the *Gentleman's Magazine* noted: 'Since the execution of the Perreaus the people appear to be as much divided in their opinions about the guilt or innocence of Robert Perreau as about the American cause.'[43] It added that although the question was perplexing, it was 'in the power of one person to solve the difficulty'. Caroline did not respond.

In the *Morning Post* of 26 January a reporter noted that a Mr Harrison had mentioned the Perreau brothers in a lecture on Saturday, cautioning his listeners that the root of all their trouble was 'a non-conformity to the condition of life in which God had placed them'. The *London Magazine* also piously wished that 'their situation may be of advantage to others, to keep them from unlawful connexions – from ambition – from gambling in the Alley – and from ways which end in *Death*'.[44]

Robert was generally considered a more suitable object for moral lessons than Daniel, who had been sunk in depravity even before he met Caroline. 'Alas! poor Robert Perreau,' wrote a *Morning Post* hack:

> Thou art no more! but it is to be hoped that thy untimely end will prove an useful lesson to those apothecaries who keep carriages and live elegantly; such men may dazzle the eyes of the public, live a few years in splendor, and leave their families beggars, or otherwise become bankrupts, which has been the case with more than one within a short time. Our correspondent says it is a certain fact, that those apothecaries who drive about in their carriages do not do the most business; as he knows several whose prudence dictates to them to walk to their patients, are much esteemed, and do more business in the course of the year than many of the chariot gentry.[45]

The Perreaus' fate became the excuse for a great deal of purple prose. 'Hurried on by the false glare of grandeur, they precipitated themselves into an abyss of inevitable destruction: ostentatious parade and fastidious grandeur bewildered them; and they pursued the *ignis fatuus* of Pomp, till they were plunged into inextricable misery.'[46]

Something good did come out of their deaths, for their story sharpened public interest in the whole question of capital punishment and the irregularities of its application. The following year another high-profile execution for forgery, that of William Dodd, raised even more interest in reform. Dodd had written some eloquent *Prison Thoughts* whilst in confinement,* dwelling on the miserable state of the condemned criminal, and Samuel Johnson took up the

---

*The diarist Charlotte Papendiek, who in 1780 visited Newgate and there saw the three rooms in which Dodd had been imprisoned, claimed that Caroline had occupied the same rooms, and indeed had given them something of a makeover: 'they were neatly furnished by Mrs Rudd'.

cudgels on his behalf. George III apparently countered Dodd's appeal by saying that if he granted him mercy, people would think he had murdered the Perreaus. Eventually cases such as these brought about a change in the law: death sentences became more consistently applied once pronounced, but far less likely to be given in the first place.

And then, with the Perreaus dead and buried, and Caroline withdrawn from the public eye, life went on. The newspapers found other things with which to amuse their readers: by the Wednesday following the executions the city's most interesting spectacle was the Tahitian Prince Omai skating on the frozen Serpentine, and with wonderful proficiency 'considering the short time he has practised'.[47]

Henrietta was granted an allowance from the Crown of £100 a year, as emergency support for herself and the children. It was a poor substitute for Robert's lost business earnings, but at least it protected them against absolute poverty.[48] The *Morning Post* tried to shame the Society of Apothecaries into organizing a collection among its members to provide extra help, but there is no sign that they did so.

Mrs Perreau was to survive her husband by many years, dying in 1809 at the age of seventy-six. The children received a respectable upbringing and education, but were always grimly marked by their father's name. Indeed, one of them – Robert Samuel Perreau – turned out to be a rogue who was described by his father's former acquaintance William Hickey as a 'greater thief and scoundrel than either his father or his uncle'. Hickey was in a position to know, for he was one of the young man's victims. Robert was caught embezzling money from a Calcutta insurance company; the debt was cleared and the matter hushed up by a number of friends – including Hickey, who was Robert's lawyer at the time. By way of thanks, Robert vanished, 'leaving a multitude of creditors completely in the lurch'. Hickey lost over £500, and although he tracked Robert down to the Indian colony of Bencoolen and wrote to him several times, not a penny of the money was ever returned. Robert died not long after these events, but Hickey still nursed a grudge against him when writing his autobiography many years later. His letters to Robert proposing partial repayment on generous terms had been greeted only with 'pert and very insolent' answers, and Hickey had been powerless to get at him. And so, 'being out of the jurisdiction of the court in which I could attack him, I had only the poor satisfaction of telling him by letter he was a despicable scoundrel, and deserved a halter quite as much if not more than his father and uncle'.[49]

CHAPTER
TEN
◆
TO END THE SUM

The Perreaus were dead, Caroline was lying low and the newspapers had new scandals to occupy them – but the three protagonists and their story lived on in a larger, simpler dimension: they became creatures of myth. This was equally true of all three; the public imagination could play as freely with Caroline's memory as with that of the Perreaus, for little was known of her day-to-day life after the trial and she maintained an inscrutable silence about the case.

Like other legends of the time, especially tales of criminal derring-do, the story survived not only in popular memory and rumour but also through a lively trade in words and pictures. Cheap broadsides, songs, engravings and pamphlets of all kinds were run off the press to meet the demand and were sold by booksellers and street vendors all over the city. Among the most sought after was Villette's account of the brothers' behaviour at the execution, immediately issued as a separate pamphlet and later worked up into a more detailed chapter for the *Annals of Newgate*. Then there were the brothers' final statements of their innocence, which were quickly met by a pro-Caroline attempt to discredit them.[1] Transcripts of the trials also enjoyed a renewed sales boost. Caroline's letter to Viscount Weymouth was published;

its editor claimed to be on Caroline's side, but it probably did as much to turn people against her as anything.

Astute publishers made bumper compilations, adding trial transcripts to accounts of the Perreaus' dying words, excerpts from Caroline's 'Case', and other bits and pieces. *Prudence Triumphing over Vanity and Dissipation* collected material from so many incompatible sources that it contradicted itself at almost every turn. And somewhere in London the anonymous author of the two-volume *Authentic Anecdotes of the Life and Transactions of Mrs Margaret Rudd* was already scribbling away at this much longer account of Caroline's life, assembled from all the worst rumours ever told about her.

Naturally people were eager to see what the three celebrities looked like, and there was a thriving trade in cheap engravings posing them against suitable backgrounds: the stony walls of a Newgate cell, or the dock at the Old Bailey. The Perreaus were shown together in profile, to emphasize their identical features. Those who had not been lucky enough to glimpse the two brothers or the glamorously dressed Caroline in court were able to marvel over these simple, iconic images.

Readers of a Gothic bent were catered for by an exploitative broadside called *A Particular Account of the Dreadful and Shocking Apparitions of the Two Unfortunate Perreaus, Accompanied by the Wife of Mr. Robert Perreau, Who All Appeared Like Flame of Fire in Her Bedchamber.* Here Caroline is portrayed as shaking and shuddering with terror on being confronted by her three victims' vengeful spirits – the fact that Henrietta isn't dead yet doesn't seem to impair her ability to haunt. They appear one by one in a midnight visitation somewhere between nightmare and reality, as Caroline lies sleeping 'in the Arms of a certain noble Lord'. The room lights up with an unearthly glow, as if on fire, and Daniel's ghost glides in and intones, 'By thy base Artifice, thy vile deceit / Me and my Brother's ruin did compleat.' Daniel's spirit warns Caroline that she will end in Hell, where justice will be dispensed by a God who will demand explanations. 'Oh! think on the great Judgment Day, / What you have to that awful Judge to say.'

Three groans then herald the arrival of Robert Perreau, 'with Countenance grim'. He confirms his brother's words:

> The fatal Day is very near,
>   Before the Lord you must appear,
> To give account for what you've done,
>   When that the Judgement Day does come.

An unearthly shriek is heard, and 'the ghastly Apparition' of Henrietta Perreau joins that of her husband. She holds her right hand to her left breast, indicating her broken heart, and addresses Caroline with a great many exclamation marks:

> Thou Infidel of a Woman, stop thy wicked and diabolical! Proceedings; though Wickedness you seem to take Pride in, but lo! the Time is short, when every idle Moment spent in this World, you must give an Account for in the World to come: *Remember the Cries of the Fatherless and Motherless! Vengeance cry aloud against you! Hell itself opening its Jaws to receive you!*

The three spirits disappear and Caroline screams and swoons away, waking her bed partner, who thinks she is dead. He rouses the house in alarm, but she comes to and tells him the whole story. Ever since, concludes the writer, she has 'remained in strong Fits, with small hopes of her Recovery'. The lesson is clear: 'May this be a Warning to all, not to let unlawful Love be their undoing.'

Then there were the musical versions of the story. Ballad sellers on the streets of London added tales of the Perreaus to their stock of songsheets. Amongst these was *The London Tragedy, or, the Widow and her Fatherless Children in*

Distress, a sentimental tear-jerker relating the events in considerable detail and from various points of view. 'Twin brothers were they' –

> None ever went more gay
> And much alike they say,
>   Perreau their name.
> Each stony heart would bleed,
> When they these lines do read,
> Fate had them thus decreed,
>   To die in shame.

The introductory verses cover their family background in detail, and then a second section turns to 'what caused all their woe' – Margaret Caroline Rudd. It shows her first impressing them with fantasies of her imminent grandeur, and then advising them:

> My council don't despise,
> You'll to preferment rise,
> That will be acting wise,
>   So understand,
> Here, take this note, my dear,
> 'Tis on Mr. Adair,
> The cash is ready here,
>   Seven thousand pounds.

But, as everyone knew, her plan turned out badly: the forgeries were discovered and the brothers imprisoned, and then they were killed, although 'Robert's wife did strive in vain / Their lives for to regain'. In the third part Henrietta Perreau's voice joins in, lamenting her loss and calling for vengeance:

> When I my children view,
> My sorrows do renew,

What can I for them do,
    They're fatherless.
May she that caused my woe,
Soon to destruction go,
And in the shades below,
    By devils trod.
Hell gasp thy hungry jaws,
Revenge a widow's cause,
Who here's escap'd our laws,
    Curs'd Mrs R—d.

Henrietta's plight is heart-rending and her fury justified. Yet, in the final verse, a happy ending is revealed for poets, balladeers and amateur warblers everywhere, because:

    . . . now to end the sum,
    For ages here to come,
    This story will be one,
        Time to amuse.

As with all such true-crime stories of death and injustice, amusement was what Caroline and the Perreaus' afterlife as legend was all about. It lined the pockets of engravers and printers, and gave the ever more literate, inquisitive, and talkative population of 1770s London what they craved more than anything: a thrill for both intellect and emotions, composed of equal parts of pity and delight.

It was also a perfect subject for the eighteenth century's favourite hobby: wit. The satirist William Combe included Caroline in a poem called *The Diabo-lady* in 1777, a sequel to his *Diaboliad* depicting the election of the King of Hell (the winner of which was Simon Luttrell, Lord Irnham – yet another infamous rake with whom Caroline's name was sometimes connected by rumour). In *The Diabo-lady* a second competition is held to find a consort for the King, and Caroline is among the three finalists. She introduces herself by admitting that 'her smallest crime was that of being Whore', and that she had defied both God and Man by living in adultery. Above all, as the narrator remarks:

In forgery and perjury owned such art,
She palmed the Gold, while others paid the smart.

She does not win the title of Queen of Hell, however; the crown goes to the 'Duchess of Kingston', Elizabeth Chudleigh – who after a great deal of debate had finally been convicted of bigamy in April 1776. According to contemporary estimations the Duchess was a beautiful woman, indeed more so than Caroline, but a good deal less intelligent. The contemporary social observer Hannah More said that during her trial she had 'imitated her great predecessor, Mrs Rudd, and affected to write very often', but it was all vain display. 'I plainly perceived she only wrote as they do their love epistles on the stage, without forming a letter.'[2] Caroline had started a fashion, but in aping the trappings of cleverness her imitator merely revealed her own vapidity.

And so the imaginary Caroline joined the imaginary Perreaus in the land of archetypes and amusements. But what of the real Caroline? Although keeping out of the limelight, she was still very much flesh and blood. She had returned from her holiday in Bath, retrieved some or all of her children,* and was now living in a small apartment in Queen Street in Mayfair. It was there that Boswell was to call on her for the first time in April 1776, when her calm and gentle manner made such an impression upon him. Not only had she escaped death; she had reinvented herself. As she told Boswell that evening, she believed one could be anything one pleased. And what pleased her now was to live quietly, as a woman who had endured terrible physical and mental

---

*Boswell mentioned that there were children in her home, but does not say how many, and no other source refers to them.

suffering but who had maintained her honour and delicacy intact, and indeed had even been refined by the experience.

Happily, she did not have to bear this state of spiritual perfection alone. She had a flamboyant and exciting new companion to enjoy it with.

'There is no truth whatever', the *Morning Post* had chirped soon after the trial, 'in the report of a well-known lady's being *protected* by a certain Peer, since her discharge from Newgate.'[3] *Prudence Triumphing over Vanity and Dissipation* went further towards naming the peer and even gave directions to his address: 'The moment that Mrs Rudd was acquitted, she went out of court, and found a hackney-coach waiting for her, which conveyed her down the Old Bailey, and along Fleet Street and the Strand. At the bottom of St Martin's Lane, the carriage turned up and drove to the house of a Worcestershire Lord, who of late has made a very distinguishing figure in the House of Peers.' It went on, 'That nobleman, who, to his eternal disgrace, has discarded his own lady, took this notorious wh—e into keeping, and furnished a house for her in Welbeck Street, near Cavendish Square, where she now resides.'[4] The *Morning Post* for 11 January 1776 agreed: 'An elegant house in Welbeck-street, Cavendish-square, is taken and fitting up for Mrs. Rudd.' This was not far from where she had lived with Daniel in Harley Street, or indeed from the first lodging house she had occupied on her arrival in London ten years earlier. It was also a convenient few minutes' carriage ride from the apartment in Queen Street where Boswell met her, which she maintained out of separate funds.

The 'Worcestershire Lord' was Thomas Lyttelton, and, although she denied it in conversation with Boswell, Caroline apparently lived under his 'protection' for several years. He was a good deal younger than most of her previous lovers – only thirty-one, the same age as herself. He was a charming and good-looking man, 'accomplished, witty, clever, a brilliant orator, a good debator, an amusing letter-writer, the life and delight of every circle he joined'.[5] His taste was exquisite and he frequented high society; as a Member of Parliament he tended to take sternly moralistic positions in politics – for example, he argued that the trial of the Duchess of Kingston should go ahead despite her sympathisers' objections, for bigamy was an offence of great atrocity. He led a double life, however, and was invariably dubbed 'the wicked Lord Lyttelton'. He was one of the runners-up in Combe's King of Hell competition; society gossips considered him one of the most debauched rakes and corrupters of youth in the city. As he wrote to a friend, 'When I appear, even in general society, mothers seem to be alarmed for their daughters, husbands for their wives, and fathers for their sons.'[6] Even prostitutes were nervous of him: 'the very impures of the town have refused my most generous offers, from an apprehension of my capacity for mischief'.

Lyttelton had probably been the 'friend' who had supported Caroline after her eviction by Frankland, and their relationship was certainly well established by the time he spirited her away from the Old Bailey. He had a wife, but it was not much of a marriage, and Caroline was not the first of his paramours. Almost immediately after the wedding in 1773 he had run off to Paris with a barmaid – just after publishing some 'extremely moral and insipid' verses in his wife's honour – but that relationship was equally short-lived. He was back in London by the end of that year and presumably met Caroline in either 1774 or 1775.

As Boswell remarked, gossip linked Caroline with other gentlemen besides Lyttelton. Much of what was said was probably untrue, but she can not have entirely given up her old contacts with the *demi-monde*, for in 1778 Boswell's friend the Earl of Pembroke bumped into her at what he called 'a certain house'[7] – a brothel. She maintained her independence, keeping her own home as well as Lyttelton's love nest in Welbeck Street. Yet, whether she was faithful or not, the relationship with Lyttelton remained peaceful and stable for some years. They were regularly seen at the theatre and went to all the most fashionable entertainments together: concerts, regattas, evenings in the gardens of Vauxhall and the great dome of Ranelagh, 'enlightened with a thousand golden lamps, that emulate the noonday sun',[8] where with other beautiful people they circled its strange, vast rotunda, watching and being watched.

But then the relationship came to an abrupt end, for Lyttelton suddenly died at the premature age of thirty-five in November 1779. The circumstances were dramatic and unusual – and had nothing to do with Caroline. He dreamed one night that a bird flew into his bedroom, turned into a woman and warned him that he had less than three days to live. He told several people about the dream, but by the third day he still felt fine and ceased to worry. He walked around town during the day and enjoyed a lively supper in Epsom. No one observed anything strange about him during the evening, but moments after getting into bed at eleven fifteen he had a seizure and dropped dead, a manservant witnessing the event. The general opinion was that it was a heart attack brought on by wild living and 'free use of drugs'.

Caroline was now bereft of her lover and alone again – but not for long, for she soon acquired a new protector to replace him. In her own later account in the pamphlet *Mrs Stewart's Case*, she openly acknowledged that there had been someone from 1779 to 1785, but she did not name him. Whoever he was, the affair continued peacefully for six years, making it probably the longest of her life* – but it eventually foundered. Caroline herself was to give contradictory versions of what happened: she complained in conversation with Boswell that the man had abandoned her, but in *Mrs*

---

*From wedding to final separation, she was with Rudd for just over seven years, but with numerous interruptions. Her connection with Joseph Salvador might also have continued longer than she admitted to Daniel, possibly for more than six years.

Stewart's Case she wrote that she had 'voluntarily relin-
quished a dependence, which, consistent with my better
feelings, I could no longer retain' – perhaps a face-saving
adjustment of the truth.

Even with wealthy and powerful protectors and an
apartment of her own, Caroline always found her fame – or
infamy – a problem. Seeking anonymity, she had taken the
name of Stewart in place of Rudd, Stewart being her mother's
maiden name as well as that of her other supposed noble
relations. It made little difference: rumours about her true
identity always caught up with her and made her life
impossible. The fact that she had been acquitted of all
wrongdoing was of little consquence; indeed, as she angrily
wrote, 'vulgar prejudice appeared but the more envenomed'
by it. Stigmatized and ruined, she felt herself forced to drag
out 'a wounded existence, cruelly embittered'.[9]

Now that she was truly alone for the first time in many
years, the situation was far worse. Not only was she hated
and distrusted by all, but she had no income. How could a
gentlewoman maintain her delicacy and decency under these
circumstances? It occurred to her that some of the wealthy
and noble relations with whom she had claimed kinship
might help and she approached them with her tale of woe,
but most of them refused even to listen. She needed legal
advice. Perhaps the threat of lawsuits would encourage her
relations to see her point of view – and surely she must also
have some moral claim upon her faithless ex-lover.

Friendless and vengeful, she went through her mental
address book. Who could advise her? Among the names that
rose into her thoughts was that of an old acquaintance, a
capable lawyer who had seemed very taken with her back in
1776 and who was now on the brink of celebrity himself:
James Boswell.

After those first few titillating meetings in 1776, Boswell had
apparently put Caroline out of his mind. For nine years he

did not discuss her at all in his diaries or letters, except for one brief mention in 1778 when his friend Pembroke saw her in a brothel – a piece of information which inspired Boswell to neither lust nor nostalgia. He had no reason to expect ever to see her again. But now, in August 1785, she exploded back into his life.

Boswell had been having an interesting but unsettling year. Johnson had died at the end of 1784: it had been a serious personal blow, but had also opened the way for the great biography he had been incubating for so long. It would not appear for some time yet, but already he was engrossed in the project, and he had a smaller one on the go too: polishing up his journal of a trip to the Hebrides made by himself and Johnson back in 1773. Johnson had published his own sobersides account of it two years after the journey; Boswell's version was livelier and more personal, and was at least as much about the two of them as about the Western Isles. Due to be published in October, it would be a tasty appetizer for the full *Life* to follow. Whilst planning these two books, he supplemented his income with regular journalistic titbits, notably accounts of Tyburn executions for the *Public Advertiser*. Finally, on top of all this literary activity, he was making a career for himself as a barrister in English law, which was hard work since it meant learning a completely different legal system from the Scottish one. It was the only way he could afford his heart's desire, which was to move permanently to London instead of commuting back and forth between there and his family home near Edinburgh.

And so it was an overworked and stress-ridden Boswell who woke up one morning in August 1785 to find a card delivered from a 'Mrs Stewart', requesting the honour of a visit. He knew at once who this mysterious lady was: she had mentioned her Stewart connections back in 1776 and he had probably heard talk of her new identity since. He did as the card requested, and went to call at her new address. It was less well appointed than the apartment of earlier years: the house was owned by two elderly sisters and Caroline was merely their lodger. It was immediately obvious to Boswell that she had come down in the world.

The reunion was pleasant, mixing serious discussion and friendly reminiscence, but Boswell knew very well that it was not just for old times' sake. Caroline needed something. He might have expected it to be money, but soon realized that his legal knowledge was the chief attraction. She was in trouble and in debt, and even feared being imprisoned again. Could Boswell help her to get compensation from her treacherous lover? All her long-practised talents came back into play; she charmed Boswell just as she had done nine years previously, and begged him not to forget her in her hour of need. There was something of a 'romantic scene', as he put it in his diary.

He did not commit himself at once, but a few days later he went to see her again. This time he found a different Caroline. Things had taken a turn for the better. She told him that despite her other problems she was not quite destitute after all; in fact, she had an independent living, and so 'would not form another connection unless it were very agreeable'.[10] She spoke with a highly meaningful air, making it clear that it was to him that she was offering such agreeability. Boswell was both alarmed and instantly excited. It was not, after all, to be just a matter of legal advice rewarded by harmless flirtation. He went away to think about it.

The few people he spoke to warned him off in the strongest terms. The painter Joshua Reynolds said that 'if a man were known to have a connection with her, it would sink him'.[11] William Temple, the friend to whom Boswell had sent the account of his first meeting with Caroline back in 1776, also disapproved: 'What have good principles to do with Margaret Caroline Rudd?' he asked in a letter to Boswell of 31 August.[12] In a later letter he protested piously at Boswell's having mentioned her on the same page as St Paul's cathedral and Holy Communion.[13]

Still Boswell dithered. His two recent meetings with her had been enough to turn him from indifference to an infatuation almost as intense as on their first encounter – and this time it was more dangerous, since an affair was now a real possibility. He was wealthier than he had been in 1776; she was less famous and more vulnerable. Both were older – Caroline was forty-one, Boswell forty-five. This significantly altered the balance of power in his favour.

On 10 September he said to her, ''Tis tantalizing.' She replied, 'Come and see me sometimes, and you shall not be tantalized.'[14] One or the other of them also said on this occasion, 'I should like to have a child between you and me; curious being. It would find its way in the world.' But Boswell continued to hesitate. He spent the month of October in Scotland with his family, but back in London in November he felt the attraction as powerfully as ever. He was now a public man: his *Tour to the Hebrides* had come out and proved such a bestseller that the first edition sold out almost immediately and a second one was in preparation. Although proudly aware of the new figure he cut in the world, Boswell's struggle with private temptation was as awkward and confusing as ever.

That November an odd, tensely phrased entry appears in his diary: 'Had cravings. Visited Mrs R. Indifferent. Then gross folly.'[15] Later, he crossed out the words 'Had cravings' and 'gross'. It is unclear whether the folly was committed with Caroline or with someone else as consolation for being rejected by her, but either way it was not an auspicious start.

The situation was again relieved by a lengthy absence in Scotland over the winter. Boswell was unhappy there, though, and longed to move to London for good. His restlessness owed something to the sheer excitement of London life (especially now he was famous), something to his unacknowledged desire to get away from his wife and children and not a little to the subject which constantly played on his mind: Caroline and her 'come and see me sometimes'. London meant all of this for him; yet he recognized the difference between the '*imaginary* London, gilded with all the brilliancy of warm fancy' which his own mind had created and the reality of life there – especially the financial reality. London was expensive, and far more so with a mistress to support.

The gilded fancy won. In February 1786 Boswell made the long, familiar journey down to London again and this time took up permanent residence. He stayed with a friend for the first few months, establishing himself in a new job as a barrister and hunting out permanent accommodation so his family could join him later. This took some time, and all that spring Boswell was effectively a single man. Solitude exacerbated his bouts of depression – but it also made him free to do whatever he liked.

If he had ever seriously intended to resist Caroline, the resolution did not last long. Her name appears in his diary almost immediately on his arrival in London, and is accompanied by one simple and expressive word: 'Wonderful.'[16] Boswell saw her again the next day and from then on they met regularly. The affair had begun. He wrote of her:

> Tasting wondrous tree of old made us know the difference between good and evil. Tasting thee, my Margaret, the reverse, for it confounds it, and all thy arts and all thy evil is lost in the blaze of thy charms. Thus I at first exclaimed – till through time and on a calm and steady view I found that it was true. My eyes were opened and that all the bad imputed to thee was false, and now saw thee good, generous, etc. etc.[17]

Sexually, he was more than satisfied: 'If the Roman Emperor who had exhausted delight offered a reward for the inventor of a new pleasure, how much do I owe to thee, who hast made the greatest pleasure of human life new to me.' With her, Boswell discovered a more sophisticated side to his sexuality: 'I used to look on love with feverish joy or childish fondness. All madness or folly, though delight. Thou hast shown me it rational, pure from evil. How keen the fire that thus clears the dross from the most precious ore.'[18]

For the first time since his youth, he wrote a love lyric. It was entitled 'Larghan Clanbrassil' in honour of the place where she was born, and sang of 'Margaret Caroline':

O Larghan Clanbrassil, how sweet is thy sound!
To my tender remembrance as love's sacred ground!
For there Marg'ret Caroline first charmed my sight,
And filled my young heart with a flutt'ring delight.*[19]

For a while, the affair settled down into a regular feature of Boswell's life, dutifully recorded in his diary. In the first few days of February he 'visited M.C., who was delighted to see me so well' on the Friday. He went back at midday on Saturday. That evening he could not stop himself from openly enthusing about her at a supper party to anyone who would listen. He woke up 'ill and vexed' from drinking too much wine and went at once to visit her again. And so it went on: he saw her almost every day. On Wednesday 8 February he told her of a distressing dream in which his wife was dangerously ill. Caroline implausibly reassured him that the dream meant 'all was well at home'.

But by the third week of the month the initial euphoria was already passing. On the 22nd he wrote, 'Took an impatient fit to see M.C. Visited there. Not well. No meeting for some time.' On his next visit two days later he was kept in a state

---

*This is a fragment from Boswell's manuscript M343, a collection of verses. Caroline's name in the third line is an amendment, replacing the original words 'gentle Fainelagh'. The whole poem in the 'Fainelagh' version was published under the title 'Songs to an Irish air, by the late James Boswell' in Sir Alexander Boswell's *Songs, Chiefly in the Scottish Dialect*, 1802, p. 17. There was a great deal of debate over its meaning before the full cache of Boswell's manuscripts was discovered in a cabinet and the relationship with Caroline was revealed in all its glory. See Frederick A. Pottle, *Notes and Queries*, 4 July 1925, p. 6.

of frustration: 'Sat two hours, and was assured that this was a very flattering attention, when, on account of "certain reasons best known to ourselves", there could be no gratification of one kind.'[20]

On Sunday 26th came the first serious disagreement: Boswell was severely scolded for taking too much for granted. He had visited Caroline in the late morning, and found her 'serious and pleasing and friendly'. But that evening he enjoyed a lavish dinner at which he talked with the Lord Chancellor, on whom he felt that he had made an excellent impression. It put him in exuberant spirits and as usual he drank more than was good for him. So, 'somewhat elevated by . . . champagne and claret', he decided to drop in on Caroline unannounced to prattle about his social triumphs. He was met at the door by her servant, John, with a message that she was not at home.

'Not at home!' exclaimed Boswell.

'Gone to bed.'

'Gone to bed! At this time of night?'

John relented, saying that she was in her night clothes but might be willing to see him. So Boswell rushed in. It was the wrong thing to do: he 'was reproved and hastened away'.

He went home crestfallen and brooded about it the following day, feeling that he had been badly treated. 'Troubled about M.C. and resolving to break off,' he wrote in his journal. He was inclined to sulk, but a contrary instinct impelled him to mollify her. A note to her, which he drafted on the back of a letter he'd received that day but probably did not send, reads: 'To affect anger or indifference *now* would be *falsehood*. Take then my genuine sentiments. With the warmest gratitude for your generous goodness, with the deepest concern for an inconsiderate offence, I will endeavour resolutely to submit to the severest punishment, which is never again to run the risk of giving so much pain to one for whom I shall ever retain an affectionate admiration.'

In accordance with this resolution, he visited Caroline the

next day and ate a large slice of humble pie. 'Found a gentler reception, and after some conversation, was forgiven and told this would do me good by teaching me prudence. I got into delightful spirits.'

He continued to see her regularly. On Sunday 5 March he met two interesting people at a dinner party. One was the sexually ambiguous Chevalière d'Éon, who Boswell astutely thought looked like 'a man in woman's clothes'.* The other was Lord Rawdon, with whom Boswell was eager to talk because he was intimately connected with Caroline.

Francis Rawdon-Hastings, later to become the second Earl of Moira, was the sort of larger-than-life-figure Boswell found irresistible. Tall and athletic, with a stately and impressive bearing, he had distinguished himself by great courage and a positively bloodthirsty degree of zealotry in the American war. He was now back in England and applying the same swashbuckling style to his budding political career. In matters concerning Caroline, however, Rawdon was a pussycat – at least for the moment. He had just started giving her money on a regular basis, not for sexual favours, but because she had convinced him that they were related through the Stewart line and he felt obliged to rescue her from the starvation she had convinced him would otherwise be her lot. Caroline had nevertheless confided to Boswell that she thought Rawdon was harbouring doubts about her pedigree and might be considering cutting her off. Boswell was keen to take the opportunity to check him out on her behalf.

He broached the subject by saying that he had not known of Rawdon's connection with Scotland until recently, when Mr Cummyng of the Lyon Office had mentioned his family links to the 'celebrated but unfortunate lady' Mrs Rudd. Rawdon was pleased and showed every sign of willingness to

*That was exactly what he was: the Chevalier(e) claimed to be a woman who had masqueraded for some years as a man, but was in truth the exact opposite – a fact that was not revealed until his death.

talk. The two men had a brief, friendly conversation about Caroline's maiden name and whether it should correctly be 'Young' or 'Youngson'. It seemed clear from the way Rawdon spoke that he had no reservations about her at all. Boswell was pleased and could not wait to take her the good news of 'how Lord Rawdon admitted her relationship to him'. To Rawdon he said that he had not seen Caroline for nine years and had thought she was dead, but had recently renewed his acquaintance with her and found her 'a very sensible, agreeable woman'.

Boswell made no serious attempt to conceal their affair from the world. He was a bibulous babbler and it was against his nature to keep anything secret for long. The society gossips certainly knew of it, and a scandalized Fanny Burney noted in her diary (actually after the end of the affair) that Boswell was an 'admirer and follower of Mrs Rudd! – and avows it, and praises her extraordinary attractions aloud!'[21] Boswell himself wrote that on Tuesday 7 March, at another party, he had 'raved' about her to a Mrs Margaret Stuart (no relation). Mrs Stuart replied that in principle she had no objection to Caroline's lifestyle, but thought she should conform to convention if she wished to live in respectable society. Yet she also admitted to being impressed by Caroline's 'extraordinary talents'. Her husband, Colonel James Stuart, overheard and butted in. He 'swore at all this and said he would think of her only as a w—re'. Boswell was shocked by his harshness.[22] It was a strange reversal of normal reactions, since men were generally more sympathetic to Caroline than women, who disbelieved her stories of suffering and judged her harshly. Mrs Stuart was an unusually jovial type, though: when she picked Boswell up in her carriage the next day to go into town and saw that he was hungover and haggard, she said with amusement, 'I wish Margaret Caroline saw you now.'

The following day, when he was feeling better, Boswell did visit Caroline. He was entranced: 'Never shall I forget the scene. So good, so generous, was she. Elegantly dressed: satin *couleur* de rose; her hair in perfect taste – not to be discomposed.' Boswell was a great fan of the towering hairstyles of the age and Caroline always had a taller and more elaborate construction than anyone else. The only disadvantage for Boswell was that he had to be careful not to demolish it in his ardour.

Later that month he had to go away on legal business; whilst away he discovered in himself unmistakeable signs of venereal disease. He had reason to think that he had caught it from someone other than Caroline and did the honourable thing by her, writing at once to confess it. (He made no comparable admission to his wife, but she was still in Scotland and they were meeting only on his occasional trips there, so he probably hoped that she would not be at risk and need never know.) Caroline sent back a 'spirited, romantic, and kind' reply.[23] After returning to London, he restrained himself with difficulty from visiting until he was sure he was quite free of the ailment. He sought advice and medicines from a doctor on 14 April and felt reassured, but could not resist seeing a favourite prostitute, Polly Wilson, on the same day.[24]

After a week of treatment he felt better, and arranged to visit Caroline on Sunday 23 April. He had been longing to see her and was very excited about the meeting, but some subterranean shift must have taken place in his emotions during the enforced separation, for he discovered that in place of the usual combination of lust and admiration he felt a peculiar unease in her presence. In his account of the evening he wrote: 'Dined with M.C.: boiled fowl and oyster sauce, cold roast mutton and salad of her dressing. Dumb waiter. (Damascene tart by her maid). Porter, white wine, port. Felt strangely. Then coffee.'

After dinner, they went with friends to visit the Magdalen Hospital for Penitent Prostitutes, a fashionable way to spend the evening. ('To leave her there?' a friend of Boswell had quipped when told of the plan.) They listened to a sermon given by a Dr Harrison – probably the same who had lectured on the downfall of the Perreaus back in 1776 – and Caroline told Boswell that she had previously heard him preach at St Martin-in-the-Fields. 'But I don't go now,' she said. 'You know who is buried there.' He realized that she was speaking of Daniel Perreau. It was an unpleasant reminder of the past and of her equivocal character. He 'was struck', but said to her, 'You are an affectionate creature.' Yet her remark preyed on him throughout the remainder of the sermon.

Afterwards they walked back to her house, but Boswell knew that it was over for him. The visit to the Magdalen and the mention of Daniel had crystallized the 'strangeness' he'd been feeling over the port and coffee. He finished his account of the evening with the remark, 'I disliked this *low* association. Home.'

And that was all. Boswell never saw her again.

Caroline's name appears just one more time in his diary. He made a single, failed attempt to call on her the following year, in May 1787. He had dreamed the night before that his wife and Caroline were fighting over him. 'This heated my fancy', he wrote, 'and the flame being increased by wine, I very improperly ... called at the house to which she had removed.'[25] She was not there, however – 'fortunately', Boswell added. Although he did not see her, he did learn something of the difficulties she had been experiencing in the past year. The elderly sisters who owned the house gave him a 'sad account': Caroline had fallen deeply into debt and was now in Fleet Prison. The sisters were obviously among her creditors, for they 'complained much of her' and were eager to know who Boswell was in case he was likely to pay her debt. Was his name Rawdon, by any chance? Boswell said no and left, asking them to tell Caroline that 'Mr Parr' had called – the first false name that came into his mind.

He did not repeat the visit. Eventually he confessed the

affair to his wife, long after it was over, and promised her that nothing of the sort would ever happen again. She was not entirely reassured by his vows, knowing that his feelings for Caroline had been strong. It had been far more than the simple sexual lust that usually motivated him, for Caroline's character and history engaged his intellect and imagination as well. (A modern writer, Gordon Turnbull, has noted that the fascination she held for Boswell sprang from the conjunction of two qualities which were equally compelling for him, but normally opposites: 'unique greatness and illicit sex'.)[26] Boswell and his wife talked about the affair on several occasions, and on 9 November 1788 he had to write reassuring her that 'the creature to whom you allude . . . was totally dismissed from my attention, and I solemnly protest that I have not corresponded'.[27] The topic came up again four months later: 'It pained me to think that after your humane and generous conduct you should be agitated with any suspicions that what I am truly sensible was very bad indeed is not totally at an end. Be perfectly assured that it is and that you shall have every proof that can possibly be given of sincere regret. You really do not know me well enough; otherwise you would give more credit to me.' Of course the problem was that she knew her husband all *too* well. Nevertheless, he was true to his word this time. 'I consider it to be my serious duty to be for ever sorry for it and to be more and more upon my guard,' he told her.[28]

He was reminded of his former lover just once more when, after his *Life of Johnson* was eventually published to huge acclaim in 1791, an anonymous fan wrote to him suggesting that he write an account of the infamous Mrs Rudd. 'A narrative written by you, or some person as capable, would be extremely acceptable to the generality of readers, and let me add to minds of a higher order than the generality.'[29] Whether the writer of this letter actually knew of the affair is not certain. Caroline's story promised to make sensational copy and Boswell was now the most fashionable biographer of his day. However, it was also true that his connection with her was no secret, and the letter-writer might have found it amusing to tease him. In any case, despite no longer having to worry about hurting his wife (she had died in 1789), Boswell chose discretion for once and declined to write the book.

Although she still complained of the difficulties attending her notoriety, the public Caroline was now fading into obscurity, her story a vague scandal from the past rather than a living piece of gossip. The Perreaus had come to a definite end before the eyes of 30,000 people; instead, she had continued with her life amid a general feeling that she ought long ago to have met her come-uppance. This feeling expressed itself through persistant reports of her death, usually depicted as occurring in deep poverty and misery. Boswell certainly heard such stories, for he had told Rawdon that he had thought her dead until she contacted him in 1785. The rumours had circulated at least since 1779, when the first obituary appeared in the *Gentleman's Magazine*, together with a note that she had been 'in very distressed circumstances'.[30] When the editors realized their mistake, they printed a correction, but similar reports continued – to the point that they became a subject of satire for her favourite newspaper, the *Morning Post*, which wryly reported in November 1786 that 'the celebrated Mrs. Rudd, who has been so often killed by the newspapers, was on Monday night at Covent Garden theatre'.[31]

The year after that she did in fact disappear from the world's view for some time, though not permanently. As her landladies had told Boswell, she spent a long spell in prison for debt in 1787. Under the name of 'Caroline Stewart' – the authorities apparently being unaware of her former identity – she was confined in Fleet Prison on 16 March following arrest for three different debts, and was not released until February 1788. The Fleet was quite a different experience from Newgate, where she had had celebrity status and was comfortably insulated by money. She was now in a prison specializing in the ragged poor and almost entirely without amenities; even basic food had to be paid for with what few pennies she could scrape together. As a middle-aged woman who had been used to far better, it was hard for Caroline. The fate of her (now teenaged) children during this period is not recorded; she may once again have been separated from them, perhaps permanently. She later described her year in the Fleet as a 'gulph of wretchedness', and wrote that she suffered there 'the *extremes* of penury, sorrow, and sickness'.[32] As the *Gentleman's Magazine* would have put it, her circumstances were distressed.

But Caroline was never one to endure distress without blaming it on someone else and devising a scheme to alleviate it. In her opinion the person responsible for the disaster this time was Lord Rawdon. After Boswell's first meeting with him, and contrary to Caroline's fears at the time, he had continued to support her for well over a year, believing it to be his family duty. At the beginning of 1787, however, someone put him right and he immediately cut off the contributions. No matter how fervently Caroline pleaded with him, he refused to have anything to do with her ever again or to give her a penny more from the family coffers, even when she was in prison. He could have saved her from the Fleet, but he did not do so.

The debts were still there after her release in 1788 and new ones continued to accumulate, since she had no income. Her recently won freedom was therefore likely to be taken away at any moment. In desperation she returned to Rawdon, once more beseeching him to do what she insisted was his duty. He ignored her, as did the rest of the family. And so, to try to shame them into changing their minds, she wrote her final vitriolic pamphlet, *Mrs Stewart's Case*, detailing her sufferings and haranguing her neglectful kin. She had lost none of her old panache with the pen, and this time her tone was one of high dudgeon throughout.

First she went through her officially authenticated pedigree, to show exactly why Rawdon was obligated to her. 'This pedigree proves me lineally descended from Graham Earls of Montieth, and Stewart Earls of Galloway, whose common ancestor and mine was Alexander the Sixth Lord High Steward of Scotland, father to Robert the Second, first monarch of the name of Stewart.'[33] The peerage was dormant owing to the lack of male heirs, she added in a footnote, but there were still two daughters, one of whom was the great-grandmother of Lord Rawdon. 'Consequently Mrs Stewart and Lord Rawdon are presumptive claimants to this dormant Peerage.'

She added haughtily, 'Vain is the folly of hoping that the ties of affinity can engage, or the plea of misfortune avail, where callous prosperity reigns; where the sense of humanity is stifled by sordidness; and the pampered insolence of superior fortune leads the possessors to conceive, that they may neglect the obligations of propriety, and the duties of kindred.' Several pages recounting her difficulties over the previous few years followed, mentioning the poverty that had followed the loss of her protector in 1785, the help she had hoped to receive from her relatives and the appalling miseries of the imprisonment that had followed when they let her down.

Admittedly, she said, Lord Rawdon had once been most generous – but that only made it more of a shock when he abandoned her so abruptly. Insult had followed injury and he had turned his entire family against her. After his betrayal she had approached a cousin of his, 'imploring that I might only be extricated from the impending danger of arrest', but he too rejected her with 'an almost incredible obduracy'. Another relative, Keith Stewart, not only failed to help, but treated her 'with something very like the vulgarity of a clown'. When Caroline sent 'two ladies' to appeal to Rawdon on her behalf, he heard them out and then replied, 'So far from thinking it an act of humanity to serve Mrs Stewart, I should think that, in giving her any assistance or countenance, I was committing a *sin*, and an *imposition* upon the world.'

Caroline blamed him for turning other people against her too. When a creditor of hers had gone directly to Rawdon, complaining of his own hardship and hoping that a relation of Caroline's would help, Rawdon told him, 'Mrs Stewart!! – *the Stewarts* were not *his* family!' As a result of this outburst, the creditor took Caroline to be an impostor, and said so to everyone he knew – resulting in further miseries for her.

Rawdon never responded to her pamphlet and he did not relent. However, her return to the limelight of controversy did not go entirely unnoticed. The *Morning Post* soon thereafter carried two attacks on her, one signed 'Justice' on 9 January 1789, and the other signed 'Scourge' three days later. The first read:

To Mrs. Margaret Caroline Rudd, alias Stewart.
Madam,
   Considering the load of disgrace which hangs on your character, it was hardly to be imagined that you would ever have ventured to obtrude yourself upon the public notice again. Whether it be fortitude, or a quality of a less respectable description, that has impelled you to emerge from that obscurity into which your conduct has deservedly cast you, the public will be at little loss to determine. That your imprudent return to the notice of the world will be as ineffectual as it is ridiculous, cannot be doubted. Lord Rawdon relieved your distress with the benignity which marks an exalted character; and because he is able to find more proper objects for his liberality, he is to be the object of your malevolent ingratitude. Your attack, however, is as weak as the motives are evidently despicable; and the only ground upon which the public will be led to censure his Lordship at all is, that he should ever have been so far deceived as to suppose you an object of compassion.

Retire, Madam, into perpetual obscurity; suffer not your vanity to delude you into an opinion, that your literary talents are deserving the notice of the public, or that though the mildness of the law has secured your impunity, mankind are in the least mistaken with respect to the true nature of your character.

Justice.[34]

The letter from 'Scourge' followed the same line, approving Rawdon's refusal to be baited and castigating 'the affected scurrilities of the amiable Mrs Rudd, who has lately started from her ignominious obscurity'.[35]

Caroline claimed that both letters were written by Rawdon himself.[36] It is possible, but if so the reference to his own 'exalted character' would display a strange lack of even feigned modesty. It is more probable that the letters were written by one of her old enemies returning to the fray. Sir Thomas Frankland could not have been the author, for he had died in 1784. The most likely suspect is the writer who had signed himself 'Justice', 'No Puffer' and 'Jack Spy' back in 1775 – Colonel Kinder.

Either age had mellowed her, or she simply knew when she was beaten. She did not respond publicly to the two letters and the battle subsided as quickly as it had begun.

'Justice' had commanded her to retire into obscurity, and that was exactly what Caroline now did. In the 1790s very little news of her surfaced in the press, apart from further unsubstantiated reports of her death. She spent more time living behind stone walls, although not on her own account. The *Carlton Magazine* reported in 1794 that 'Mrs Rudd of Perreau memory! whose adventures have so often been the subject of publick curiosity, seems fated to end her career in Newgate. She is now absolutely living in that wretched prison with a man whose appearance bespeaks misery in the extreme! He is confined on the debtor's side, and she seldom stirs out of the place in which they sleep.'[37] It was then common for women who were unable to support themselves alone in the outside world to join imprisoned menfolk in their cells. Caroline, who was now fifty years old and had descended a great deal from her former glories, had presumably fallen into this predicament.

After jumping the gun in 1779, the *Gentleman's Magazine* now trailed behind the times. It reported her as dying in 1800, but in truth she probably died some years before. The magazine's obituary announced that she had died in Hardingstone, Northamptonshire,[38] and added that 'for some years she gained a competent living by writing for the Reviews'.[39] This is a pleasing thought, and consistent with her skill in wielding the pen for many different purposes – but alas, this must have been a different Mrs Rudd. The woman buried in Hardingstone had the full name Mrs William Rudd, which bears no relation to any of Caroline's former identities.[40]

On 4 February 1797, instead, *The Times* announced simply that 'the once celebrated Mrs Rudd died a short time since in an obscure apartment near Moorfields'.[41] No entry appears in the burial records of parishes in the area, but this is the most likely of the reports and it is probably as close as we can get to knowing the year and circumstances of her death.* And although *The Times* gives no further details, the location suggests that these circumstances were indeed ones of financial distress.

And so, in darkness and decline, the life of this extraordinary woman came to an end. It had been a strange life indeed. Almost the only person ever to take an entirely generous view of it in either contemporary or later accounts was Caroline

---

*She may have adopted yet another name, perhaps that of the man with whom she lived in Newgate, with the rumour of her true identity somehow reaching the finely tuned ear of a *Times* journalist. Her children, too, appear to have changed their names or moved far from their mother's territory.

herself, in her eloquent, self-serving pamphlets and letters. Yet it was not a life entirely without sense, or beyond understanding.

There is no doubt that Caroline was naturally astute and strong-willed, but she had also met with tough experiences early on, which helped set the lines of her personality. Her childhood was one of extreme loneliness and alienation. An only child orphaned at such a young age that she barely knew her parents, she was brought up alternately by two relatives – her grandmother and her uncle – who were equally unable to handle her. Being clever, she was bored by the facile feminine curriculum at her school and became involved in the mysterious sexual scandal for which she was expelled in disgrace and anathematized by the whole town of Lurgan. By the age of seventeen, therefore, she had completely lost her place in the interwoven structure of family, school and community, and was destined instead to be moulded only by her own interests and her sense of separation from others.

The English soldiers garrisoned in the town offered the obvious escape route to a wider world; they adored her, but the more eagerly they fell at her feet the more she despised them for it. Nor did she like women any better, although they were less easily manipulated; her later comments about Henrietta Perreau show how deeply she resented female piety and hypocrisy. By the time she married Valentine Rudd, the main features of her attitude to life had been established: a low opinion of others, a defiant attitude to established morality and a flinty sense of self-reliance. Her painful adventures in London – the episodes of street vagrancy and prostitution, and the violence she suffered at her husband's hands – added the final ingredient: a brutalized, hardened heart.

There is no getting away from the fact that the fully fledged Caroline became a bad woman – or at least a dangerous one to know. Even so, it is impossible to feel entirely unsympathetic towards her. Above all, there is the fact of her exceptional and magnetic intelligence. The men who fell for her found this far more attractive than her physical beauty, which was only average. Boswell was one of these men, and a typical letter to the *Morning Post* from another admirer marvelled that 'her vivacity is always awake, her wit inexpressibly refined, her apprehension active, her memory astonishing'.[42] Caroline had *wit* in the full eighteenth-century sense of the term: insight, intellect, adaptability, cynicism and the ability to use language as a deadly weapon.

Yet she also had something else in her make-up: a bizarre recklessness, bordering on folly. Again and again, she would fling herself pointlessly into situations from which she then needed all her mental powers to escape. Even when earning good money, she rarely bothered to pay her rent – a minor oversight which got her into all sorts of difficulties. The games she played with Joseph Salvador were amusing, but risked wiping out her most valuable source of income. In particular, the scheme of serial forgery was one that no rational person could have expected to work for long. She simply chose to ignore the dangers and, as with many of her escapades, the forgeries were probably prompted as much by sheer restlessness as by cool calculation. The two sides of her fitted awkwardly together, creating a constant tension.

Caroline springs vividly to life in her writing. She was a person of incredible vitality and power, and one cannot read her words without feeling the force of her personality reaching across the centuries. Yet in the end she remains mystifying, in a way that Boswell, for example, does not. Admittedly Boswell left a greater physical volume of information about himself: his journals, notes and letters amount to an entire library full of self-revelation. The real difference between them, however, is that Boswell was devoted to uncovering the truth about himself, however unpalatable some of it may have been, whereas Caroline was every bit as set on concealing it. She told so many lies about herself that one cannot quite believe anything she says, even in moments of the greatest emotional poignancy. This atmosphere of mendacity affected all around her; almost everyone involved was either hiding something or simply did not know the truth. Honesty – Boswell's god – was no friend to Caroline. Her story, and that of the Perreaus, is the story of an enigma wrapped in a mystery and set at the centre of a labyrinth of false paths.

One word in particular resounds again and again in the sparse documents of the last years of Caroline's life: 'obscurity'. It meant not only poverty and retirement from the public eye, but also – especially for those who wished it upon her as a punishment – a kind of moral exile, shut away from the community of ordinary people. For the author of the *Authentic Anecdotes*, it summoned up a black and soulless future. 'A sense of religion and a future state, have never entered into her creed; she therefore leads a mere animal life, and like the beasts that perish, will insensibly sink into obscurity.'[43]

Caroline may have palmed the gold, but, with her uncertificated and apparently unlamented death in the 'obscure' Moorfields apartment, she also paid the smart. There remained only a final question mark, a trio of lost children with altered identities, and a fading myth.

Yet she also left other traces behind, in her own publications and in the vivid impression she made upon those who met her in her prime. And through these she rises again and emerges from her darkness, as smart, wicked and luminous as ever.

Notes and References

1 'Not a robber but a thief'

1   The account of the meeting, which Boswell eventually sent to his friend William Temple instead of his wife, is reprinted in *Boswell: The Ominous Years, 1774–1776*, pp. 355–61. The dialogue in this chapter is all taken from Boswell. He recorded most of the conversation exactly as he remembered it, but a few lines which he gave in indirect speech have been converted to the direct form.

2   William Temple, letter to Boswell, 7 May 1776. Pottle et al., eds, *Catalogue of the Papers of James Boswell at Yale University*, no. C2769, vol. 3, p. 954.

3   Boswell, 'The execution of Gibson and Payne', originally published in *The Publick Advertiser*, 26 April 1768; reprinted in Jefferson, D.W. ed., *Eighteenth-Century Prose 1700–1780*, Harmondsworth: Penguin, 1956, p. 48.

4   Journal, 28 November 1762, *Boswell's London Journal, 1762–1763*.

5   Journal, 15 March 1776, *Boswell: The Ominous Years, 1774–1776*.

6   Journal, 14 January 1763, *Boswell's London Journal, 1762–1763*.

7   Journal, 14 December 1762, ibid.

8   Journal, 30 March–1 April 1776, *Boswell: The Ominous Years, 1774–1776*.

9   Journal, 31 August 1774, *Boswell for the Defense, 1769–1774*.

10 Journal, 21 September 1774, ibid.

11 Journal, 22 March 1776, *Boswell: The Ominous Years, 1774–1776*.

12 Boswell, *Life of Johnson*, p. 696.

13 Ibid., p. 776.

14 Quoted in, D.B. Wyndham Lewis, *James Boswell: A Short Life*, 2nd edn, London: Eyre & Spottiswoode, 1952, p. 98.

15 Journal, 16 May 1776, *Boswell: The Ominous Years, 1774–1776*.

2   Adventures

1   See the family tree in *Boswell: The Ominous Years, 1774–1776*, chart IV, p. 377.

2   Ibid.

3   Rudd, 'The Case of Mrs Rudd, Related by Herself'.

4   Letter from John Stewart, reproduced in *The True Genuine Lives, and Trials &c*, p. 24 and other sources.

5   *Authentic Anecdotes of the Life and Transactions of Mrs Margaret Rudd*, vol. 1, p. 14.

6   *Genuine Memoirs of the Messieurs Perreau*, 2nd edn, pp. 126–7.

7   M. Dorothy George, *London Life in the Eighteenth Century*, Harmondsworth: Penguin, 1966, p. 109.

8   *Nocturnal Revels*, vol 1, p. 42.

9   This is confirmed by the army list for that year; he appears for the first time in the half-pay section of *A List of the General and Field-Officers, as They Rank in the Army . . .*, London: J. Millan, 1766, p. 209.

10 *Prudence Triumphing over Vanity and Dissipation*, p. 40.

11 *Authentic Anecdotes*, vol. 1, p. 47.

12 Ibid., p. 59.

13 *Daily Advertiser*, 8 November 1767. Quoted in ibid., pp. 61–2.

14 This story is from ibid., vol. 1, pp. 73–80.

15 After leaving Rudd, Caroline showed her deeply bruised arms to a potential landlady to prove that her story of fleeing a violent husband was true. Ibid., p. 104.

16 Rudd, 'Narrative', in her *Facts*, p. 18. The 'Narrative' was originally published in the *Morning Post*, 1–14 July.

17 Lord Deloraine. See *Authentic Anecdotes*, vol. 1, p. 107.

18 Ibid., p. 133.

19 Ibid., pp. 125–30. Christian Hart's *Letter . . . to Mrs Margaret Caroline Rudd* tells a similar story on p. 42, naming the landlady as a Mrs Hunt.

20 Ibid., vol. 2, p. 4.

21 See entry for Granby in the *Dictionary of National Biography*.

22 *Morning Post*, 3 October 1775.

23 Bleackley, *Some Distinguished Victims of the Scaffold*, p. 48.

24 *Genuine Memoirs of the Messieurs Perreau*, 2nd edn, p. 129.

25 *Prudence Triumphing over Vanity and Dissipation*, p. 46.

26 *Genuine Memoirs of the Messieurs Perreau*, 2nd edn, p. 130.

27 *Town and Country Magazine*, 1775, p. 481.

28 *Authentic Anecdotes*, vol. 2, p. 60. The anecdotes in the following paragraph come from the same source.

29 This story is told in ibid., p. 61, *Genuine Memoirs of the Messieurs Perreau*, 2nd edn, p. 133 and *Eccentric Biography*, pp. 287–8.

3   The Macaroni

1 The twins' baptism and that of five of their siblings is listed in the 'Register of the parish of St. Thomas, Middle Island, St. Christopher, 1729–1823', transcribed by John Bromley, published as a supplement to *Caribbeana*, vol. 4, 1915–16.

2 The marriage (1688) and the two daughters named Esther (baptised 1691 and 1696 respectively) are listed in *The Registers of the French Church, Threadneedle Street, London*, ed. T.C. Colyer-Ferguson, Aberdeen: Huguenot Society of London, 1906. There is a slight degree of conjecture in concluding that these are also the parents of Daniel and Susannah, but it seems highly likely. The dates match; the names run consistently through the family; Susannah mentions having one sister as well as a brother in her will; and the

Genuine Memoirs of the Messieurs Perreau states that on the twins' grandfather's death the family contained two girls and a boy.

3   *Genuine Memoirs of the Messieurs Perreau*, 2nd edn, p. 12.

4   *Genuine Memoirs* says that there were twenty-two children, which is unsubstantiated by the St Kitts registers. However, there do seem to have been more children than the seven listed in the registers, two of whom died young: the first daughter, Elizabeth, in infancy and a boy named Sam in a shipwreck (this is according to the *Genuine Memoirs*; but there was indeed a Samuel in the baptism register). The wills of two other members of the family, Susannah Perreau and Sarah Blomer (née Perreau), between them reveal a minimum of eight Perreau siblings surviving in the 1760s. For details of the wills, see Henry Wagner's transcript of Huguenot wills in the Huguenot Society Library (for which I am indebted to the very kind help of Stephen Massil, the Society's librarian), and the Court of Chancery records for the case of Jackson v. Perreau in the Public Record Office.

5   *Genuine Memoirs of the Messieurs Perreau*, 2nd edn, pp. 55–76.

6   Ibid., p. 44.

7   Ibid., p. 47.

8   *Prudence Triumphing over Vanity and Dissipation*, p. 10.

9   *Genuine Memoirs* mention a 'Mr. Jollie'; the names of Daniel and a Martin Jollie appear together in a lawsuit following Daniel's return to England in 1765. See records of the case in the Court of Exchequer's archives at the Public Record Office.

10 *Genuine Memoirs of the Messieurs Perreau*, 2nd edn, p. 117.

11 George Stevens, *Adventures of a Speculist*, London: S. Bladon, 1788, pp. 54–63.

12 *The Stocks; or, High Change in Change Alley*, London: [1760?].

13 *Town and Country Magazine*, April 1775, pp. 121–3.

14 See in particular Rudd, *Mrs. M.C. Rudd's Genuine Letter to Lord Weymouth*, pp. 13, 23–4, and a letter in the *Morning Post* signed 'A.B.', 3 May 1775, asserting that Robert had enticed Daniel into the gambling life rather than the other way round.

15 Perreau, *Mr Daniel Perreau's Narrative of His Unhappy Case*, p. 1, and *Authentic Anecdotes*, vol. 2, p. 36.

16 *Genuine Memoirs of the Messieurs Perreau*, 2nd edn. p. 121–39.

17 Rudd, 'Narrative', in her *Facts*, p. 20.

18 Ibid., p. 9.

19 Ibid., pp. 8–9.

20 *The True Genuine Lives, and Trials &c*, p. 18.

21 Perreau, *Mr. Daniel Perreau's Narrative of His Unhappy Case*, p. 1.

22 *Authentic Anecdotes*, vol. 2, pp. 32–3.

23 A letter supposedly written to a Mr Wrightson; quoted in *Authentic Anecdotes*, vol. 2, pp. 33–4.

24 From Boswell's account of his meeting with Caroline, *Boswell: The Ominous Years, 1774–1776*, p. 357.

25 *Gentleman's Magazine*, 1809, p. 581.

26 *Authentic Anecdotes*, vol. 2, p. 56, and *Town and Country Magazine*, 1775, p. 481.

27 Perreau, *Mr. Daniel Perreau's Narrative of His Unhappy Case*, p. 21.

28 Hart, *A letter from Mrs. Christian Hart to Mrs. Margaret Caroline Rudd*.

29 Ibid., p. 45. Subsequent quotations come from the same source, pp. 45–67.

30 'The Narrative of Mrs Rudd Written by Herself', *Morning Post*, 1 July 1775.

4 Danger

1 *Annual Register*, 1775, p. 222.

2 See Paul Baines, *The House of Forgery in Eighteenth-Century Britain*, Aldershot: Ashgate, 1999, p. 10, and John Howard, *The State of the Prisons in England and Wales*, 3rd edn, Warrington: W. Eyres, 1784, pp. 382–3.

3 *Prudence Triumphing over Vanity and Dissipation*, p. 178.

4 The financial details in this chapter are principally taken from two sources: *Prudence Triumphing over Vanity and Dissipation* and *Authentic Anecdotes of the Life and Transactions of Mrs. Margaret Rudd*. Other contemporary sources also give

useful, but slightly less detailed, accounts of the various forgeries.

5 *Prudence Triumphing over Vanity and Dissipation*, p. 103.

6 *The Gazetteer and New Daily Advertiser*, 22 July 1775. The plain letter 'l.' has been changed to a modern pound sign for ease of reading.

7 *The Life, Trials and Dying Words . . .*, p. 3.

8 Stephen Roe, *The Ordinary of Newgate's Account of . . . John Ayliffe*, 1759, pp. 19–20, quoted in Paul Baines, *The House of Forgery in Eighteenth-Century Britain*.

9 See entries for both Frankland and Pye in the *Dictionary of National Biography*.

10 *Prudence Triumphing over Vanity and Dissipation*, pp. 212–13.

11 Ibid., p. 115.

12 'The Narrative of Mrs. Rudd Written by Herself', *Morning Post*, 1 July 1775.

13 This and subsequent dialogue comes from the testimony of Robert and Henry Drummond at Robert Perreau's trial, as transcribed in *The Trials of Robert and Daniel Perreau's*.

14 Bleackley, *Some Distinguished Victims of the Scaffold*, p. 68.

15 *Morning Post*, 10 January 1776.

16 Rudd, 'Narrative', in her *Facts*, p. 61.

17 *Morning Post*, 21 March 1775.

18 *Prudence Triumphing over Vanity and Dissipation*, p. 65.

5 Suffering Merit

1 *The True Genuine Lives, and Trials &c*, p. 12.

2 *Morning Post*, 16 March 1775. The quotes which follow come from the same source.

3 *Daily Advertiser*, 17 March 1775.

4 *Morning Post*, 18 March 1775.

5 Rudd, *Facts*, pp. 42ff. The quotes which follow come from the same source.

6 *Morning Post*, 18 March 1775.

7 *Daily Advertiser*, 20 March 1775.

8 Hickey, *Memoirs*, vol. 1, p. 335.

9 Daniel's account was originally intended to be used as a

defence statement in his trial. It was never read out in court, but he worked it up into a longer version and published it as *Mr. Daniel Perreau's Narrative of His Unhappy Case.*

10 *Prudence Triumphing over Vanity and Dissipation*, p. 68.

11 Ibid., p. 112.

12 Ibid., pp. 227–30.

13 Letter from Walpole to Rev. William Mason, 14 April 1775. *The Letters of Horace Walpole*, vol. 6, p. 202.

14 *Genuine Memoirs of the Messieurs Perreau*, p. 145.

15 Letter from M.C. Rudd, *Morning Post*, 10 April 1775.

16 Ibid.

17 'The Case of Mrs. Rudd Related by Herself', *Morning Post*, 27 March 1775.

18 *Morning Post*, 29 March 1775.

19 Ibid., 4 April 1775.

20 The letter is reproduced in the *Authentic Anecdotes*.

21 Letter from M.C. Rudd, *Morning Post*, 10 April 1775.

22 Letter from M.C. Rudd, ibid., 18 August 1775.

23 M.C. Rudd's letter to Sukey Perreau, *Authentic Anecdotes*.

24 Letter from 'S.L.', *Morning Post*, 30 March 1775.

25 Letter from John Stewart, *Morning Post*, 13 April 1775.

26 Perreau, *Mr. Daniel Perreau's Narrative of His Unhappy Case*, pp. 93–4.

27 Letter from 'X.Y.', *Morning Post*, 6 May 1775.

28 *Genuine Memoirs*, pp. 201–5.

29 Letter from M.C. Rudd, *Morning Post*, 10 April 1775.

30 Hickey, *Memoirs*, vol. 1, p. 336.

31 *Morning Post*, 22 May 1775.

32 Rudd, 'Narrative', in *Facts*, p. 29.

6   The Perreaus on Trial

1 *Morning Post*, 2 June 1775.

2 Rudd, *Mrs M.C. Rudd's Genuine Letter to Lord Weymouth*, pp. 31–3.

3 The account of the trials in this chapter is taken primarily from the transcriptions in the Old Bailey sessions papers, *The Whole Proceedings on the King's Commission of the Peace*

... *1–6 June 1775*, and in *The Trials of Robert and Daniel Perreau's*.

4 *Annual Register*, vol. 18. 1775, p. 224.

5 Cumberland, *Memoirs*, p. 295. The subject of Robert Perreau's speech and its authorship is discussed in W.T. Lowndes, *The Bibliographer's Manual of English Literature*, new edn, London: G. Bell, 1871, vol. 3, p. 1833, and by Horace Bleackley in *Notes and Queries*, 10th series, IV, 1903, p. 186.

6 Daniel's trial is reported in the same sources as Robert's. In addition, some of the following description is taken from the *Annual Register*, vol. 18, 1775, p. 226.

7 Perreau, *Mr. Daniel Perreau's Narrative of His Unhappy Case*, p. iii.

8 *London Magazine*, 1775, p. 307.

9 Letter signed 'Neitherside', *Morning Post*, 25 September 1775.

10 *Morning Post*, 6 July 1775.

11 Letter from 'R.S.', *The Gazetteer*, 1 July 1775.

12 'Marcellus', *A Letter to the Right Hon. Earl of Suffolk in Which the Innocence of Robert Perreau Is Demonstrated*, p. 26.

13 *London Magazine*, 1775, p. 429.

14 *Mrs. Marg. Car. Rudd's Case Considered, Respecting Robert Perreau*, p. i.

15 Ibid., p. 27–8.

16 Letter from 'Nobody', *Morning Post*, 10 June 1775.

17 *Mrs. Marg. Car. Rudd's Case Considered*, p. 5.

7 'Her present dreadful situation and misfortune'

1 Letter from M.C. Rudd, *Morning Post*, 12 June 1775.

2 Hart, *A Letter from Mrs. Christian Hart*, pp. 8–9.

3 Papendiek, *Court and Private Life in the Time of Queen Charlotte*, vol. 1, p. 125.

4 Walpole, letter to Sir Horace Mann, 17 December 1775, in *Letters*, vol. 9, p. 298.

5 Letter from M.C. Rudd, *Morning Post*, 14 July 1775.

6 Marcellus, 'Advertisement to the Reader', *A Letter to the Right Hon. Earl of Suffolk*.

7   Ibid., p. 66.
8   Letter from M.C. Rudd, *Morning Post*, 12 June 1775.
9   Preface to M.C. Rudd's 'Narrative', in her *Facts*, p. vii.
10 Letter from M.C. Rudd, *Morning Post*, 12 June 1775.
11 Letter from 'Achates', ibid., 4 July 1775.
12 Ibid., 20 June 1775.
13 *Gazetteer*, 4 July 1775. The following account of this hearing is taken from reports in the *Gazetteer* and the *Morning Post*.
14 Ibid.
15 *Morning Post*, 4 July 1775.
16 Ibid., 7 July 1775.
17 Beattie, *Crime and the Courts in England, 1660–1800*, p. 368.
18 *Morning Post*, 7 July 1775.
19 Ibid., 22 July 1775.
20 Ibid., 30 August 1775.
21 This and the rest of the account of this hearing is from the *Gazetteer*, 17 July 1775.
22 Letter from 'A Student', *Morning Post*, 26 July 1775.
23 *Gentleman's Magazine*, 1775, p. 349.
24 Letter from Hannah Dalboux, *Morning Post*, 14 August 1775.
25 Letter from M.C. Rudd, ibid., 18 August 1775.
26 Boswell's account of their first meeting, April 1776.
27 Letter from J. Cummyng, *Morning Post*, 27 October 1775.
28 *She Is and She Is Not*, p. 2.
29 Ibid., p. 106.
30 The account of this hearing is taken from the report in the *Morning Post*, 18 September 1775.
31 Letters from 'Neitherside', 25 September, and from 'Viator', 27 September, both in ibid.
32 Letter from 'Humanity', ibid., 29 September 1775.
33 Letter from 'Viator', ibid., 30 September 1775.
34 Letter from 'W.D.', ibid., 13 September 1775.
35 Ibid., 11 November 1775.
36 *Gentleman's Magazine*, September 1775, p. 443.
37 Ibid., October 1775, p. 492.
38 *Morning Post*, 1 January 1776.
39 Ibid., 19 September 1775.
40 Ibid., 21 September 1775.

8 Trial

1 Villette, *The Annals of Newgate*, vol. 4, p. 417.
2 Angelo, *Reminiscences*, vol. 1, p. 470.
3 Bleackley, *Trial of Henry Fauntleroy*, p. 181.
4 Villette, *The Annals of Newgate*, p. 421. Walpole, letter to Sir Horace Mann, 17 December 1775, *Letters*, vol. 9, p. 298.
5 *The Whole Trials, at Large, of Robert Perreau, Daniel Perreau, and Margaret Carolina Rudd*, [sic] *Rudd* p. 47. The account of Caroline's trial in this chapter is taken from this source and from the Old Bailey sessions papers, *The Whole Proceedings on the King's Commission . . . 6–11 December 1775*.
6 The summing up comes from the *Town and Country Magazine*, 1775, p. 632.
7 Angelo, *Reminiscences*, vol. 1, p. 470.
8 Walpole, letter to Sir Horace Mann, 17 December 1775, *Letters*, vol. 9, p. 298.
9 *Annual Register*, 1775, vol. 18, p. 231. The following quotes are from the same source.

9 Unhappy Fate

1 *Prudence Triumphing over Vanity and Dissipation*, p. 341.
2 Walpole, letter to Sir Horace Mann, 17 December 1775, *Letters*, vol. 9, p. 298.
3 Trusler, *Memoirs*, p. 167.
4 Letter from 'Amator Justitiae', *Morning Post*, 9 June 1775.
5 Boswell's description of his first meeting with Caroline, 22 April 1776, *Boswell: The Ominous Years, 1774–1776*, p. 356.
6 Hart, *A Letter from Mrs. Christian Hart*, p. 6.
7 Ibid., p. 26.
8 Ibid., p. 19.
9 Ibid., pp. 35–9, for this and the following quotes from Mrs Hart's relation of the story.
10 Walpole, letter to Sir Horace Mann, 17 December 1775, *Letters*, vol. 9, p. 298.
11 *Prudence Triumphing over Vanity and Dissipation*, pp. 7–8.
12 Ibid., p. 148.
13 Knapp and Baldwin, *The Newgate Calendar*, vol. 3, p. 16.
14 *Morning Post*, 6 January 1776.

15 *Gentleman's Magazine*, 1776, p. 44.

16 Ibid., p. 23.

17 Ibid., p. 44.

18 Papendiek, *Court and Private Life in the Time of Queen Charlotte*, vol. 1, p. 124.

19 *London Magazine*, 1776, p. 53.

20 Letter from 'A.E.', *Morning Post*, 12 January 1776.

21 *Gentleman's Magazine*, 1776, p. 22.

22 *Morning Post*, 12 January 1776.

23 Letter from D. Perreau, *Morning Post*, 12 January 1776. See also *Prudence Triumphing over Vanity and Dissipation*, pp. 347–8.

24 *Prudence Triumphing over Vanity and Dissipation*, p. 351.

25 Rudd, *Mrs. M.C. Rudd's Genuine Letter to Lord Weymouth*, pp. 5–11. Also reprinted in *Prudence Triumphing over Vanity and Dissipation*, pp. 340–5.

26 Villette, *Annals of Newgate*, vol. 4, p. 412.

27 *Morning Post*, 18 January 1776.

28 Ibid.

29 Hart, *A Letter from Mrs. Christian Hart*, p. 40.

30 *Annual Register*, vol. 18, 1775, p. 232.

31 *Morning Post*, 19 January 1776.

32 *London Magazine*, 1776, p. 54.

33 *Morning Post*, 18 January 1776.

34 *Town and Country Magazine*, 1776, p. 53.

35 *Gentleman's Magazine*, 1776, p. 44.

36 *Morning Post*, 18 January 1776.

37 This and most of the remainder of the description of the execution is from the *Annual Register*, vol. 18, 1775, pp. 232–3.

38 Knapp and Baldwin, *The Newgate Calendar*, vol. 3, p. 14.

39 *Morning Post*, 18 January 1776.

40 This and most of the remainder of the description of the funeral is from the *Morning Post*, 24 January 1776.

41 Ibid., 26 January 1776.

42 See Bleackley in *Notes and Queries*, 10 s., VIII, p. 361.

43 *Gentleman's Magazine*, 1776, p. 45.

44 *London Magazine*, 1775, p. 356.

45 *Morning Post*, 19 January 1776.

46 *Nocturnal Revels*, vol. 1, p. 132.

47 *Morning Post*, 24 January 1776.

48 Ibid., 19 January 1776, also mentioned in *The London Tragedy*.

49 Hickey, *Memoirs*, vol. 4, pp. 324, 449.

10 To End the Sum

1 *Mrs Marg. Car. Rudd's Case Considered.*

2 Hannah More, letter to her family, 1776, in *Memoirs of the Life and Correspondence of Hannah More*, ed. W. Roberts, 3rd edn, 1835, vol. 1, p. 82.

3 *Morning Post*, 25 December 1775.

4 *Prudence Triumphing over Vanity and Dissipation*, p. 339.

5 T. Frost, *The Life of Thomas Lord Lyttelton*, London: Tinsley, 1876, p. v. See also Lyttelton's entry in the *Dictionary of National Biography*.

6 Ibid., p. 250.

7 Boswell, journal, 21 April 1778, *Boswell in Extremes, 1776–1778.*

8 Lydia Melford's description in Tobias Smollett's *Humphry Clinker.*

9 Rudd, *Mrs Stewart's Case*, pp. 6–7.

10 Boswell, journal, 14 August 1785, *Boswell: The Applause of the Jury, 1782–1785.*

11 Ibid., journal, 28 August 1785.

12 Letter from Temple to Boswell, 31 August 1785. Quoted in Pottle et al., eds, *Catalogue of the Papers of James Boswell at Yale University*, no. C2835, vol. 3, p. 968.

13 Letter from Temple to Boswell, 15 July 1786, ibid., no. C2841, vol. 3, p. 970.

14 Journal, 10 September 1785, *Boswell: The Applause of the Jury, 1782–1785.*

15 Journal, 24 November 1785, *Boswell: The English Experiment, 1785–1789.*

16 Journal, 4 February 1786, ibid.

17 M258 in Pottle et al., eds, *Catalogue of the Papers of James Boswell at Yale University*: a fragmentary page of text.

Quoted in Brady, *James Boswell: The Later Years, 1769–1795*, p. 319.

18 Ibid.

19 Pottle et al., eds, *Catalogue of the Papers of James Boswell at Yale University*, no. M343, vol. 1, p. 131.

20 Journal, 24 February 1786, *Boswell: The English Experiment, 1785–1789*.

21 Brady, *James Boswell: The Later Years, 1769–1789*, p. 295.

22 Journal, 7 March 1786, *Boswell: The English Experiment, 1785–1789*.

23 Journal, 1 April 1786, ibid.

24 Journal, 14 April 1786, ibid.

25 Journal, 29 May 1786, ibid.

26 Turnbull, 'Criminal Biographer: Boswell and Margaret Caroline Rudd', *Studies in English Literature*, vol. 26, 1986, p. 521.

27 Letter from Boswell to his wife, 9 November 1788, *Boswell: The English Experiment, 1785–1789*.

28 Letter from Boswell to his wife, 9 March 1789, ibid.

29 Letter from 'an anonymous correspondent' to Boswell, 10 December 1792, *The Correspondence and Other Papers of James Boswell Relating to the Making of the Life of Johnson*, ed. Marshall Waingrow, New York and Toronto: McGraw-Hill, 1969, vol. 2. pp. 504–8. Quoted by Turnbull in 'Criminal Biographer', p. 511.

30 *Gentleman's Magazine*, 1779, p. 327.

31 *Morning Post*, 29 November 1786. See Bleackley in *Notes and Queries*, s. 8, VIII, 9 November 1907, p. 361.

32 Rudd, *Mrs Stewart's Case*, 1788, pp. 12–13.

33 Ibid., p. 4.

34 *Morning Post*, 9 January 1789.

35 Ibid., 12 January 1789.

36 Rudd, 'Appendix' (1789) to *Mrs Stewart's Case*.

37 *The Carlton Magazine*, vol. 3, p. 569, January 1794. See Bleackley in *Notes and Queries*, 10 s, IX, 9 February 1908, p. 114.

38 *Gentleman's Magazine*, 1800, pt 1, p. 188.

39 Ibid., p. 483.

40 See Bleackley in *Notes and Queries*, s. 8, VIII, 9 November 1907, p. 361.
41 *The Times*, 4 February 1797. The notice also appeared in the *True Briton*, 4 February 1797.
42 Letter to *Morning Post*, 21 September 1775.
43 *Authentic Anecdotes of the Life and Transactions of Mrs. Margaret Rudd*, vol. I, p. 143.

Select Bibliography

1 Newspapers and Journals

Daily newspapers gave Margaret Caroline Rudd and the Perreaus considerable coverage between March 1775 and January 1776 and are a key source, particularly the *Morning Post and Daily Advertiser* and the *Gazetteer*. Others that paid close attention to the story included the *Public Advertiser*, the *Daily Advertiser*, the *Morning Chronicle*, the *London Chronicle* and the *Lloyd's Evening Post*.

The *Morning Post* serialized Caroline's 'Case' from 27 March to 10 April 1775 and the 'Narrative of Mrs Rudd Written by Herself' from 1 to 14 July 1775. The *London Chronicle* also published the 'Case' from 28/30 March to 4/6 April and part of the 'Narrative' on 1/4 July.

Caroline's death was reported in *The Times* and the *True Briton* on 4 February 1797.

The *Gentleman's Magazine* published accounts of the arrests, trials and executions in 1775–6, as well as other miscellaneous notes relating to the case. It also reported Caroline's death twice, once in 1779 and once in 1800.

The *London Magazine*, the *Town and Country Magazine*, the *Annual Register* and the *Westminster Magazine* all gave detailed accounts of the arrests, trials and executions in 1775 and 1776.

Discussion of the case by Horace Bleackley and others appeared in several issues of the journal *Notes and Queries* 8 s, XI, 1897, pp. 148, 232–3, 279; 10 s, IV, 1903, p. 186; 10 s, VIII, 1907, p. 361; 10 s, IX, 1908, p. 114.

2 Books and Pamphlets

Angelo, Henry, *Reminiscences of Henry Angelo*, London: H. Colborn, 1828, vol. 1, pp. 468–71.

An authentic account of the particulars which appeared on the trials of Robert and Dan. Perreau, on Thursday 2d, and Friday 3d instant, London: E T Carpenter [etc.], [1775].

Authentic Anecdotes of the Life and Transactions of Mrs Margaret Rudd . . . Addressed in a Series of Letters to the Now (by a Late Act of Parliament) Mrs Mary Lovell, 2 vols, London: J. Bew, 1776.

   The woman to whom it is addressed, Mary Lovell, is described as a long-term friend and accomplice of Caroline's in 'prostitution, forgery and intrigue'.

Bailey, John, *The Trial at Large of Mrs Margaret Caroline Rudd, at the Old Bailey, on Friday, December the 8th, 1775 . . . with the Particulars of Her First Commitment to Tothill-Fields-Bridewell, on the Eleventh of June Last*, London: [T. Bell], 1775,

   The author was Caroline's lawyer.

Beattie, J.M., *Crime and the Courts in England, 1660–1800*, Oxford: Clarendon Press, 1986, p. 368.

Bleackley, Horace, *Some Distinguished Victims of the Scaffold*, London: Kegan, Paul, Trench, Trübner, 1905, pp. 39–73.

Bleackley, Horace, *Trial of Henry Fauntleroy and Other Famous Trials for Forgery*, Edinburgh and London: W. Hodge, 1924, pp. 173–84.

Boswell, James (*Journal*), published as part of the *Yale Editions of the Private Papers of James Boswell*. The following volumes are referred to in the text:

Boswell's London Journal, 1762–1763, ed. F.A. Pottle, New York: McGraw-Hill, 1950.

Boswell for the defense, 1769–1774 ed. W.K. Wimsatt and F.A. Pottle, New York: McGraw-Hill, 1959.

Boswell: The Ominous Years, 1774–1776, ed. C. Ryskamp and F.A. Pottle, New York: McGraw-Hill, 1963.

Boswell in Extremes, 1776–1778 ed. C. McC. Weis and F.A. Pottle, New York: McGraw-Hill, 1973.

James Boswell: The Applause of the Jury, 1782–1785, ed. I.S. Lustig and F.A. Pottle, New York: McGraw-Hill, 1981.

Boswell: The English Experiment, 1785–1789, ed. I.S. Lustig and F.A. Pottle, New York: McGraw-Hill, 1986.

Boswell, James, *Letters of James Boswell to the Rev. W.J. Temple*, ed. T. Seccombe, London: Sidgwick & Jackson, 1908, pp. 182–6; 189; 191.

Boswell, James, *The Life of Johnson*, ed. R.W. Chapman, rev. edn, Oxford: Oxford University Press, 1970; paperback edn, 1980, pp. 696, 776, 977.

Brady, Frank, *James Boswell: The Later Years, 1769–1795*, New York: McGraw-Hill, 1984.

The Case of Margaret Caroline Rudd, from Her First Commitment to Newgate, on Thursday the 1st of June Last, to Her Final Acquittal at the Old Bailey, Friday, December 8, 1775. By a Barrister at Law, London: printed for J. Bew, 1775.

Combe, William, *The Diabo-Lady, or, a Match in Hell: a Poem Dedicated to the Worst Woman in Her Majesty's Dominions*, London: Fielding & Walker, 1777, pp. 3–4.

The Criminal Recorder, or, Biographical Sketches of Notorious Public Characters . . . by a Student of the Inner Temple, London: J. Cundee, 1804–9, vol. 2, pp. 226–43.

Cumberland, Richard, *Memoirs of Richard Cumberland, Written by Himself*, London: Lackington, Allen, 1806, p. 295.

Dictionary of National Biography, ed. L. Stephen and S. Lee, London: Smith, Elder, 1908–9.

Eccentric Biography, or, Memoirs of Remarkable Female Characters, Ancient and Modern, Worcester: I. Thomas, 1804, pp. 285–9.

    Mostly concerns Caroline's relationship with Joseph Salvador, and calls her 'Mary Catharine Rudd'.

An Explicit Account of the Lives and Trials of the Twin Brothers, Messieurs Daniel and Robert Perreau, now under Sentence of Death . . . and the Remarkable Case of Mrs Rudd (Written by Herself); Likewise the Whole Proceedings on the Case of Mrs Rudd, at the Old Bailey . . . on Saturday, September 16th, 1775 [London: 1775].

The Female Forgery; or, Fatal Effects of Unlawful Love: Being a Minute and Circumstantial Account of the Late Extraordinary Forgery, London: sold by J. Bew, 1775.

Forgery Unmasked, or, Genuine Memoirs of the Two Unfortunate Brothers, Rob. and Daniel Perreau, and Mrs. Rudd, London: A. Grant [1776?].

  Includes Caroline's 'Case'.

Genuine Memoirs of the Messieurs Perreau. By a Gentleman Very Intimate with the Unfortunate Families, London: G. Allen [1775?]; 2nd edn, London: G. Kearsley, 1775.

  The main text of the memoirs is signed 'Theodosia'; the 'Postscript' is signed 'Horatio'. A detailed if unreliable source on the early lives of Caroline and the Perreau brothers.

Gurney, T., *An Account of the Arguments of Counsel . . . Whether Mrs. C. Rudd Ought to Be Tried*, London: M. Gurney, 1775.

Hart, Christian, *A Letter from Mrs. Christian Hart, to Mrs. Margaret Caroline Rudd, Elucidating Several Circumstances Which Did Not Appear on the Trial: Refuting Particular Falsities and Mal-aspersions Asserted by that Notified Lady, and Relating a Circumstantial Account of Her Transactions during the time Mrs. Hart lived servant with her*, London: J. Williams, 1776.

Hickey, William, *Memoirs of William Hickey*, ed. A. Spencer, London: Hurst & Blackett, 1913–25, vol. 1, pp. 333–7; vol. 4, pp. 324, 449.

Knapp, Andrew and Baldwin, William, *The Newgate Calendar*, London: J. Robins, 1824–8, vol. 3, pp. 5–16.

Langbein, John H., *Shaping the Eighteenth-Century Criminal Trial*, Chicago: University of Chicago Press, 1983, pp. 91–6.

Law Observations Relating to the Case of Mrs Rudd; in the Course of Which, the Legality of Her Admission by the Magistrates of Bow-Street, as an Evidence on the Part of the Crown Will Be Clearly Demonstrated. By a Gentleman of the Inner Temple, London: T. Bell [1776?].

The Life, Trials and Dying Words of the Two Unfortunate Twin Brothers, Robert and Daniel Perreau, Who Was Executed on Wednesday, January 17th, at Tyburn; . . . To Which Is Added, the Genuine Life, and Trial of Mrs. Marg. Caroline Rudd,

Whose Trial Lasted Near 12 Hours ... When She Was Honourably Acquitted, London: F. Foresight, [1776].

Includes Caroline's 'Case'.

The London Tragedy, or, the Widow and Her Fatherless Children in Distress [London]: printed and sold at no. 30, King-Street, West Smithfield [1776].

Malefactor's Register; or, the Newgate and Tyburn Calendar, London: A. Hogg, 1779, vol. 5, pp. 161–85.

Marcellus [pseud.], *A Letter to the Right Hon. Earl of Suffolk ... in Which the Innocence of Robert Perreau is Demonstrated*, London: T. Hookham, 1775.

Mrs. Marg. Car. Rudd's Case Considered, Respecting Robert Perreau: in an Address to Henry Drummond, Esq. and the Gentlemen of the Jury Who Tried Mr. R. Perreau: with a Comparative View of His Trial and His Last Solemn Declaration, London: J. Wilkie, 1776.

A reply to Marcellus's *Letter to the ... Earl of Suffolk*.

Nocturnal Revels; or, the History of King's-place, and Other Modern Nunneries. By a Monk of the Order of St. Francis, 2nd edn, London: M. Goadby, 1779, vol. 1, p. 132.

Observations on the Trial of Mr Robt. Perreau. With Mr. Perreau's Defence, as Spoken, on His Trial, in Which Many Unaccounted-for Omissions in the Sessions-Paper are Supplied, from a Copy Sent to the Author by Mrs. R. Perreau, an Address to the Jury on Mr. R. Perreau's Trial, and Such Remarks on Mrs. Rudd's Narrative as Tend to Confirm the Justness of These Observations, London: S. Bladon, 1775.

Papendiek, C.L.H. *Court and Private Life in the Time of Queen Charlotte, Being the Journal of Mrs Papendiek*, ed. Mrs Vernon Delves Broughton, London: R. Bentley, 1887, vol. 1, pp. 124–5.

A Particular Account of the Dreadful and Shocking Apparitions of the Two Unfortunate Perreaus, Accompanied with the Wife of Mr. Robert Perreau, Who All Appeared Like Flame of Fire in Her Bedchamber [London, 1776].

Pelham, Camden (pseud.), *The Chronicles of Crime, or, The New Newgate Calendar*, London: T. Tegg, 1841, vol. 1, pp. 244–50.

Perreau, Daniel, *Mr Daniel Perreau's Narrative of His Unhappy Case*, London: T. Evans, 1775.

Perreau, Daniel, *A Solemn Declaration of Mr. Daniel Perreau,*

Addressed to the Public. Written by Himself, and Delivered to a Friend in the Cells of Newgate, on Sunday, Jan. 14, 1776, Published at His Dying Request, London: T. Evans, 1776.

Pottle, Frederick A., editorial note introducing Boswell's account of his first meeting with Caroline, in *Boswell: The Ominous Years, 1774–1776*, pp. 352–5 (see above).

Pottle, Marion S., Abbot, Claude Colleer and Pottle, Frederick A., *Catalogue of the Papers of James Boswell at Yale University*, Edinburgh: Edinburgh University Press, 1993.

Prudence Triumphing over Vanity and Dissipation, or the History of the Life, Character and Conduct . . . of Mr. Robert and Mr. Daniel Perreau, and Mrs. Rudd. The Whole Compiled from Authentic Records, Communicated to the Editor, by a Person Well Known in the Literary World, London: printed for the author, 1776.

    Apparently compiled from alternative versions of the same events.

Radzinowicz, L., *A History of English Criminal Law and Its Administration from 1750*, London: Stevens, 1948–68, vol. 1, pp. 462–3n.

Register of the Parish of St. Thomas, Middle Island, St. Christopher, 1729–1823. Transcribed in St. Kitts by John Bromley, published as supplement to *Caribbeana*, ed. Vere Langford Oliver, vol. 4, 1915–16.

Rhodes, H.T.F., *Clues and Crime*, London: John Murray, 1933, pp. 161–5.

    Advances the interesting but ultimately unconvincing theory that the alleged forgery might have been a plot by the Adairs.

Rudd, Margaret Caroline, 'The Case of Mrs Rudd Related by Herself', originally published in the *Morning Post* (27 March–10 April 1775) and in the *London Chronicle* (28/30 March–4/6 April 1775). Reprinted in *An Explicit Account, Forgery Unmasked*, M.C. Rudd's *Facts*, and *The True Genuine Lives . . . of the Two Unfortunate Brothers*.

Rudd, Margaret Caroline, *Facts, or, a Plain and Explicit Narrative of the Case of Mrs. Rudd, Published from Her Own Manuscript, and by Her Authority in Which, the Particular Transactions of Messrs. Perreaus; the Public and Private Conversations and Consultations of Mr. H— D—; the Impartial View of the*

Character of Colonel —; the Answer to Mr. Daniel Perreau's Defence; and the Circumstantial Account of the Proceedings from the Time of Committment till this Present Hour Will be Faithfully Related; and the Invidious and Sillogistical Arguments of a Hireling Refuted, London: T. Bell, [1775].

Includes her 'Case' and 'Narrative'.

Rudd, Margaret Caroline, *Mrs. M. C. Rudd's Genuine Letter to Lord Weymouth, with Several Authentic Anecdotes of the Late Messrs. Perreaus, Together with an Explanation of the Conduct of a Certain Great City Patriot*, London: G. Kearsly, 1776.

The 'patriot' is John Wilkes.

Rudd, Margaret Caroline, *Mrs Stewart's Case, Written by Herself*, London: J. Kerby; Scatcherd & Whitaker, 1788. Reissued with an appendix, pp. [29]–38, dated February 1789.

Rudd, Margaret Caroline, 'Narrative of Mrs Rudd Written by Herself'; originally published in the *Morning Post*, 1–14 July 1775; reprinted in her *Facts*.

Select Criminal Trials at Justice-Hall in the Old Bailey, Edinburgh: P. Hill; London: Longman & Rees, 1803. Appendix, pp. 1–11.

Discusses the legal implications of Caroline's trial.

She Is and She Is Not: a Fragment of the True History of Miss C. de Grosberg, Alias Mrs. Potter, &c. &c. . . . Dedicated to Mrs. M–t C–e R–dd, London: J. Bew, 1776.

An attempt to identify Caroline with Caroline de Grosberg.

The Trial of Margaret Caroline Rudd for Forging a Bond for 3500 l. . . . Taken in Shorthand by Joseph Gurney, and Revised by John Glynn [London?, 1776].

The Trials of Robert and Daniel Perreau's, on the King's Commission of the Peace, Oyer and Terminer and Gaol-Delivery, Held for the City of London, &c. Before the Right Hon. John Wilkes [etc.], London: T. Bell, 1775.

The True Genuine Lives, and Trials &c. of the Two Unfortunate Brothers, R. and D. Perreau . . . Also an Authentic Narrative of Mrs Rudd, London: J. Miller, 1775?

Includes Caroline's 'Case'.

Trusler, John, *Memoirs of the Life of the Rev. Dr. Trusler*, Bath: J. Browne, 1806, pp. 167–8.

Turnbull, Gordon, 'Criminal Biographer: Boswell and Margaret

Caroline Rudd', *Studies in English Literature*, vol. 26, 1986, pp. 511–35.

Villette, John et al., *The Annals of Newgate, or, Malefactors Register. Containing a Particular and Circumstantial Account of the Lives, Transactions, and Trials of the Most Notorious Malefactors ... from the Commitment of the Celebrated John Sheppard, to the Acquittal of the Equally Celebrated Margaret Caroline Rudd*, London: J. Wenman, 1776, vol. 4, pp. 399–421.
The Ordinary of Newgate's account.

Villette, John, *A Genuine Account of the Behaviour and Dying-Words of Daniel Perreau and Robert Perreau, Who Were Executed at Tyburn, on Wednesday, the 17th of January, 1776, for Forgery*, London: printed for the author and sold at his house, no. 1, Newgate Street, [1776].

Walpole, Horace, *The Letters of Horace Walpole*, ed. Mrs Paget Toynbee, Oxford: Clarendon Press, 1903–5, vol. 9, pp. 181, 253, 298.

Wheatley, Henry B., *London, Past and Present: A Dictionary of Its History, Associations, and Traditions*, London, John Murray, 1891, vol. 2, p. 122; vol. 3, p. 416.

The Whole Proceedings on the King's Commission of the Peace, Oyer and Terminer, and Gaol Delivery for the City of London; and also the Gaol Delivery for the County of Middlesex, Held at Justice Hall in the Old Bailey London, 1775.
Old Bailey sessions papers. Relevant sessions are 1–6 June, 13–19 September and 6–11 December 1775.

The Whole Trials, at Large, of Robert Perreau, Daniel Perreau and Margaret Carolina [sic] *Rudd; for Divers Forgeries ... Revised and Corrected by Serjeant Glynn, Recorder of London*, [London]: T. Walker, 1776.

Index